PUNISH OR TREAT?

MEDICAL CARE IN ENGLISH PRISIONS

1770–1850

PETER McRORIE HIGGINS

Printed in Victoria, BC, Canada. Printed on paper with minimum 30% recycled fibre.
Trafford's print shop runs on "green energy" from solar, wind and other environmentally-friendly
power sources.

PUBLISHING

Offices in Canada, USA, Ireland and UK

Book sales for North America and international:
Trafford Publishing, 6E–2333 Government St.,
Victoria, BC V8T 4P4 CANADA
phone 250 383 6864 (toll-free 1 888 232 4444)
fax 250 383 6804; email to orders@trafford.com
Book sales in Europe:
Trafford Publishing (UK) Limited, 9 Park End Street, 2nd Floor
Oxford, UK OX1 1HH UNITED KINGDOM
phone +44 (0)1865 722 113 (local rate 0845 230 9601)
facsimile +44 (0)1865 722 868; info.uk@trafford.com
Order online at:
trafford.com/06-1910

10 9 8 7 6 5

CONTENTS

List of Illustrations

List of Tables

Acknowledgements

My thanks are due to the staff at the Record Offices at Gloucester, Norwich, Preston and Leigh and to the staff at the House of Lords Archive, all of whom gave all the help one could have wished for in the pursuit of research for this work. Similar thanks are due to staff at the Bodleian Library, the Wellcome Library, the Gloucestershire Collection and the Bingham Library (Cirencester).

When the project was in its infancy I received considerable encouragement from my Open University M.A. tutor, Dr Joe Coohill, but most of all thanks are due to Dr Debbie Brunton, my supervisor, for her unflagging enthusiasm and help in the preparation of my PhD thesis. Valuable critical input was provided by my other internal supervisor, Dr Jim Moore. I am grateful to the Wellcome Trust for awarding a grant which covered a substantial part of the costs of travelling and maintenance when visiting Record Offices and the House of Lords Archive.

I would like to express my thanks to the following sources of illustrative material and for permission to reproduce: the Wellcome Library, 2, 3, 8, 9, 10, 11, 14, 16, 17, 18, 20, 21, 22, 23, 24, 25, 26, 28 and 29; the Mary Evans picture library, 5, 6, 7, 19, 27, 30 and 32; the Gloucestershire Collection, 4; and 12 is reproduced by kind permission of the President and Council of the Royal College of Surgeons of England.

I am immensely grateful to our daughter Charlotte, who has devoted much of her scarce and precious spare time to the tedious process of proof-reading.

Finally, and perhaps most importantly, I must also acknowledge the help given by my wife, Pamela, who has had to put up with my absences and failure to participate in activities that might normally have been expected of a husband in retirement.

1

INTRODUCTION

In 1618 Geffray Minshul, a released prisoner, wrote: '[Prison] is a place that hath more disease predominant in it, than the Pesthouse in the plague-time, and it stinks more that the Lord-Mayor's dogge-house or Paris-garden in August'.[1] This *cri-de-cœur* was echoed and embellished in 1777 by the great prison reformer John Howard – his words indicating that not much had changed in 160 years:

> I beheld in many of them [the houses of correction and city and town gaols], as well as in the *County-Gaols*, a complication of distress: but my attention was principally fixed by the *gaol-fever*, and the *small-pox*, which I saw prevailing to the destruction of multitudes, not only of *felons* in their dungeons, but of *debtors* also. ... These effects are now so notorious, that what terrifies most of us from looking into prisons, is the gaol distemper so frequent in them.[2] ... some [prisoners] are grievously affected with scorbutic distempers: others have their toes mortified, or are quite rotted from their feet; many instances of which I have seen.[3]

---

[1] Geffray Minshul, *Essayes and Characters of a Prison and Prisoners* (Edinburgh: Ballantyne, 1821, reprinted from 1618), pp. 14-15. Minshul was incarcerated in the King's Bench prison, probably for debt. Paris-garden: a bear garden at Bankside, Southwark.

[2] John Howard, *The State of the Prisons in England and Wales, with Preliminary Observations and an account of some Foreign Prisons* (1st edn., Warrington: Eyres, 1777), pp. 2-3. Howard (1722-1790) became High Sheriff of Bedfordshire in 1773. He promoted several parliamentary bills on prison reform and from 1777 published a series of reports on prisons, strongly influencing the reform process.

[3] Ibid., p. 39.

Minshul's comments fell on deaf ears but Howard was riding the wave of a mood for prison reform. Consequently, sixty years later in 1836, prison inspector Bissett Hawkins was moved to pen this eulogy:

> In all the County Gaols which I have entered, a remarkable degree of cleanliness and neatness has reigned throughout, equalling that which is usually maintained among the middle class in England, and largely surpassing the standard which generally prevails in the most splendid residences in Continental Europe. ... The rate of mortality is, in most of these abodes [the principal gaols], so remarkably low, that I can confidently affirm, that in very few situations in life is an adult less likely to die than in a well-conducted English prison.[4]

Later, William Guy in more measured tones, wrote:

> In reference to this class of prisons, the work which John Howard set himself to do seems to have been fully accomplished. The prisoner not only undergoes no punishment beyond that which the law awards him, ... not only is he not exposed to the gaol fever, the small-pox, and other fatal maladies which decimated our prisons less than a century ago, but his health is carefully protected against every cause of injury not inseparable from the state of imprisonment ....[5]

Even discounting some of Hawkins' hyperbole as to the desirability of English prisons for those seeking longevity and allowing for a certain amount of exaggeration by Howard as to their awfulness (see chapter two), the later years of the eighteenth century and the first half of the nineteenth century without doubt saw a marked improvement in the health of those confined in English prisons.

The object of this book is to provide a complete reassessment of the part played by prison medical officers in this transformation. The starting date of 1770 was chosen because it is roughly that at which reform of the English prison system is agreed to have begun; the closing date of 1850 because it is roughly the start of a new era of change: when central government took over the powers previously exerted by local authorities and when most prisons became staffed by full-time, rather than part-time medical attendants.[6] The central features of prison medical care: a much healthier environment, the employment of a surgeon and the provision of <u>some sort of infirmary accommodation</u>, were introduced into the larger

---

[4]   *First Report Inspector of Prisons, Southern and Western Districts*, PP 1836, XXXV, 269, pp. 1-2.

[5]   William A. Guy, *Results of Censuses of the Population of Convict Prisons in England taken in 1862 and 1873* (London: Eyre and Spottiswoode, 1875), p. 26. Guy was medical superintendent at Millbank prison and in 1869 became Professor of Hygiene at King's College. A humanitarian, he was keenly interested in public health and statistics and by seeing to the provision of potatoes for all prisoners helped abolish scurvy in prisons.

[6]   An 'Act for the Better Governance of Convict Prisons (13 & 14 Vict. c. 39)' was passed in 1850. McConville dates the start of the change to 1835 when central government began to play a part in the financing of local prisons. Sean McConville, *A History of English Prison Administration. Vol. I 1750-1877* (London: Routledge, 1981), pp 252-259.

prisons soon after 1770. Also, as it happens, there were few changes in methods of medical management between 1770 and 1850 – first, there was no real understanding of the nature of infective diseases until the second half of the nineteenth century and consequently little progress in public health measures; second, general anaesthesia and antisepsis, together allowing dramatic advances in operative surgery, did not come into general use until after 1850; and third, there were few innovations in drug usage in this period. Thus, from both penal and medical points of view, it is reasonable and practicable to look at this period as an entity.

Before reform, many prisons were decrepit slums, and sick prisoners were attended on an *ad hoc* basis: a local practitioner would be called in by the controlling authority (usually magistrates) for a poor prisoner thought ill enough and deserving enough to warrant the expense. Wealthier prisoners funded their own medical needs. With reform, there was a gradual transformation of prison environments and local general practitioners (at this time mostly carrying the designation of surgeon) were contracted (usually on a part-time basis) to take responsibility for all sick prisoners. In prisons containing both felons and debtors the latter were sometimes excepted from the contract but I have not come across any example of a debtor being refused medical care for this reason. Good health care was seen as an integral part of the reform process – the reformers, mostly comfortably-off philanthropists and physicians, were deeply concerned that prisoners should not suffer disease, and death from disease, in addition to the sentence imposed.

Many modern works on penal history contain references to medical care in prisons in the late-eighteenth and early-nineteenth centuries. J.R.S. Whiting in his history of prison reform in Gloucestershire describes the provision for health care in the new (1791) prisons in that county, paying particular attention to the management of malingering patients.[7] In another work he gives some information on medical care at the smallest of these prisons, Littledean house of correction.[8] Sean McConville, in his comprehensive history of prison administration provides factual information on the employment of surgeons and their duties.[9] Robin Evans' work on prison architecture necessarily encompasses the design measures specifically taken to overcome disease problems.[10] In her account of prison reform in Lancashire, Margaret DeLacy provides some

---

[7] J.R.S. Whiting, *Prison Reform in Gloucestershire 1776-1820* (London: Phillimore, 1975), pp. 18, 38-44.

[8] J.R.S. Whiting, *A House of Correction* (Gloucester: Alan Sutton, 1979), pp. 62-64 and pp. 99-104.

[9] McConville, pp. 15, 76, 101, 129-30, 149, 199, 398, 450-2.

[10] Robin Evans, *The Fabrication of Virtue: English Prison Architecture 1750-1840* (Cambridge: Cambridge University Press, 1982), pp. 96-116, 171.

material on medical care and also supplies comparisons of death rates in prisons with those in the general population.[11]

Although these works furnish useful narrative information, with a general acceptance that this period saw improvements in prison medical care, in none is there a serious attempt to evaluate its quality. Those few historians who have paid specific attention to the role of prison surgeons in the late-eighteenth and early-nineteenth centuries have reached mostly derogatory conclusions – prison medicine has suffered a bad press. Their criticisms are levelled in two main areas: first belittling the part played by medical men in the process of change and second, attacking medical staff for their supposed role in controlling and participating in the process of punishing the inmates, rather than in providing care. Anne Hardy states: 'Medical services to prisons were ramshackle until at least 1850', and claims that the disappearance of epidemic diseases was 'largely a tribute to the efforts of lay reformers, and not to medical men'.[12] Roy Porter is equally dismissive: 'And when prison reform came, it was not led by physicians, still less by the medical profession and its colleges and coteries. It focused not on a regime of preventive and curative medicine, but on the construction of perfectly regulated environments'.[13] This denigratory attitude is epitomised in a review of the published proceedings of a multidisciplinary conference held in 1997 on the subject: 'Incarceration, Humane and Inhumane':

> Prison medicine has stood, and to an extent still stands, on the side of barbarism. It is integrally bound up with prison discipline and to suggest otherwise is an ideological distortion. Although individual doctors have resisted, prison medicine has colluded in the generation of physical and psychological ill-health, sanctioning cruel punishments which often masquerade as treatment.[14]

Much of the material on which this conclusion is based is provided by Joe Sim, who has carried out the only comprehensive theoretical analysis of the subject of health care in prisons.[15] He 'challenges the view that medical care for prisoners has been a journey from barbarism to enlightenment' and

---

[11]   Margaret DeLacy, *Prison Reform in Lancashire 1700-1850: A Study in Local Administration* (Manchester: Manchester University Press, 1986), pp. 28-9, 80-93, 182-90. Her comparisons of death rates in prisons with those in the community will be examined in chapter six.

[12]   Anne Hardy, 'Development of the Prison Medical Service', in *The Health of Prisoners: Historical Essays*, ed. by Richard Creese and others (Amsterdam: Rodopi, 1995), p. 59.

[13]   Roy Porter, 'Howard's Beginning: Prisons, Disease, Hygiene', in *The Health*, ed. by Creese and others, p. 16.

[14]   Diana Medlicott, review of 'Incarceration, Humane and Inhumane: Human Values and Health Care in British Prisons', ed. by Stuart Horne and Meg Stacey, (London: Nuffield Trust, 1999), in *The Howard League Magazine*, 19, (2001), p. 18.

[15]   Joe Sim, *Medical Power in Prisons: The Prison Medical Service in England, 1774-1989* (Milton Keynes: Open University Press, 1990), passim.

describes those staffing the prison medical service as 'front line controllers' who 'rather than operating from a perspective bereft of ideology and politics have been intimately involved in reinforcing the discipline of penality, attempting to create the well adjusted individual from the undifferentiated mass of criminals living dangerously behind penitentiary walls'.[16] Even popular historian A.N. Wilson sees medical men in general as part of the control system:

> The increase in social status of the doctor, from village sawbones – often the very same person as the barber – to lofty professional, exactly follows the growth of Benthamism from private fad of the Philosophic Radicals in the Regency period to the underlying ideology of the whole Victorian state machine. Doctors were essential officers of control.[17]

In discussing medical involvement in the prison dietary, Philip Priestley is moved to poetic language:

> The doctors patrolled the narrow straits that separate hunger from starvation and punishment from outright cruelty, hauling aboard the life raft of their dispensations this drowning soul or that, and repelling, with brute force if necessary, the efforts of the others to climb to safety. In so doing, they lent to the work of preserving their employers' reputations whatever dignity and authority their emerging profession possessed – and lost it.[18]

Sim pursues a similar argument: 'The disciplinary strategies which lay at the heart of penality were legitimised by the interventions which Medical Officers made'.[19] His work is concerned with the time-span 1774-1989 but he uses instances from the early part of the period to support accusations that imprisonment has been (and still is) used not only *as* punishment but *for* punishment, and that medical staff were (and are) intimately involved in the latter process.[20] Prison medical officers are accused of providing less than adequate care: 'The will to discipline has had a profound impact on the level of medical care that prisoners have received since the end of the eighteenth century with deleterious and sometimes fatal consequences for a number of them.[21] He supports his conclusions by citing instances (many taken from Whiting's work on prison reform in Gloucestershire) of surgeons subjecting prisoners to cold baths, the strait-jacket, and electric shocks in cases of real or feigned insanity. He suggests that prison doctors

---

[16]   Ibid., p.x.
[17]   A.N. Wilson, *The Victorians* (London: Hutchinson, 2002), p. 309.
[18]   Philip Priestley, *Victorian Prison Lives: English Prison Biography 1830-1940* (Methuen: London, 1985), p. 190.
[19]   Sim, *Medical*, p. 40.
[20]   Ibid., p. 24.
[21]   Ibid., p. x.

colluded in enforcing the hardships of solitary confinement. He criticises medical failure to do more to improve the diet of prisoners, their use of blistering as a punishment, and what he sees as the casual attitude of doctors and coroners to deaths in prisons. He quotes figures purportedly demonstrating a high death rate in prisons, and condemns the apparent lack of medical staff concern at an outbreak of so-called scurvy at Millbank penitentiary in the early 1820s.[22] So far as the last episode is concerned, he argues that it was an example of medical officers using their privileged position to experiment with the health of prisoners. He cites the instance of a prisoner at Ilchester county gaol who, during an illness, had to sit in rooms that were at least six inches deep in water.[23]

A lone voice counters this chorus of vilification – that of Martin Wiener: '... prison medical officers have become villains in the accounts of penal failure by critical revisionists ... revisionists have often donned blinkers of their own in assuming that the only proper role for the prison medical officer was oppositional, to put forth the claims of 'care' against 'punishment'. He goes on to argue that prison doctors were motivated in various ways; that they were perfectly capable of balancing 'one social aim – health – ... against other, equally legitimate, social aims [that is] the Benthamite principles of lenity, severity and economy'.[24]

In all but the last of the works so far cited, prison surgeons are seen as participants in a comprehensive system of punishment – cogs in a complex machine designed to dominate the masses. Mostly they are positioned in an essentially Foucauldian framework: part of a control mechanism pervading society and based on the regimentation and documentation of each and every individual. Michel Foucault's views on penality were proposed in his influential book "Discipline and Punish", first published in 1975.[25] His archetype is a society based on conditioning mechanisms modelled on those initially imposed in religious institutions, enforced at school, in the workplace, in hospitals, and specifically, in prisons.

Michael Ignatieff discerns a class element in the reformative ideal – the seemingly humane reformers such as John Howard and Elizabeth Fry[26] were in fact motivated by a desire for 'what they imagined to be a

---

[22] Ibid., pp. 15, 17 & 20-26.

[23] Joe Sim, 'Prison Health Care and the Lessons of History', in *Incarceration, Humane and Inhumane*, ed. by Stuart Horner and Meg Stacey (London: The Nuffield Trust), p. 24.

[24] Martin J. Wiener, 'The Health of Prisoners and the Two Faces of Benthamism', in *The Health*, ed. by Creese and others, pp. 52-53.

[25] Michel Foucault, *Discipline and Punish: The Birth of the Prison* (London: Penguin, 1991, first published as *Surveiller et punir: Naissance de la prison* (Paris: Gallimard, 1975), passim.

[26] Elizabeth Fry (1780-1845) was a Quaker who became deeply involved with the spiritual well-being and education of women prisoners.

more stable, orderly and coherent social order ... a new strategy of class relations'; and: 'As a hopeful allegory of class relations in general, [the reformative ideal] proved capable of surviving the repeated frustrations of reality because it spoke to a heart-felt middle-class desire for a social order based on deferential reconciliation'.[27] He sees the idea of the penitentiary:

> as a system of authority and as a machine for the remaking of men, it reflected some of [the reformers] deepest political, psychological, and religious assumptions. It promised, above all, to restore the legitimacy of a legal system that they feared was jeopardized by the excessive severities and gratuitous abuse of the Bloody Code.[28]

The 1834 Poor Law Act resulted in a large increase in the number of workhouses. One aim was to draw a broad line of distinction between the classes of independent labourers and paupers. 'The prospect of a managed and disciplined existence in one of these institutions [the workhouse] would, it was contended, deter all but the truly destitute from applying for relief'.[29] As will become clear, this need for a graduation in 'diets and deprivations' as between independent labourers, paupers, and those in prison – the principle of less eligibility – often posed problems in prison management and difficulties for prison medical officers.

On the face of it, in neither the Foucauldian system of control nor in a Marxist model, would it be necessary to provide much in the way of medical care for prisoners. If prison is to be a place of terror, why should not fear of disease be part of that terror?[30] It is perhaps a paradox that Howard and other reformers, although anxious that prison should remain an object of dread, were deeply concerned to remove from punishment both the fear of disease and its reality. This (perhaps irresolvable) conflict between the need for punishment to be both severe and at the same time humane – the need to balance the Benthamite principles of 'lenity, severity and economy' – was a matter of concern to contemporaries and will be encountered regularly throughout this book.[31]

---

[27] Michael Ignatieff, *A Just Measure of Pain* (London: Penguin, 1989), p. 213.

[28] Ibid., p. 79. The "Bloody Code" is a name given to the British legal system as it existed between the late –seventeenth and the early-nineteenth centuries. Perhaps its most notorious component was the Waltham "Black Act" (9 Geo. 1, c.22) of 1723, enacted in response to poaching at Waltham and a group of bandits who operated at Wokingham with blackened faces.

[29] Felix Driver, *Power and Pauperism: The Workhouse system 1834-1884*, (Cambridge: Cambridge University Press, 1993), pp. 24-25. 'Extracts from the information received by H.M. Commissioners into the administration and operation of the Poor Laws etc.' *The Edinburgh Review*, CXXVIII, (1836), 487-537 (p. 490).

[30] And indeed, such views were widely held. McConville, pp. 61-62.

[31] For a discussion of the Benthamite approach to this problem see Wiener, 'The Health', pp. 44-58.

So far as prison medical care is concerned, a careful reading of the work of those authors I have quoted shows their conclusions to be based mostly on a reading of secondary sources or, at best, on an incomplete and inadequate appraisal of the primary sources. In contrast, this book is based on a comprehensive study of primary source material relating to the subject in the period 1770 to the 1850s, allowing a complete re-evaluation of existing assertions and filling the large gap in knowledge relating to the activities and motivation of the medical men who provided care for prisoners.

The considerable amount of primary source material I have used is found in four main areas. The first category, reports made by prison reformers, provides much information on medical matters principally for the early years, 1770-1812. Howard at the start of the period and James Neild[32] latterly, paid regular visits to nearly all prisons in the land, making comments on their state and paying attention to the quality of medical provision. The second category consists of reports of parliamentary enquiries into prison conditions and relates (intermittently) to most of the period under study. Although most enquiries were not specifically directed to medical matters, relevant information frequently emerges. Thirdly, and perhaps most valuable, are the surviving journals kept by prison surgeons – for Gloucestershire,[33] Norwich[34] and Lancaster[35] (see Table 1:1). Together these cover the years 1791-1850, and provide an unrivalled source of information on patients' complaints, diagnoses made, treatment given, the medical outcome, the attitude of surgeons to their patients, and surgeons' brushes with authority. In addition, annual or quarterly reports written by surgeons of other gaols and houses of correction in Lancashire in the 1820s and 1830s have been examined at Lancashire county record office (Preston) and these are quoted as appropriate.

Finally, resulting from a recommendation by a parliamentary select committee of 1835, the prison inspectorate was instituted. Inspectors' reports, published annually from 1836, give much additional information for later years, a period during which the move to centralised control was getting under way and when statistical information was eagerly compiled. Other sources, such as magistrates', chaplains' and prison governors' journals, and a variety of contemporary writings, are used as appropriate.

[32] James Neild (1744-1814), a long-term campaigner for the rights of debtors, became High Sheriff of Buckinghamshire in 1804 and followed in Howard's footsteps, providing an account of prison conditions in the early years of the nineteenth century.

[33] Except for Lawford's Gate house of correction, near Bristol, which in 1832 was 'attacked by a riotous and tumultuous assembly, who after liberating the prisoners confined therein, burnt and destroyed [most of] the building'. *Reports*, PP, 1833 (12), XXVIII,1, p. 90. No records survived the conflagration nor are there any surgeons' journals extant from after its rebuilding.

[34] I have also referred to medical matters noted in *Keeper's daily journal*, (NCRO, MF/RO 576/1).

[35] Wigan Archive Service, Leigh (Lancs).

Table 1.1 Surgeons' journals studied[36]

Prison	Dates	Location and reference
Gloucester county gaol	31 July 1791 – 11 March 1799	GRO[37], Q/Gc 32/1
	2 January 1809 – 12 April 1815	GRO, Q/Gc 32/2
	13 April 1815 – 10 February 1820	GRO, Q/Gc 32/3
Northleach (Glos) house of correction	20 October 1800 – 31 January 1818[38]	GRO, Q/Gn 5/1
	1 February 1818 – 27 June 1834	GRO, Q/Gn 5/2
	10 July 1834 – 30 June 1841	GRO, Q/Gn 5/3
Littledean (Glos) house of correction	17 October 1806 -19 October 1829	GRO, Q/Gli 18/1
	22 October 1829 – 7 April 1838	GRO, Q/Gli 18/2
	18 October 1842 – 4 January 1848	GRO, Q/Gli 18/3
	5 May 1844 – 24 October 1854	GRO, Q/Gli 19
Horsley (Glos) house of correction	1 January 1843 – 30 April 1844	GRO, Q/Gh 12
Gloucester city gaol and house of correction	9 March 1825 – 6 November 1837	GRO, G3/G 8/1
Norfolk county gaol and bridewell	1 January 1843 – 26 December 1846	NCRO, MF/RO[39] 576/1
	1 January 1848 – 25 February 1850	NCRO, MF/RO 576/1
Lancaster castle gaol	12 December 1843 – 30 November 1849	MMP 12

---

[36] Since reference to entries in the journals listed occur so frequently, only the prison and the entry date will be given (in the text) on each occasion.

[37] Gloucestershire County Record Office, Gloucester (GRO)

[38] Labelled as "Apothecary's Journal".

[39] Norfolk County Record Office, Norwich (NCRO).

2

PRISONS:
DEVELOPMENT AND REFORM

In order to assess the activities of those involved in the prison medical service it is necessary to understand the system within which they operated – although the use of the word "system", implying as it does a degree of organisation and coherence, is to reward this set-up with unmerited dignity. From Saxon and Norman times, prisons sprang up to serve the needs of local communities and by the time of Henry VIII most municipalities had gaols or lock-ups as adjuncts to their own courts. Additionally there were franchise prisons, held by ecclesiastical or secular lords serving a group of estates, a hundred, a manor or even a soke or liberty (zones within a larger jurisdiction having their own courts).[40] In 1795 physician and reformer John Mason Good did his best to sum up the resulting gallimaufry:

> In modern times, the buildings allotted for the reception of prisoners and the poor, and especially in this kingdom, are of such various forms, dimensions, materials and situations, with strange diversities of customs and rules, that it is almost impossible to arrange them into regular and appropriate classes. In general however, they consist of old castles, barns or monasteries, purchased by the county or district for this purpose. Sometimes, however, they are the gift of individuals, as at SHEFFIELD, where there is a prison which was granted

---

[40]   McConville, p. 7.

by the Duke of Norfolk for the confinement of debtors; and sometimes they are still private property, and subject to an annual rent for occupation: instances of which are to be found at the MARSHALSEA prison, which belongs to four landlords, and is farmed out at one hundred guineas per year.[41]

The largest English gaols were in London and, in this still predominantly pre-industrial-revolution rural society, the next-sized prisons were county gaols, usually located in the county town. Town and borough gaols tended to be smaller – sometimes very small indeed. Until the first quarter of the nineteenth century there was no national prison system, apart from the Tower of London (used only for special prisoners), the Savoy (for military offenders), some parts of the large debtors' prisons in London, and – from 1776 – the prison hulks; but Newgate, although the property of the City of London, gradually came to be recognised as the leading criminal prison in the country, taking state and religious prisoners as well as those guilty of notorious crimes. It was among the oldest in the country: 'This gate hath of long time been a gaol, or prison for felons and trespassers, as appeareth by records in the reign of King John ...'.[42] Only the Fleet prison was older. It was always seen as being 'for the worst type of criminal in the City of London and the county of Middlesex', and, since it was also seen as being secure, for prisoners from other parts of the country.[43] There was no truly national prison until 1816 when Millbank penitentiary opened, taking prisoners from every part of England and Wales, until provision could be made for confining such offenders in penitentiary houses elsewhere.[44]

Confinement had been part of the disciplinary system in England since the ninth century. The extent to which imprisonment *per se* was used as punishment in the early years is arguable,[45] but there is general agreement that its primary purpose was to hold those awaiting sentence or its execution, as well as for the coercion of debtors.[46] By the late-eighteenth century imprisonment had evolved into something like its modern punitive function; most prisons held both felons and debtors – male and female alike – often with little separation by class of offence committed, and sometimes not even by sex. In London there were several large prisons purely for debtors; such specialisation was rare elsewhere.

[41] John Mason Good, *A Dissertation on the Diseases of Prisons and Poorhouses* (London: Dilly, 1795), pp. 21-22.

[42] Stow, p. 34.

[43] Anthony Babington, *The English Bastille: A History of Newgate Gaol and Prison Conditions in Britain 1188-1902* (London: Macdonald, 1971), pp. 1, 14, and 15.

[44] George Holford, *An Account of the General Penitentiary at Millbank*, (London: Rivington, 1828), p. 26. He states that prisoners came from Scotland also.

[45] McConville, pp. 1-4.

[46] Allan Brodie, Jane Croom & James O. Davies, *English Prisons: An Architectural History* (Swindon: English Heritage, 2002), pp. 10-11.

Among these prisons was a category first materialising in 1556, at the former royal palace of Bridewell.[47] This was defined as a house of correction and Sir Edward Coke (1552-1634) stated its function was 'to punish rogues, vagabonds, and sturdy beggars, and other idle and disorderly persons by provid[ing] mills, turns, cards, and suchlike instruments, for setting idle persons to work'.[48] According to McConville: 'Bridewell can truly be treated as the first example of modern imprisonment, certainly in Britain and probably in Europe'.[49] Before long other towns followed suit: Oxford (1562), Salisbury (1564), Norwich (1565), Gloucester (before 1569), and Ipswich (1569). Eventually there may have been as many as two hundred houses of correction in England.[50] Similar institutions were established in cities throughout northwestern Europe. The principle of reform through work was (reputedly) carried to its logical conclusion at the *Rasphuis* in Amsterdam where recalcitrant offenders were placed in a cell below the level of the water table. They had a free choice: work the pump in the cell or drown.[51]

Despite the reformatory ideal, by the mid-eighteenth century many houses of correction in England became squalid and little used hovels. Towards the end of the eighteenth century the worst closed but some were enlarged and improved, and new ones built. In the last category was Horsley (Gloucestershire) and its list of prisoners is probably fairly representative of bridewell occupants (in others the proportion of vagrants and from the local industry would vary). Between 8 February 1792 and 8 February 1807 1,104 prisoners were committed. They included 52 deserters, 182 for theft of potatoes, fuel or corn, 264 for breach of service, 167 for woollen manufactory offences, 48 for poaching, 15 lewd women, 7 men and 5 women for swearing, 15 for selling beer without a licence, 77 vagrants, 62 for leaving families chargeable to the parish, 20 for breaches of the peace, 43 for bastardy and 85 debtors. The average stay was ten weeks and two days.[52] The rather strange term "lewd woman" referred to someone who had given birth to an illegitimate child she could not support and she was usually imprisoned for one year, not because the offence was seen as particularly heinous, but because, according to Whiting this was a way of transferring the financial

---

[47] "Bridewell" was used as a generic term for this type of prison well into the nineteenth century. For a comprehensive account see Joanna Innes, 'Prisons for the poor: English bridewells', in *Labour, Law, and Crime: A historical perspective*, ed. by Francis Snyder & Douglas Hay (Cambridge: Tavistock, 1987)' pp. 42-122 (passim).

[48] G.O. Paul, *Address to His Majesty's Justices of the Peace for the County of Gloucester assembled at their Epiphany General Quarter Session* (Gloucester: Walker, 1809), p. 58.

[49] McConville, p. 22.

[50] Ibid., pp. 38-39 & 42.

[51] Simon Schama, *The Embarrassment of Riches: An Interpretation of Dutch Literature in the Golden Age* (London: Fontana, 1991), pp. 22-24. Schama admits that most of the evidence for this practice is hearsay.

[52] *Justices Journal*, GRO, Q/Gli 1/1.

burden of her support from the parish to the county.[53] Sir G.O. Paul strongly deprecated this practice 'as a cunning calculation of parish economy', which he considered more prevalent in Gloucestershire than elsewhere.[54] More exotically, Hannah Williams aged 46 and Hosiah Willaims aged 20 were each imprisoned for a month on the grounds that they 'did wander abroad in the habit of an Egyptian endeavouring to take in the unwary in pretending to tell their fortunes'.[55] As time went by a greater proportion of offences warranting bridewell imprisonment were for minor crimes against property and for poaching; longer sentences were given and the distinction between the occupants of gaols and bridewells in terms of crimes committed became more and more blurred. However those committing the more serious offences such as burglary or murder were normally confined to a gaol, as were those awaiting transportation (of which more later).

In the larger towns (particularly London) debtors were confined in specialist prisons but where such institutions did not exist, they went into the local (county or town) gaol or bridewell, most of which had wards solely for debtors. Until the late-eighteenth century many prisons were self-financing through fees charged upon prisoners – for admission, removal of fetters, privileged treatment, and even in order to obtain release when the time came for discharge. In addition, keepers enjoyed a lucrative sideline in the sale of food and ale to their charges. A statute of 1577 had authorised the payment to felons of a county allowance for food – funded by a levy of 6*d*. to 8*d*. on each parish. For debtors this was discretionary only; they were less affected by the eighteenth century reform process and their obligation to pay fees continued well into the nineteenth century – long after prison staff had become salaried and felons were in general no longer subjected to this kind of extortion.[56] In most county gaols debtors were saved from starvation by being given the "county allowance" of food if destitute, and were provided with medical care.

Many gaols allowed debtors a considerable measure of self-government[57] with their own systems of extortion. New arrivals were required to pay fees to their fellows such as "garnish" and "chummage" – which were then divided amongst the other inmates or used to finance a dinner. Failure to pay resulted in auction of the unfortunate arrival's clothes and other items. DeLacy paints a vivid picture of the state of affairs at Lancaster castle (the county gaol):

---

53   Whiting, *Prison Reform*, pp. 108 and 174.
54   Paul, *Address to His Majesty's Justices etc.*, pp. 129-130.
55   *Governor's Register of Prisoners*, 1 August 1816, GRO, Q Gn 4
56   Abuses continued (illegally) in some of the larger London prisons. McConville, pp. 230-231.
57   For what is probably a fairly typical situation, see DeLacy, pp. 31-34.

On the whole, the condition of debtors changed little in the course of a hundred years. As late as 1835, debtors on the county allowance still received their pound of bread a day and ten pounds of potatoes a week; the only addition had been two pounds of oatmeal a week. They still lived in Norman towers, although a few new rooms and an arcade had been added for their benefit. They could still bring in their own bedding, now subject to inspection for cleanliness, and they still cooked over the open fires in their rooms. They still, if they wished, pursued a multitude of trades and shopped for meat, vegetables, and fish at the market held within the Castle. As they were not clothed by the county, many were still to be seen in rags ....[58]

Discipline was usually lax; at King's Bench prison Howard noted: 'at my first visit there was a Wine-Club and a Beer-Club; and one can scarcely ever enter the walls without seeing parties at skittles, mississippi,[59] portobello,[60] tennis, fives, etc'.[61] Conditions were not always so jolly; the four debtors in the Chesterfield gaol 'were almost starved: one of them said, with tears in his eyes, "he had not eaten a morsel that day"; it was afternoon. Their meagre sickly countenances confirmed what they said'.[62] Debtor numbers declined from about half the total prison population in the 1770s to less than an eighth by the 1840s. In absolute terms the decline was by only about one quarter (figure 1), so that throughout the period of study, medical staff were involved in the care of this group of prisoner.

In theory all prisons were under the authority of the King; in practice, from Norman times, county gaols were governed by the sheriff. By the late-eighteenth century, justices of the peace had largely assumed responsibility – they exercised control and appointed staff [63] – and it was they who were empowered to collect rates in order to finance this exercise. As Christopher Hill points out: 'Justices of the Peace, through control of wages and poor relief, ... enjoyed great power over the masses of the population who 'existed only to be ruled'; and this power was virtually independent of [the] government ...'.[64] Hill is writing about the seventeenth century but if anything, the magistrates' power had increased by the turn of the nineteenth century: particularly with regard to the dispensation of summary justice. They could imprison for vagrancy, desertion of family, bastardy, disobedience and embezzlement in most trades, theft of field produce, taking firewood, minor game-law offences etc.[65] Assize judges could intervene in the management of county gaols but rarely did so.

---

[58]   DeLacy, pp. 192-193.
[59]   Mississippi: a game similar to bagatelle (OED).
[60]   Portobello: perhaps a game resembling billiards (OED – the only reference given is to Howard).
[61]   Howard, *The State* (1st edn.), p. 198.
[62]   Ibid., p. 286.
[63]   Occasional disputes between sheriff and magistrates over staff appointments continued into the nineteenth century. McConville, pp. 318-321.
[64]   Christopher Hill, *The Century of Revolution 1603-1714* (London: Routledge, 1980), p. 87.
[65]   Ignatieff, p. 25.

**Figure 1 Changes in the prison population of England and Wales
1775-1843**[66]

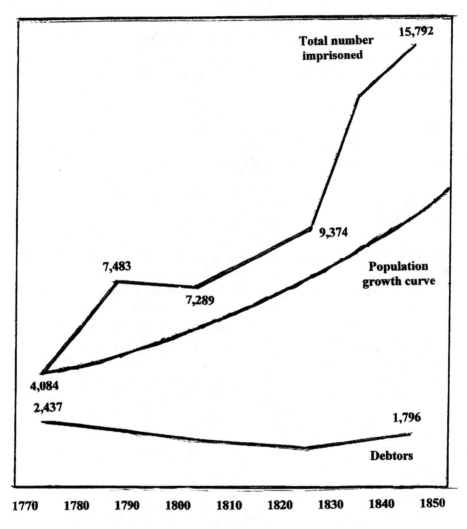

Total number
imprisoned

15,792

9,374

7,483

7,289

Population
growth curve

4,084

2,437

1,796

Debtors

1770   1780   1790   1800   1810   1820   1830   1840   1850

[66] Adapted from Evans, *The Fabrication*, p. 421. The reasons for the increase in prisoners after 1820 are complex and cannot be discussed at length but were partly economic (rising when unemployment or food prices rose), partly due to a changed attitude to property crime and poaching in the nineteenth century (resulting in more prosecutions), and perhaps also because the improved environment in prisons made magistrates and judges more ready to use imprisonment as a punishment: 'The increase in crime was not the only cause which led to prison crowding; their own improved state had tended to the same result. Small-pox and fever no longer decimated the prisoners, and judges, now that their sentences did not involve the certainty of disease, and the probability of death, were less chary of committing to Gaol'. W.L. Clay, *The Prison Chaplain: A Memoir of the Rev. John Clay, B.D.*, (London: Macmillan, 1861), p. 68 (f.n.).

In towns, gaol management was less well defined: responsibility was often divided between the various municipal officials.[67] Consequently, matters there were less well arranged; as late as 1835 the Royal Commission on Municipal Corporations noted that administration in these prisons (and there were many of them) was much more irregular than that of county gaols, with the governing magistrates 'often selected from a class incompetent to the discharge of judicial functions'.[68] Clay described the one hundred and forty prisons belonging to local and corporate jurisdictions in the late 1820s as 'the filthiest and most abominable in the Kingdom and containing about eight thousand inmates'.[69] Worst of all were several semi-private gaols for debtors, described as: 'miserable filthy dens for the most part, where the wretched debtor, without any allowance from the county, without the means of wringing his alimentary sixpence a week from his creditor [in theory, the creditor applying for the debtor to be imprisoned was obliged to provide for the latter's sustenance – in practice this rarely seems to have happened] was left to starve'.[70]

Many municipal authorities eventually closed their own prisons, paying to use the county gaol or bridewell; some boroughs built satisfactory new gaols. In any event, the days of the smaller prisons were numbered. Acts of Parliament in the late 1830s led to the closure of many of them, and of those remaining a proportion were used for remand prisoners only.[71] Legislation allowing the closure of franchise prisons did not come until 1850 but 'By mid-century, the local prisons, in common with many other English institutions, had undergone an administrative transformation. Most of the very small prisons had been closed. Although many variations in policy and regime persisted, prisons were more thoroughly regulated than ever before'.[72] Finally, the Prisons Act of 1877 transferred the responsibility for all prisons to the Home Secretary.

REFORM

Until the early modern period, discipline for criminals was carried out either by means of fines or was directed to the body – such as exposure in the stocks, beating, mutilation, or execution. In the seventeenth and eighteenth centuries the general appetite for brutal forms of retribution and deterrence began to diminish. More were reprieved – in the ten

---

[67] McConville, pp. 6-7.
[68] Ibid, pp. 225-226.
[69] Clay, p. 98.
[70] Ibid., p. 99.
[71] McConville, pp. 232-3.
[72] Ibid, p. 259.

years 1749-58 in London and Middlesex, from 527 capital convictions 365 (69.3%) were executed whereas between 1799 and 1808, 804 capital convictions resulted in 126 (15.7%) executions. Additionally, although under the "Bloody Code" over two hundred offences were punishable by death (fifty of these added by the Waltham "Black Act"), in practice those accused were often not convicted. Prosecutors and juries accepted that a crime did not warrant death, many offenders went unpunished and consequently the better-off members of society began to perceive that draconian laws were not delivering the protection their persons and their property deserved.[73] Self-interest was also evident in the fear that gaol fever would spread to the population at large. A well-known example was that of Mr Clerk (a prisoner at Newgate), tried at the Old Bailey in April 1750. During the trial, attendants were struck by a 'noisome smell' in court. A week later fifty people were dead – and not just *hoi polloi*. The toll included an alderman (a former Lord Mayor), an undersheriff, a baron of the Exchequer, a Justice of the Common Pleas, two barristers at law, and twelve others (among these an apothecary and a surgeon).[74] Of course, in an era when contagious disease – frequently in epidemic form – was all too common, there was no certainty that these infections had originated in the prison. Indeed, according to Charles Creighton writing of the Old Bailey episode, 'there was no sickness in the goal more than is common is such places'.[75]

Whatever the reason, the seeds of reform were sown and the soil, made fertile by the efforts of utilitarians and evangelicals[76] was further nourished by the writings of Cesare Beccaria, whose essay on crime and punishment (translated from the Italian in 1767) was well received in England.[77] He argued against unduly harsh punishments, pointing out that it was not severity of punishment which deterred potential criminals so much as its certainty, and he insisted that the interval between crime and retribution should be as short as possible.[78]

The slow process of change was given a considerable fillip by the activities of John Howard – long regarded as being foremost amongst the reformers. As Porter points out, he was not alone: '... far from being

[73] Robert Hughes, *The Fatal Shore: A History of Transportation of Convicts to Australia, 1787-1868* (London: Pan, 1988), pp. 29-36.
[74] *Gentleman's Magazine*, Vol. XX (1750), pp. 233-235.
[75] Charles Creighton, *A History of Epidemics in Britain*, Vol. II, (Cambridge: Cambridge University Press, 1894), p. 93.
[76] McConville, p. 84.
[77] Cesare Beccaria (1738-1794), born in Milan of a reasonably wealthy noble family. He wrote on reform of the penal system and also on fiscal and tax reform.
[78] Richard Bellamy, *Beccaria: On Crimes and Punishment and Other Writings* (Cambridge: Cambridge University Press, 1995), pp. 63 & 48.

a solitary reformer a prophet crying in the wilderness, Howard was on a wave of prison reform, itself part of the late-Enlightenment tide of opinion impatient to reconstruct all manner of institutions – gaols, madhouses, barracks, orphanages, workhouses, hospitals – to meet the need of modernity'.[79]

Reform might well have come sooner had there not emerged early in the seventeenth century a convenient alternative to execution – transportation to the American colonies. In the years leading up to 1775 when the total number of criminals in British gaols averaged about 4,000 there were some 960 transportations per annum.[80] It is estimated that between 1750 and 1770 there were about ten transportations for every execution.[81] The transportation system worked reasonably well, reducing the prison population to manageable proportions but this changed dramatically in the 1770s and 1780s when three factors combined to cause a large growth in prison population. First was the ready availability of a cheaper form of labour (slaves) in the American plantations (it is estimated that 47,000 African slaves arrived annually in America at this time[82]); secondly, British defeat in the American war of independence completely closed this outlet (although, 'Shortly after the American wars, the British government rather ingenuously attempted to revive transportation to that country along former lines'[83]); and thirdly, increased unemployment and hardship in post-war Britain resulted in a rise in the number of offenders convicted (figure one). This increase focused attention on places of confinement which by general consent were insecure, squalid, and unhealthy. Typifying this concern with the problem of health is an anguished letter from the Bridgwater magistrates addressed to the Home Secretary on 6 August 1783: 'owing to the great number of convicts confined in our County gaol at Ilchester under sentence of transportation, a very malignant Disorder has prevailed and notwithstanding the greatest care has been taken, no less than Eleven Prisoners have died'. They go on to point out that the number of inmates is likely to increase even more at the next Assizes. Similar letters were sent by the justices at Salisbury, Maidstone and Winchester,[84] and by the High Sheriff and Grand Jury of Berkshire.[85] On the same theme is a letter written by Thomas Bayley to all members of parliament for Lancashire with a

[79] Porter, 'Howard's', p. 5.
[80] Howard, *The State (1st edn.)*, p. 39 (f.n.).
[81] Evans, *The Fabrication*, p. 119.
[82] Hughes, p. 41.
[83] Wilfred Owen, quoted in McConville, p. 106.
[84] PRO, HO 42 3 & 42 4.
[85] Peter Southerton, *The Story of a Prison* (Reading: Osprey, 1975), p. 15

John Howard visiting prisoners in gaol. Drawing, circa 1780.

copy to Lord Sydney:[86] 'The gaols are now crowded beyond Example and a pestilential Fever, peculiar to these Mansions of Misery, prevails in very many of them, which threatens Danger to the whole Nation'.[87] He went on – echoing the mood of the time – to make a plea for wholesale reform in the prison system.

Medical men played an important part in the process: 'Gaol fever frightened the justices, but they would not have chosen rebuilding [of the prisons] as a remedy unless doctors had begun to suggest that this was the best preventative'.[88] A more broad-brush view is taken by Porter: 'Not from philosophies, prison reform arose from practicalities, and it was generated from below, in the localities, amongst cabals of sheriffs, lords lieutenants and JPs. It arose out of local crisis, it proceeded piecemeal'.[89]

Howard's concern with health is apparent in the preamble to the Health of Prisoners Act (14 Geo. III c. 59) which he promoted in1774:

> Whereas the malignant Fever, that is commonly called *The Gaol Distemper* is found to be owing to a Want of Cleanliness and fresh Air in the several gaols in England and Wales, and the fatal Consequences of that Disorder, of which there has been of late, too much Experience, might be prevented, if the Justices of the Peace were duly authorised to provide such Accommodation in gaols as may be necessary to answer this salutary Purpose ...[90]

Under the act, magistrates were empowered to order scraping and whitewashing of prison walls at least once a year, along with regular washing and cleaning. Howard recommended that satisfactory ventilation should be provided; there should be adequate rooms available for the sick; and that infirmaries should be separate from other gaol buildings, raised on arcades, with a grate in the floor for ventilation as well as being provided with hand-ventilators.[91] Magistrates were allowed to appoint 'an experienced Surgeon or Apothecary ... a man of repute in his profession' to attend the prison, paid from the rates; one of his duties being to report to the justices on the prisoners' health. He was to order removal of the sick to the infirmary where their irons would be cut off and they would receive appropriate medication

---

[86] Lord Sydney, Home Secretary in the 1780s. Thomas Butterworth Bayley, born 1744, perpetual chairman of the Lancashire quarter sessions and prominent prison reformer. DeLacy, pp. 70-74.

[87] *Letter dated 26th January 1784*, PRO, HO 42/4.

[88] DeLacy, p. 82. She describes conditions in Lancashire, but similar relationships between reformers and physicians existed elsewhere.

[89] Porter, 'Howard's', p. 15.

[90] McConville, p. 87. A bill to allow payment from the rates for clergy to attend prisons– at up to £50 per annum – had been passed in 1773. Ibid., p. 86.

[91] Howard, *The State*, (1st edn.), p. 45. Healthy blasts of fresh air were unwelcome to prisoners and staff alike with the result that the architectural purity of the building could be tarnished – for instance by means of rags stuffed in unglazed windows.

and diet.[92] This Act was to be displayed in every gaol – Howard himself paid for copies to be distributed.[93] However, this legislation was permissive: little would have happened had there not been a general perception of the need for reform, particularly so far as prisoners' health was concerned.

Indeed, many reformers saw a direct link between crime and disease. Jonas Hanway wrote that crime issues 'from the same source as disease, from the squalid, riotous and undisciplined quarters of the poor'; similar views were held by others including the Edinburgh physician David Hartley, and in London by Drs. Fothergill and Good. Dr Good emphasised the importance of separation of prisoners from one another: 'Great advantages to health result from private and solitary cells'.[94]

A spurt in the building of new prisons ensued, all based on a shift away from the practice of confining prisoners together in large wards, with their in-built propensity to both moral and physical contamination, to the cellular system. The county gaol which opened at Horsham in 1779 went part way in that it had separate night cells, but still communal day wards. This prison employed a chaplain at a salary of £50 and a surgeon at £5 per annum.[95] A completely new county gaol opened at Bodmin (Cornwall) soon afterwards.[96] The new house of correction at Petworth, (1789), had two infirmary rooms to serve its thirty-two cells – and here the principle of separation was rigorously applied.[97] Perhaps the most marked spurt of building came in Gloucestershire – apparently almost entirely the result of the efforts of one man: Sir George Onesiphorus Paul.[98] According to Ignatieff: 'Next to Howard, he [Paul] was the most influential institutional reformer of his generation – a relentless, dictatorial administrator who single-handedly made Gloucester penitentiary the model for prisons across the country'.[99] In his crusade he echoed Howard's emphasis on health: 'putrid distemper is a natural and almost necessary consequence, to which a full gaol, with its present defects in construction, must subject

---

[92] Ibid., p. 56.

[93] McConville, p. 87.

[94] Good, p. 107.

[95] There was nearly always a disparity in the salaries of chaplain and surgeon although the difference in favour of the chaplain was not usually as marked as in this instance.

[96] Brodie and others, p. 37. For details of Stafford county gaol (1793), see Anthony John Standley, 'Medical Treatment and Prisoners' Health in Stafford Gaol during the Eighteenth Century', in *The Health*, ed. by Creese and others, pp. 38-39.

[97] McConville, pp. 94-96.

[98] Paul (1746-1820) was High Sheriff of Gloucestershire. The original Onesiphorus lived in Ephesus, provided hospitality for St. Paul, and – very much to the point – visited and succoured St. Paul when he was imprisoned in Rome. 2 Tim. I. 16-18. Paul took advantage of Acts passed in 1784 empowering county councils to borrow on the security of the rates – 'a device developed by Paul in Gloucestershire', DeLacy, p. 75. His reforming efforts took their toll:, he claimed that prison duties 'wore out his constitution and a large part of his fortune'. McConville, p. 126 (f.n.).

[99] Ignatieff, p. 99.

John Howard bringing fresh air into a prison. Watercolour 1787

its inhabitants'.[100] He went on: 'No sentence, under the British dispensation, is so cruel as to condemn a man to die by famine, to languish in disease, or to become a prey to filth and vermin'.[101] He gave instances of diseases spreading from prisons to the population at large and quoted examples from his own experience of those who had been discharged after imprisonment for minor offences infecting – often with fatal consequences – other family members. Paul's audience was convinced – funds became available for a completely new county gaol for Gloucester, along with four smaller houses of correction distributed through the county – all in the year 1791.[102] Criminal prisoners each had a day cell for work and a night cell for sleep; separation was enforced as far as possible. The same design principles were adopted in the construction of most new prisons built subsequently in other counties. The attempt to avoid moral contamination extended to the intention that prisoners should be classified and the different classes kept separate.

THE IMPACT OF REFORM

An idea of the speed with which improvement in health care provision took place can be obtained by reading the surveys carried out first by Howard and in later years by James Neild (1744-1815). The former covered some 25,000 miles between 1773 and 1782 in Great Britain and Ireland[103]; his reports providing an outline of the structure of each prison; detailing any fees payable by the prisoners and any charitable trusts which had been set up to provide relief; and stating the name of the surgeon or apothecary (if any) and their salaries. The institutions visited were mostly small: in his first report (1777) only six (King's Bench (debtors), Newgate (mostly felons), Fleet (debtors), Marshalsea (mostly debtors), and Clerkenwell house of correction) – all in London – and York county gaol (felons and debtors) held more than 100 prisoners each, whilst 130 prisons held fewer than ten inmates each.[104]

In 1812 Neild reported on a similar series of tours.[105] Altogether, he visited in England (at least once) some 79 town, borough, or city gaols, 72 houses

---

[100]   G.O. Paul, *To the Gentlemen of the Grand Jury for the County of Glocester[sic] at the Summer Assizes 1783* (Gloucester: Walker, 1783), p. 9.

[101]   Ibid., p. 25.

[102]   At a total cost of £46,437 11s. 4d. made up as follows: Gloucester £25,891 18s. 6d., Horsley £6,180 17s. 10d., Northleach £5,111 6s. 4d., Bristol (Lawford's Gate) £4,990 17s., Littledean £3,308 16s. 6d., and general items £953 15s. 2d. G.O. Paul, *An Address delivered to a General Meeting of the Nobility, Clergy, etc.* Gloucester: Walker, 1792, p. 3. For architectural details of these prisons see Brodie and others, pp. 40-52.

[103]   John Howard, *The State of the Prisons*, (Everyman's Library, London: Dent, 1929), p. xi.

[104]   Howard, *The State*, (1st edn.), pp. 147-452.

[105]   James Neild, *State of the Prisons in England etc.* (London: Nichols, 1812), passim. Another collector of information between 1802 and 1812 was Dr Lettsom (1744-1815). His reports came out piecemeal in *The Gentleman's Magazine* and have been collected into four volumes held in the Wellcome Historical Collection. Their content does not differ greatly from that of Neild's book.

The old county gaol, Gloucester, with its replacement built in 1791.

of correction or bridewells, 23 county gaols, 15 combined county gaols and bridewells, 6 county bridewells, 27 combined town gaols and bridewells, and 7 with miscellaneous titles, including the apparently oxymoronic "Liberty Gaols" at Ripon (owned by the Archbishop of York) and at St Albans (owned by the Marquis of Salisbury).[106] In addition to the above he visited 13 provincial debtor prisons, and another 13 prisons for felons and debtors in London.

Howard found that his 1774 Bill had borne early fruit – most of the county gaols and major London prisons for felons employed a salaried surgeon although it has to be admitted that some were reluctant to expose themselves to risk. At Worcester county gaol: 'Mr *Hallward* the Surgeon caught the Gaol-Fever some years ago, and has ever since been fearful of going down into the dungeon: when any Felon is sick there, he orders him to be brought out'. Dr Johnstone, a physician 'whose humanity had led him to attend the prison' had been 'carried off' by gaol fever.[107] Mr Rule, surgeon at the "High Gaol" at Exeter told Howard 'that he was by contract excused from attending in the Dungeons any Prisoner that should have the Gaol-Fever'.[108] Keenly interested in ventilation, Howard was pleased to find that Worcester county gaol possessed:

> a Hand Ventilator for airing the Men-felons dungeon, which is twenty-six steps under ground ... the felons work on the Ventilator cheerfully about quarter of an hour before they go down, and as long when they come up; for it freshens and cools the air amazingly; we could hardly keep our candle burning below when it was working.[109]

There were considerable variations in both physical conditions and prisoners' health, both of which were poor on occasion. Nevertheless, in expressing his conclusions Howard allowed himself the liberty of exaggeration. The statements: 'my attention was principally fixed by the *gaol-fever*, and the *small-pox* which I saw prevailing to the destruction of multitudes'; and: 'Some are seen pining under diseases, "*sick and in prison*"; expiring on the floors of pestilential fevers, and the confluent small-pox', lack little in dramatic force.[110] In fact these words applied to few of the prisons he visited. At the Savoy prison for soldiers he saw 'many sick and dying ... of the Gaol

---

[106] A Liberty was of course an administrative entity: either a district within a county but having freedom from the jurisdiction of the sheriff; or a district extending beyond city boundaries but subject to municipal authority.

[107] Howard, *The State*, 1st edn., p. 322.

[108] Ibid., p. 372. Howard reported several other instances of prison staff (including surgeons) dying from gaol fever.

[109] Ibid., p. 322.

[110] Howard, *The State*. (1st edn.), pp. 2-3.

Distemper'[111] and sick prisoners lay on the floor at a few others, such as Southwark county gaol, and St George's Fields and Clerkenwell bridewells.[112] At the last of these, prisoners complained that their feet were sore and were, according to the Turnkey, 'quite black'. This discolouration could conceivably have been due to gangrene but was probably ingrained dirt. Only at the Savoy, Monmouth, Marlborough, Gloucester and Launceston did Howard actually see cases of gaol fever.[113] At a number of other prisons evidence of outbreaks of gaol fever and smallpox was hearsay, usually relating to small numbers.[114] These instances were culled from total of 546 prison visits: in fewer than 1% of his visits did he actually witness anything approaching *'gaol-fever* and *small-pox* prevailing to the destruction of multitudes', otherwise the evidence of serious outbreaks of disease is mostly from the past and is anecdotal – garnered from witnesses who knew what Howard was looking for and were anxious to demonstrate the efficiency of the current regime as opposed to that which had operated in the past. It is hard to escape the conclusion that Howard, whom we cannot blame for making his case for prison reform as powerful as possible, indulged in a certain amount of embellishment in the introduction to his book – relying on the fact that few readers would attempt a close analysis of his findings.[115] When he started his surveys in the mid-1770s prisons were subject to epidemics, particularly of typhus, brought in from the community by new committals, but these episodes were not as frequent as might have been expected. He admits as much in one of his later reports: 'In 1782 I did not find a single person labouring under [gaol-fever] in the whole kingdom'.[116]

By the time of Neild's report in 1812, conditions were still bad in some smaller prisons, their only saving grace being that generally the worst held few, if any, prisoners. Carlisle city and county gaol, with neither infirmary nor bath, was typical of these: 'this Prison is in a very ruinous, dilapidated

---

[111] Prisoners of war often fared even worse. For mortality among Spanish prisoners at Winchester in 1780 see John Coakley Lettsom, *Memoirs of John Fothergill M.D.* (London: Dilly, 1780), p. 152. Mortality amongst French and Americans at Dartmoor 1809-1811 was truly appalling. Justin Atholl, *Prison on the Moor: The Story of Dartmoor Prison* (London: Long, 1953), pp. 14-78. On the other hand statistics provided by Howard for American, French, Spanish and Dutch prisoners 1777-1782 suggest that the mortality amongst these men was no higher than would have been expected in any English prison at that time. Howard, *The State*, pp. 142-146. Howard's later visits to the Savoy in 1779, 1782 and 1783 showed a much healthier state of affairs. Ibid., p. 178.

[112] Howard, *The State* (1st edn.), pp. 192, 233, 236 & 186-187.

[113] Ibid., pp. 192, 340, 365, 344 & 383.

[114] Ibid., pp. 217, 219, 226, 244, 267, 270, 277, 293, 314, 316, 354 & 364.

[115] The impression of relatively healthy prisons is borne out by figures relating to Lancaster castle gaol collected by Margaret DeLacy. Apart from 1715, the year of the Jacobite rebellion, when the prison contained many wounded rebels, the average number of deaths among prisoners in the gaol between 1690 and 1755 was 2.36 per annum and only 1.88 between 1756 and 1820. In only two years: 1728 and 1729 were there more than ten deaths. DeLacy, p. 29.

[116] Howard, *An Account of the Principal Lazarettos*, pp. 231-232.

condition';[117] and at Hereford city gaol:

> there is likewise one room, justifiably denominated *The Black-Hole*, which if
> not impenetrably dark, has no light nor ventilation, save what is faintly admitted
> through a small aperture in the door. It is supplied with a barrack bedstead and
> loose straw; and in this wretched sink-hole was found a poor deranged Man, in
> the most filthy and pitiable state that it is possible to conceive.[118]

Peterborough bridewell was described as a 'wretched place ... The whole
Bridewell must be more unhealthy, and is not much cleaner, than a pig-sty';
Plymouth town gaol was perhaps ever worse: 'The whole prison is dirty in
the extreme: the lowermost cells were filthy beyond conception, with urine
and excrement'; at Taunton county bridewell there was 'one Woman, sick,
yet lying on straw upon the floor. Those Prisoners who have beds pay one
shilling per week'; and at Warrington town bridewell, prisoners 'are never
permitted to come out of their wretched and offensive cells except when
the Town Constable thinks proper and finds it convenient to attend them'.[119]
Clearly some small, poorly administered prisons, with at best minimal
medical supervision, continued to be unsatisfactory.

Such terrible conditions were relatively unusual and in many instances
praise was bestowed. Singled out was the surgeon at Lancaster county gaol:
'Mr Baxendale, the humane Surgeon, is frequent in his visits, and particularly
attentive to the sick. He makes a regular entry of the state of his patients, in a
book kept for that useful purpose'.[120] Paul's achievements in Gloucestershire
were noted; of Littledean house of correction: 'The whole building is clean
and well-ventilated, and the same excellent Rules and Regulations are here
established and observed, as in all the other Gaols of this exemplary County
of *Gloucester*'.[121]

Similar statements could not possibly have been made with regard to
what were then among the largest prisons in the land – the London debtor
prisons. In these, health care provision, of which detailed accounts are given
in parliamentary enquiries held in 1814 and 1818,[122] was very much a hit-
or-miss affair. At King's Bench (with about 440 confined and 220 'within

---

[117] Neild, p. 111. This prison held 13-28 debtors and 5-16 felons but a new building was under construction.
Mr Blaincre the surgeon was paid 'two guineas for making his Report, and paid for medicines'.

[118] Ibid, p. 269.

[119] Ibid., p. 477, p. 479, p. 555 and p. 571.

[120] Ibid., p. 329. Mr Baxendale received £84 and medicines were provided by the county. By provincial standards, this was a large prison with (three visits) 74-116 debtors, 58-97 felons etc. and 0-5 'lunaticks'.

[121] Ibid., p. 151.

[122] *Report from the Committee on the King's Bench, Fleet and Marshalsea Prisons*, PP, 1814-15, IV, 533;
*Report from the Commissioners appointed to inquire into the state, conduct, and management of the
Prisons and Gaols of The Fleet etc.*, PP, 1819, XI, 325.

the rules'[123]) health care for the poor was left to any medical man who, coincidentally, happened to be a prisoner. Thus Mr Gilbert Burnett, surgeon, confined four or five months, provided care *gratis*, and had even 'given them money to pay for their medicines ... sometimes the chymist [sic] has sent the money back again, as I sent him so many prescriptions'.[124] He claimed to have seen to twenty or thirty patients per day; one of his current patients was quite seriously ill: 'an inflammation of the lungs and a pleurisy, but now it assumes the appearance more of a typhus fever'. The prison was clean at the moment, very offensive piles of dirt having been taken away (the cart 'pulled by a white horse and a chestnut horse' – Mr Burnett had an artist's eye for detail) about a month previously. But parts of the prison were still very offensive due to 'persons in the habit of throwing slops out of their windows' (Mr Burnett said 'I have been ducked twice myself') and he feared the risk of typhus if the prison were not kept clean.[125]

A similar situation applied at Fleet (18 March 1814: 209 confined and 52 within the rules) where, fortuitously, an apothecary, Edward Williams, was an inmate. He was able to provide some sort of care *gratis* but his eleemosynary instincts had perforce been curtailed: 'I have a family of eight children myself'.[126] He was unhappy about the 'state of morality' in the prison, citing a case of miscarriage he had been called to see where the patient was in bed with her husband, another couple in another bed, and a man in a third bed; all in the same 'common-sized room' although 'they went out when I went to attend to her'.[127] In 1818, no medical man had been careless enough in his financial affairs to become an inmate of Fleet prison. The deputy warden stated that he paid for medical care from 'his own private pocket'.[128]

Neild summed up the general situation as regards debtors:

> ... poor Debtors are often the most pitiable objects in our British Gaols. The same complaint, want of food, and of work whereby to earn it, still exists in many of our Gaols, whilst in others, to the honour of Philanthropy, a Generous Allowance is afforded. In some Prisons within or near the Metropolis, as well as in other far remote, the *Debtors* have no *Bread*, although it is granted to the *Highwayman*, the *Housebreaker*, and the *Murderer* ...[129]

---

[123] 'The Rules' allowed certain prisoners freedom of movement within a specified distance (usually a mile or two) outside the prison walls. This privilege was purchased and allowed the prisoner to conduct business.

[124] *Report*, PP, 1814-15, IV, 533, p. 137.

[125] Ibid., p. 138.

[126] Ibid., p. 163.

[127] Ibid., p. 164. Elsewhere (p. 163) he gives his opinion that 'in young cases of miscarriage, persons are competent to assist themselves'.

[128] Ibid., p. 21.

[129] Neild, p. 599.

PENAL SYSTEMS: TRANSPORTATION AND PRISON HULKS

As has already been described, transportation – an integral part of the British penal system – was halted in the 1770s. An alternative was offered by an Act of 1776 (16 Geo. III cap 43) allowing prisoners to be confined in hulks and to labour on local river and dockyard works. This, after the government had rejected as alternatives both transportation to the Gambia, and 'Mr Eden's fantastical proposal that the surplus convicts should be given to the Mohammedan pirates of Algiers and Tunis in exchange for more honest Christian captives'.[130] Although intended as a temporary expedient, hulks continued to have an important role as holding prisons for those awaiting transportation, and their use did not finally cease until 1857. By this time there were just two hulks still in use, at Woolwich, occupied mostly by prisoners deemed unfit to make the voyage to Australia.[131]

**The prison hulk *York* at Woolwich, prisoners going aboard.
Engraving, 1829.**

A more far-seeing solution to the problem of prisoner disposal was proposed

---

[130] Edward Cadogan, *The Roots of Evil* (London: Murray, 1937), p. 156. Another proposal had been that prisoners should be used as slaves in the herring industry – five to a vessel – so as to be able to undercut the Dutch. Sidney Webb and Beatrice Webb, *English Prisons under Local Government* (London: Longmans, 1922), p. 44.

[131] Charles Campbell, *The Intolerable Hulks: British Shipboard Confinement 1776-1857* (Maryland: Heritage, 1994), pp. 203-204.

in the "Hard Labour" bill of 1779. This advocated building two large national penitentiary prisons (one for 600 males, one for 300 females) to which less serious offenders would be sent, and where the dual objectives of correction (through work) and reformation would be pursued – only the most 'atrocious and daring' offenders would be sent to the hulks. The same bill allowed the hulks to be kept in use for another five years. Although the penitentiary scheme was conceived in 1779 its gestation period was prolonged. Jeremy Bentham's ambitious schemes having aborted,[132] building of the new penitentiary at Millbank did not begin until 1812. Constructed at the vast expense of £458,000 ('It may be doubted whether the Taj at Agra, the Cloth Hall at Ypres or the Cathedral at Chartres had cost anything like this sum'[133]) it opened to the first of its inmates in 1816. Capable of holding 600 males and 400 females as a penitentiary it was never used to full capacity: its population varied between 400 and 700. Although originally intended to serve Middlesex and London, in the event suitable prisoners (those deemed by the sentencing judge most susceptible to reform) originated from all parts of the country and were sent there as an alternative to transportation.

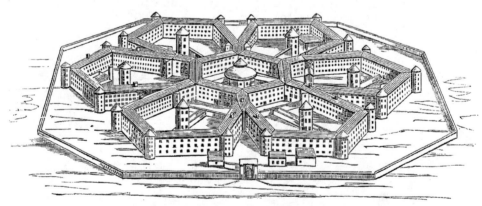

BIRD'S-EYE VIEW OF MILLBANK PRISON.
(Copied from a Model by the Clerk of the Works.)

A bird's eye view of Millbank prison. Engraving.

In the meantime – and well beyond – hulks and transportation continued to play an important role, a bill of 1784 having allowed the removal of prisoners

[132] George Holford, *An Account of the General Penitentiary*, (London: Rivington, 1828), pp. 8-27.
[133] Webb and Webb, p. 49.

to anywhere in the world. As early as 1779 Joseph Banks suggested the newly discovered Botany Bay as a suitable destination for convicts but when the 1784 bill was passed it seemed more probable that prisoners would be heading for Gibraltar or the west coast of Africa – it was not until 1787 that the first batch of 736 convicts set sail for Australia.[134] In all, between then and January 1868 when the last ship sailed, the British penal system disposed of some 165,000 prisoners in this way – an average of nearly 2,000 per year.[135] Smaller numbers were sent to Bermuda (closed 1863) and Gibraltar (closed 1875).[136] Nonetheless, as shown in figure one, the numbers of prisoners held in the prisons of England and Wales continued to increase.

PENAL SYSTEMS: SEPARATION AND THE PROVISION OF WORK

The reformers' main objectives had been that prisoners should be separated from one-another and should work. Separation aimed to minimise moral contamination; the prisoner 'exposed solely to the good influence of the chaplain and governor, who made their rounds each day, and to the watchful eye of the medical officer who visited the cells somewhat less frequently'[137] would also be encouraged to self-reform through introspection. Employment aimed at providing useful training, stimulating the work ethic and, to some extent, financing the prison. These objectives were usually thwarted – the sheer impracticability of maintaining any sort of separate system meant looser arrangements came into being in most prisons, and provision of profitable work was an ongoing problem. The Webbs describe some early-nineteenth century prisons: 'becoming regular factories dominated by the hum and clatter of their scores of looms in constant work, and earning a profit which defrayed a large proportion of the cost of the prison's maintenance [where] there were busy scenes of cheerful industry'; from which: 'Prisoners were discharged with more money in their possession than they could have saved in the same time by free labour'. A notable example was Preston house of correction where the net cost of each prisoner to the county was reduced to less than 3*d*. daily. The county took 40% of earnings, the taskmaster 10% with the remainder going to the prisoners – part paid at once and part on discharge.[138] The good earners were treated tolerantly: 'The discipline, lax generally, was very lax indeed in the case of lucrative felons'.[139] This

---

[134] Hughes, pp. 57, 64-65 & 70-72.

[135] Ibid., p. 143.

[136] McConville, pp. 393-396.

[137] Peter Dickens, Sean McConville and Leslie Fairweather (eds.), *Penal Policy and Prison Architecture*, (Chichester: Barry Rose, 1978), p. 43.

[138] Webb and Webb, pp. 83-85.

[139] Clay, p. 105.

happy scenario of contented and industrious prisoners earning good money (which in any event was very unusual) did not attract universal approval, and the comment by Baron Western in 1821 that 'our gaols and Houses of Correction, are generally considered by offenders of every class as a sure and comfortable asylum whenever their better fortunes forsake them, a sort of refuge of the unfortunate of their profession', was a not untypical reaction.[140] Eventually, the practice of productive labour was largely abandoned in favour of the (usually) unproductive treadwheel.

Treadwheels of various descriptions had been in use as lifting gear in Europe for centuries[141] but, until the 1820s in only one English prison: at Bury St. Edmunds, used since about 1810, grinding barley meal for pigs.[142] This was the traditional type with prisoners pedalling inside the wheel, but in 1818 William Cubitt, a civil engineer from Ipswich, patented a much more efficient model with steps on the outside.[143] Cubitt's machine was intended to grind corn and was seen as a commercial proposition whereby prisoners' labour would be used as an alternative to water or wind power. Other regimented methods of prison labour such as the capstan, the hand-crank (invented in 1846, particularly useful for the enforcement of a completely separate system since the device could either be contained completely within the prisoner's cell or the regulatory machinery could be placed just outside), breaking stones, or picking oakum were used, but the tread-wheel proved most popular by far with the authorities. Some indication of the numbers employed in various ways can be gained from figures given for Exeter county house of correction where, on 22 July 1840, there were 152 males and 33 females (85 felons, 49 misdemeanours, 22 soldiers sent by court-martial and 29 vagrants). Of the men, 93 were on the tread-wheel, 6 cookery, 6 cleaning, 5 picking oakum, 5 tailoring, 4 being treated for itch, 6 in the infirmary, 17 at school and 12 in solitary cells. As well as the 10 being treated for itch or in the infirmary, 3 were unable to work on the wheel because of rupture and 2 because of lameness. [144] In most prisons the use of the treadwheel was on a relatively small scale, with machines taking from ten to thirty prisoners, but at Coldbath-fields in 1831 there were thirty-six treadwheels, each capable of holding eleven prisoners.[145] Initial good intentions concerning productive activity gradually faded and although as prison inspectors' reports make clear, it was still used wherever possible for grinding corn or occasionally for pumping water, eventually in most prisons its function became largely punitive. In such

---

[140] Webb and Webb, p. 87.

[141] A fourteenth century example may be seen by anyone willing to climb to the base of the spire at Salisbury cathedral.

[142] Neild, p 88.

[143] Evans, *The Fabrication*, pp. 295-296.

[144] *Sixth Report of Inspector, Southern and Western District*, PP, 1841 Sess. 2, V, 177, p. 147.

[145] *Second Report of Inspector, Home District*, PP, 1837 (89) XXXII, p. 76. In addition to the treadwheel they worked at picking oakum or coir, painting or washing, and general odd jobs.

instances, the resistance could be increased by the warder tightening a screw – hence the origin (reputedly) of the slang term.

PRISONERS WORKING AT THE TREAD-WHEEL, AND OTHERS EXERCISING, IN THE 3RD YARD OF THE VAGRANTS'
PRISON, COLDBATH FIELDS.
(From a Photograph by Herbert Watkins, 179, Regent Street.)

Prisoners on the treadmill at Coldbath-fields house of correction. Others exercise. Engraving, Mayhew, *Prisons of London*, 1860.

The significance of the treadwheel in relation to the activities of prison medical staff in such areas as injuries, discipline, diet, and malingering, will become clear in later chapters but as regards its value in reforming prisoners, the last word can safely be left to George Holford:[146] 'The Treadmill is a useful engine of punishment, but it is no instrument of reform, and it would be a strange conceit to imagine that a change would be worked in the heart of any man by exercising his legs and feet'.[147]

PENAL SYSTEMS:
A RENEWED ENTHUSIASM FOR SILENCE AND SEPARATION

Although circumstances (particularly overcrowding) in the early-nineteenth century had necessitated a shift away from the strict enforcement of separation, a deep-seated belief in its reformative potential never entirely vanished and the principle re-surfaced with the 1835 Prisons Act, allowing the introduction of a much tighter system of separation than seen before.

---

[146] George Holford (1767-1839), an M.P. from 1803 to 1826, was keenly interested in prison management and reform and was a key member of the management committee of Millbank Penitentiary for many years.

[147] Holford, *An Account*, p xli.

In reality, the physical lay-out of most existing prisons and the numbers of prisoners they contained precluded use of the separate system. A second-best alternative was the silent system, the aim of which was to prevent communication thus providing the benefits of separation without the expense of rebuilding or converting older prisons. As prison inspector William J. Williams noted: 'The affinity between this discipline and that of monastic institutions has been remarked, and relied on as an argument in its behalf'. Williams did not accept the validity of this argument, seeing a world of difference between silence voluntarily accepted and silence imposed.[148] Introduced at Coldbath-fields (then the largest prison in England with 417 cells and at times as many as 1245 prisoners[149]) and Westminster houses of correction and elsewhere, it brought both the need for an increase in supervisory staff[150] and a surge in the number of transgressors punished.[151] The newly built Home Office convict prison at Pentonville, opened (despite opposition from Charles Dickens who had been greatly disturbed by a short visit to the Eastern Penitentiary in Philadelphia where the separate system was rigorously enforced[152]) in December 1842, was the temple to the separate system. It held up to 520 young (18-35 years of age) prisoners, mostly first offenders sentenced to transportation and thought physically strong enough to cope with separate confinement (initially of up to eighteen months) and the purification process. Even in the regular chapel sessions prisoners were screened from one another, and masks were worn during exercise.

Early signs were encouraging: in 1844, with average daily occupancy 456, there were only three deaths (0.7%) and there was 'No case of insanity, hallucination or mental disease of any kind' despite the presence of 'hereditary predisposition to insanity among 23 of the prisoners received into the Penitentiary'.[153] This early optimism proved ill-founded, and although prisoners remained physically healthy (the serious national outbreak of cholera in the late 1840s did not affect the prison), in 1850 G. Owen Rees, M.D., visiting physician, wrote: 'On examining the returns relating to mental disease, it will be seen that the past year shows a most unfavourable result'. There had been 'frequent suicidal attempts', three of which were serious, one successful, and, 'with respect to the general mental

[148] *Third Report of Inspector, Northern and Eastern District*, PP, 1837-38, XXXI, 1, p. viii. As already noted, Foucault traces the origin of the control system he describes to that imposed in monastic orders. Foucault, p. 149.

[149] *First Report of the House of Lords Committee Appointed to Inquire into the Present State of the several Gaols etc.*, PP, 1835, XI, 1, Appendix, p. 148.

[150] Such was the need for extra staff that 'prison monitors' were recruited from the inmates. Clay, p. 184.

[151] In the year 1836 there were 5,138 punishments at Coldbath-fields for talking and swearing. Webb and Webb, p. 123.

[152] Philip Collins, *Dickens and Crime* (London: Macmillan, 1962), pp. 117-139.

[153] *Third Report of the Commissioners for the Government of the Pentonville Prison*, PP, 1845, XXV, 53, p. ix.

condition of the prisoners, there is an irritability observable which I never before noticed among men confined at Pentonville, and which has frequently been the source of anxiety to me'.[154] In the following year's report, the gaol's surgeon, C. Lawrence Bradley, disputed the significance of these figures but there is no doubt that the solitary/silent system, imperfectly applied as it was (unless enforced with draconian rigour, the system represented no more than a challenge to the prisoners' ingenuity in inventing other means of communication) resulted in an unacceptably high level of suicides and psychiatric illness. The removal rate at Pentonville for lunacy between the years 1842 and 1855 was 17.3 per 10,000 ('... lest a prolonged detention under the separate system should prove permanently detrimental to them ...')[155] as compared with 5.8 per 10,000 for other prisons. Consequently the system was modified and by 1853 prisoners at Pentonville spent no more than nine months alone in their cells and the use of masks was abandoned.

Another innovation was the opening of a prison for juveniles, in 1838 at Parkhurst, with the hope this would offer a better deterrent than the threat of transportation and result in reform. Originally it had been intended that prisoners should spend four months in strict separate confinement '... to habituate him to control ... to moderate the wilful and turbulent dispositions that are more or less found in all such criminals'. Such a degree of isolation was found unnecessary and later they were brought together for school and exercise – though still forbidden contact.[156] Almost inevitably the reformative hopes at both prisons were not realised.[157]

Confinement in the hulks and transportation continued to be mainstays of the punitive system until 1855 when the passing of the Penal Servitude Act shifted the emphasis to the use of specified terms of confinement with hard labour in British prisons. New large convict prisons for public works were opened at Portland, Portsmouth and Chatham; Brixton house of correction was converted into a prison for women convicts, and derelict buildings at Dartmoor (last used for French and American prisoners-of-war) were re-opened as an invalid prison.

Although separation was only intermittently and imperfectly applied in English prisons throughout this period, the principle was sufficiently strongly established that (with the exception of the hulks, as we shall see later) rarely again were prisoners herded together in conditions of squalor. Clearly this underlying ethos carried important implications for prisoners' health.

---

[154] *Eighth Report of the Commissioners for the Government of the Pentonville Prison*, PP, 1850, XXVIII, 1, p. 23.

[155] *Report of the Directors of Convict Prisons on the Discipline and Management of Pentonville Prison*, PP, 1852, XXIV, 197, p. 14.

[156] *Report of the Directors of Convict Prisons, Parkhurst Prison*, PP, 1852, XXIV, 197, p. 48.

[157] McConville, pp. 208-209.

As regards all these changes in the approach to penality, we may sympathise with an exasperated commentator looking back from the vantage point of 1853, who conveys a flavour of the problems experienced in this era by those interested in reform and penal policy:

> A sustained clamour has long existed as to punishment in general, and every kind of system enforcing it has been canvassed, adopted, and abandoned in turn. The hanging system, the hard-labour, the solitary, the silent, the separate, and the transportation systems, with their various modifications, have all been taken up and thrown down, with such astonishing rapidity as to make one doubt whether there is anything called experience, or whether it is of any use.[158]

---

[158] John T. Burt, 'Results of the System of Separate Confinement as Administered at the Pentonville Prison', *The Quarterly Review*, XCII, (1852-53), 487-506 (p. 487).

3

PRISON SURGEONS: TRAINING, STATUS AND WORKING PRACTICES

The spotlight now falls on those men occupying centre stage in this book – prison surgeons, particularly their education, remuneration, and status in society. Working practices in prisons will be closely scrutinised with an emphasis not on clinical matters (covered in the next chapter) but on the provision of essential adjuncts to care provision such as availability of infirmaries in prisons, nursing, and the surgeons' role in maintaining a healthy environment. It will become clear that prison surgeons, although not inhabiting the social top drawer, were well educated and highly motivated in the pursuit of their duties.

SURGEONS' TRAINING AND STATUS

Medical care in prisons was usually provided by general practitioners working part-time – it was not until large national penitentiaries opened after 1816 that full-time prison medical officers were appointed. Most were designated as surgeons (initially in some instances as apothecaries, in rural areas their function being much the same).

These general practitioner-surgeons were completely distinct from physicians – the latter were university educated with the degree of M.D. A contemporary description (by a surgeon) reads: 'The physician, in those days, was distinguished from the common mass by an imposing exterior – He moved in a measured step and affected a meditating abstraction of countenance, with a pomposity of diction and manner which served to keep the vulgar at a respectable distance'.[159] The more down-to earth surgeons were typically grammar school products with some Latin and a little Greek, receiving most of their medical education by means of an apprenticeship, often with a family member. This was usually followed by pupillage to a hospital surgeon and attendance at privately run courses providing instruction in a variety of medically related subjects.[160] The training of Richard Owen (born 1804) was fairly typical. At the age of six he enrolled at Lancaster Grammar School and then aged sixteen was apprenticed to one of the Lancaster surgeons. His indenture provided that his (widowed) mother would provided 'meat, drink, washing and lodging, and also decent and suitable cloathes [sic] and wearing apparel' and his master to teach him 'the arts, businesses, professions and mysteries of a surgeon, apothecary and man midwife, with every circumstance relating thereto.' After his apprenticeship he enrolled first at Edinburgh University and then at St Bartholomew's Hospital (London), passing his M.R.C.S. in 1826. Fortuitously, one of his Lancaster teachers was surgeon to the county gaol where the fact that all prisoners who died were subjected to post-mortem examination (prior to an inquest) gave him the opportunity to develop an interest in anatomy. This led on to the study of (and a career in) comparative anatomy and it was he who, in 1842, coined the neologism "dinosaur" (dinos – fearfully great; sauros – lizard).[161]

The 1815 Apothecaries Act introduced a degree of uniformity into the training requiring five-year apprenticeships, attendance at courses of lectures (in anatomy, physiology, theory and practice of medicine, *materia medica*, and chemistry), six months' attendance at a hospital or dispensary, and then the passing of the (oral) examination for licentiate of the Society of Apothecaries.[162] In addition to the L.S.A. it was usual to obtain the diploma

---

[159] Mary E. Fissell, *Patients, Power, and the Poor in Eighteenth-Century Bristol*, (Cambridge: Cambridge University Press, 1991), p. 62.

[160] Irvine Loudon, *Medical Care and the General Practitioner 1750-1850*, (Oxford: Clarendon, 1986), pp. 29-35.

[161] Richard Owen, *The Life of Richard Owen* (2 volumes), (London: Murray, 1894), passim.

[162] Loudon, p. 167. The oral examinations took from one and a half to one and three quarter hours and were generally thought to be fair and comprehensive. S.W.F. Holloway, 'The Apothecaries' Act, 1815: A Reinterpretation', *Medical History* 10 (1966), p. 233.

RIDING HIS HOBBY.

Sir Richard Owen riding his hobby.
Cartoon by F. Waddy in *Once a Week*, 1873.

of member of the Royal College of Surgeons (M.R.C.S.).[163] Clearly, in a
system relying heavily on apprenticeship, the quality of training depended
largely on that part of the learning process. Given a tutor who took his
responsibilities seriously, the average surgeon, already well educated in a
general sense, acquired a good grasp of such medical knowledge as was
available in this period.[164] Despite the designation surgeon, most carried out
few operations beyond such emergency procedures as setting broken limbs,
opening abscesses, or pulling teeth: the basis of their work was general
practice – which usually included midwifery. The more ambitious embarked
on further training, obtained a hospital post with the opportunity to carry
out the full range of surgical procedures then undertaken, and concentrated
on the practice of surgery.[165]

For their income surgeons relied on fees charged for visits (3s.–5s. after
about 1750[166]) and for the medications they prescribed, made up – and sold
– to the patient.[167] In the second half of the eighteenth century the average
rural surgeon/apothecary could expect to earn about £400 per annum in
mid-career, but from 1815 onwards an over-supply of practitioners resulted
in lower earnings – perhaps £150-250 in the country and £300-500 in a
town.[168] Although some city surgeon/apothecaries became wealthy (Thomas
Baynton of Bristol who died in 1820, made £3,000 per annum and left
£33,000[169]) a Lincolnshire practitioner complained that, after thirty years
of toil: 'I will not maintain myself, wife and six sons and daughters as
gentlemen and ladies'.[170] Despite this statement it seems that most surgeons
maintained comfortable middle-class status with servants, a horse and
possibly a carriage, and enjoyed a life-style similar (in a relative sense)

---

[163] Loudon, pp. 225-6. The M.R.C.S. was not a legal requirement but by convention was necessary. Holloway,
      pp. 224, 235.

[164] For more information see Joan Lane, 'The Role of Apprenticeship in Eighteenth Century Medical
      Education in England', in *William Hunter and the Eighteenth Century Medical World*, (Cambridge:
      Cambridge University Press, 1985) ed. by W.F. Bynum and Roy Porter, pp. 57-103.

[165] For an example see: V. Mary Crosse, *A Surgeon in the Early Nineteenth Century: The Life and Times of
      John Green Crosse* (Edinburgh: Livingstone, 1968), passim. Most better known hospital surgeons had
      obtained an M.D. as their first qualification.

[166] Loudon, pp. 66-68.

[167] This was not necessarily true in London where prescriptions would normally be made up by an apoth-
      ecary or a druggist.

[168] Anne Digby, *Making a medical living: Doctors and patients in the English market for medicine, 1720-
      1911* (Cambridge University Press, 1994), pp. 136-137. By the 1840s overproduction had led to levels of
      medical density of 10.7 per 10,000 inhabitants and 'competition from druggists, chemists, sectarians and
      other irregulars was fierce'. Toby Gelford, 'The History of the Medical Profession' in *Companion History
      of the Encyclopaedia of Medicine, Vol. 2*, ed. by W.F. Bynum and Roy Porter (London: Routledge, 1993),
      p. 1134.

[169] Loudon, p. 74.

[170] Digby, *Making*, p. 136.

to that of the modern general practitioner.[171] However, they ranked low in the social scale: 'naval surgeons were warrant, and not commissioned officers',[172] and had even been defined – by law – as "inferior tradesmen". This was the result of a 1757 judgement in the King's Bench Division. An Act of William and Mary (c. 23, s. 10) had forbidden trespass by hunting on the part of 'inferior tradesmen, apprentices and other dissolute persons'. The defendant in the case in question, a surgeon, was fined 1*s*. with 40*s*. costs for transgressing this law but went to appeal, where the fine was confirmed (by a 2-1 majority) since a surgeon, having no university education, fell into the inferior tradesman category. The presiding judge said he regretted having to give this decision for:

> In my own private opinion a surgeon is the fittest person in the world to be in the field with gentlemen a'hunting, for I remember the master of a pack of hounds had his neck dislocated by a fall from his horse when out a'hunting, and if a surgeon had not been near him when the accident happened, who pulled his neck right, the gentleman would certainly have lost his life.[173]

Their status was significantly below that of a clergyman and is astutely summed up in *Middlemarch* (set in the early 1830s), when the formidable Lady Chettam contrasts the newly arrived Lydgate with his predecessor Hick:

> Mr Brooke says he is one of the Lydgates of Northumberland, really well connected. One does not expect it in a practitioner of that kind. For my own part, I like a medical man more on a footing with the servants; they are often all the cleverer. I assure you I found poor Hick's judgement unfailing; I never knew him wrong. He was coarse and butcher-like, but he knew my constitution.[174]

REMUNERATION OF PRISON SURGEONS

As already mentioned, before the period of reform medical care in prisons was provided on an *ad hoc* basis, and some early records of payment exist. In 1631 the London Bridewell made provision for 'A Surgeon to view the bodies of such as are brought in diseased or lame within the house and

---

[171] Loudon, pp. 100-107. For an example of a surgeon living beyond his means see George Eliot, *Middlemarch*, (London: Penguin, 1985), passim, and particularly pp. 633-635 and pp. 892-893. Lydgate – or rather Rosamond – over-spent; his: 'five hundred [pounds] chiefly in unpaid entries' was insufficient.

[172] Charles Bateson, *The Convict Ships 1787-1868* (Glasgow: Brown, 1985), p. 54.

[173] Buxton v. Mingay, 3 Wilson 70, Vol. XCV, XXIV, pp. 691-693. This distinction still rankles. British surgeons, despite their unvarying tranquil consciousness of effortless superiority, adhere – as a form of inverse snobbery and causing endless confusion to most of their patients – to the designation mister.

[174] Eliot, *Middlemarch*, pp. 117-118.

to cure such as be suddenly hurt who receiveth yearly xl.s.'.[175] The City of London records note: 'In 1674 a Dr. Hodges was paid ten pounds: "to inform himself of the gravity of the distemper in Wood Street compter",[176] and approval was granted for settlement of an apothecary's bills for certain medicines used in treating the disease'. The city aldermen also paid £10 'for his care of the prisoners in the compter'.[177] Later, in 1692, in response to an outbreak of gaol fever, a surgeon from St. Bartholomew's hospital assisted by an apothecary, was appointed to attend Newgate.[178] At Stafford county gaol in 1728 a surgeon was paid £2 for bleeding and purging transports before they were conveyed to Liverpool. Subsequent gaol accounts feature regular payments, each item authorised by the justices, for medical care throughout the period 1729 to 1778 after which (doubtless a result of Howard's 1774 bill) the surgeon received a salary.[179]

Other early examples of payment come from Norwich castle where the treasurers' accounts read: 'Also paid Mr John Harmer the Surgeon his bill for the cure of a poor prisoner in the Castle on the first of May 1734 £1.15s.'; and: 'Mr Thomas Ekins Surgeon, his Bill for the Cure of Mary Stephenson a poor prisoner by order £3.3s.'.[180] The apothecary's bill for Bedford county gaol in 1724 included: 'February 10th – Bleeding Jane Smith 1/- [1 shilling]; March 16th – Bleeding Jane Smith 1/-'. Jane Smith was a debtor.[181] George Weale, who had succeeded to the post of surgeon at Worcester gaol in 1755 was paid to provide 'physick' and averaged fees over a twenty-year period of £5 per quarter, suggesting that he visited the prison on a fairly regular basis.[182] Before the new county gaol was built at Gloucester, medical care had been provided by local apothecaries: until 1785 Messrs Powell and Mills "sent a bill" but following an advertisement in the *Gloucester Journal* of 16 July 1785, Messrs Mills and Pace were given a contract to supply medicines and to visit the sick daily for £30 annually, together with £5 for poor debtors.[183]

As Howard's reports confirm, the system of *ad hoc* provision of medical care changed quite quickly in the 1770s as salaried surgeons were appointed at many prisons – receiving between £5 and £60 depending on the size of

[175]   E.M. Leonard, *The Early History of English Poor Relief* (Cambridge: Cambridge University Press, 1900), pp. 352 & 355.
[176]   Compter: an archaic term for a prison.
[177]   Anthony Babington, *The English Bastille: A History of Newgate Gaol and Prison Conditions in Britain 1188-1902* (London: Macdonald, 1971), pp. 63-64.
[178]   Ibid., p. 64.
[179]   Standley, pp. 30-34.
[180]   *Accounts of the Treasurers for the Prisoners in the Castle, 1734 &1735*, NCRO, MF/RO 581/7 & 581/8.
[181]   Eric Stockdale, *A Study of Bedford Prison 1660-1877* (London: Phillimore, 1997), p. 36.
[182]   Joan Lane, *The Making of the English Patient: A Guide to Sources for the Social History of Medicine* (Stroud: Sutton, 2000), p. 144.
[183]   Whiting, *Prison*, p. 5.

A physician and a surgeon attending a woman patient. The physician stands, feeling the pulse, whilst the surgeon, on his knees, gets on with the more mundane task of resuscitating the apparently moribund patient. Painting by Mathijs Naiveu, late eighteenth century.

A surgeon bleeds a young woman, her friend catches the blood in a bowl. Etching with watercolour, Thomas Rowlandson, 1784.

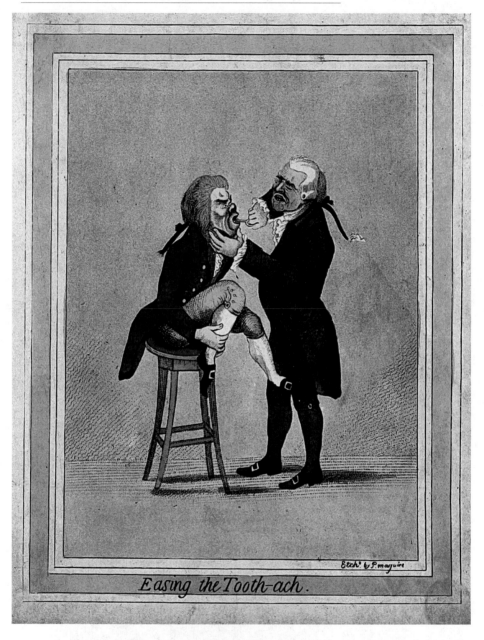

Easing the toothache. Stipple engraving with watercolour.
James Gillray, 1796.

the prison. In most instances the surgeon paid for medication out of this sum. At some county gaols and at most town and borough gaols the old system persisted: when medical care was needed the magistrates authorised payment. By the time of Neild's report in 1812 formal provision had become more widespread and he recorded some remarkably high levels of remuneration. Mr Webb at Clerkenwell (from 48 to 154 inmates) received £300 and Mr Wallett, the apothecary at Bridewell and Bethlem was paid the extraordinarily high sum of £335 (rising later to £400[184]) for the care of prisoners. Wallett was non-resident, did not have to pay for medicines and a surgeon (much less well-remunerated) also attended these two institutions, so the reason for this high level of pay is unclear. However, such a lavish reward was unusual. Although there was a general rise in the early-nineteenth century as prisoner numbers rose, most prison surgeons received modest remuneration: working out at well under £1 per annum per inmate (or probably about 5s. per patient seen). Rises in prison occupancy in the 1820s and 30s resulted in further salary increments. Fairly typical is Gloucester county gaol: £38 (plus £5 for the care of poor debtors) in 1791, £60 in 1817, £100 in 1843 and £180 by 1845.

Some received perks. The surgeon at Bristol city gaol was awarded a gratuity (of £20) in addition to his salary of £63.[185] At Huntingdon county gaol, in addition to a £20 salary there was a fee of 5s. for attending corporal punishments and ½ guinea for itch and venereal cases.[186] At Usk county house of correction the surgeon, in addition to his salary of £80 received £1.1s. per inquest (there were three in the years 1843-1845[187]) and probably this was the norm. At Worcester county gaol the surgeon was allowed one guinea for each midwifery case. The surgeon at Oxford county gaol received the same sum for midwifery, and 'For operations he is paid according to their severity: for one, amputation of the breast, he received two guineas and a half'.[188] The county funded trusses, leeches and bandages.[189]

The system whereby surgeons paid for medicines out of salary gave rise to problems. An entry in the Gloucester county gaol Justices' Journal (15 April 1817) recognises this: 'From the immense number of prisoners which have been lately in the Gaol, and the quantity of Medicines which has been requisite for them, it is my opinion that a considerable sum of money

---

[184] *Report*, PP, 1818, VIII, 297, p. 159.

[185] *Sixth Report of Inspector, Southern and Western District*, PP, 1841 Sess. 2, V, 177, p. 133.

[186] *First Report of Inspector, Northern and Eastern District*, PP, 1836, XXV, 161, p. 34.

[187] *Tenth Report of the Inspector, Southern and Western District*, PP, 1845, XXIV, 565, p. 85.

[188] For a graphic account of the horrors of pre-anaesthetic mastectomy see Kate Chisholm, *Fanny Burney: Her Life 1752-1840* (London: Chatto & Windus, 1998), pp. 214-217.

[189] *Fourth Report of Inspector, Southern and Western District*, PP, 1839, XXII, 215, pp. 179 and 195.

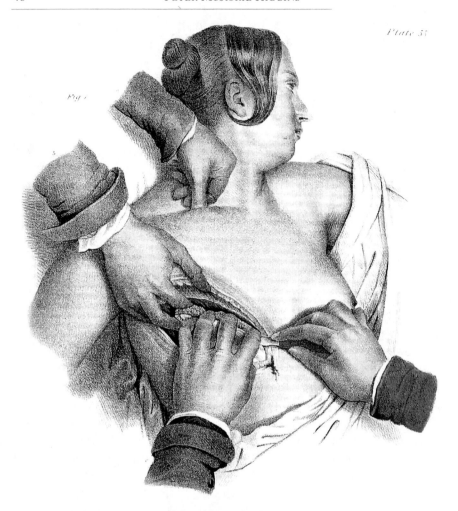

**Amputation of a breast. Illustration in *A Treatise of Operative Surgery*
by Joseph Pancoast, 1846.**

should be allowed to Mr Wilton [the surgeon] in addition to his salary of sixty pounds. [signed] T.J.H. Baker'. Another example was noted at Peterborough city gaol:

> The surgeon's salary is inadequate. He attends and finds the medicines both here and at the House of Correction, for 15 guineas a year. He informs me that during this year (1835) a case of low fever occurred at the House of Correction which lasted between two and three weeks, requiring daily attention and medicines. This single case swallowed up his little remuneration.[190]

[190]   *First Report of Inspector, Southern and Western District*, PP, 1836, XXXV, 269, p. 46.

In 1818 the surgeon at Newgate who received £300 per annum from which he had to pay for medicines, claimed these cost him £50 per quarter; when he had paid £40 to his assistant he was left with only £60 for a year's work. Even this sum, he said, was whittled away by additional costs incurred in making up medicines, sending them, and stationery. [191] He asserted his duties at Newgate and at other prisons (Borough and Gilt Street compters) were quite onerous: 'it has injured my [private] practice a great deal the last two years'.[192] The surgeon at Marshalsea debtors' prison received £50 per annum, plus a fee of 1s. from each person discharged, amounting to about £9 annually. From this £59 he paid 'for everything that belongs to the class of medicines; linen rag, and lint and trusses, and cupping, are paid for extra'.[193] He was not happy with this claiming that his net profit was:

> not … more than £12 counting everything; I am liable to be called up in the night and to find every thing if a woman is taken in labour here, either myself or my assistant is obliged to go; that is a branch of the practice we did not contract for; if children of the prisoners are ill, I should forfeit my reputation if I did not attend them.[194]

The reference to his reputation is significant and provides a clue as to why prison surgeons were motivated to maintain high standards.

An exhaustive analysis of expenditure on medicine and medically prescribed extras (table 3:1) drawn up by the surgeon at Lancaster castle in the 1820s gives some idea of the size of the problem:

Table 3:1 'A Table exhibiting the <u>Average annual Cost</u> of Medicine, Wine, Ale, Groceries, Milk and all other extra allowances for the different Prisons of the County collected from the published reports of the <u>last six Years</u>. [and in the last four columns] Average Annual Cost <u>per Man per Annum</u>'.[195]

Prison	Prisoner Numbers	Medicine	Wine, Ale & Spirits	Groceries	Milk & Mutton	Total	Drugs	Wine, Ale & Spirits	Mutton, Milk & Groceries	All Extras & Drugs
Lancaster	352	£106.16s.8d	£16.2s.8d.	£11.4s.4d.	£20.2s.9d.	£154.6s.7d.	6s0d.	1s.6d.	2s.11d.	10s.6d.
Preston	170	£35.19s.11d.	£32.16s.0d.	£8.17s.6d.	£16.6s.0d.	£93.19s.6d.	4s.2d.	3s.10d.	2s.11d.	11s.0d.
Salford	596	£178..2s.8d.	£76.1s.0d.	£32.9s.0d.	£49.15s.7d.	£336.8s.3d.	5s.11d.	2s.6d.	2s.9d.	11s.3d.
Kirkdale	541	*	*	*	*	£285.2s.7d.	5s.1d.	3s.4d.	2s.1d.	10s.6d.

[191] *Report*, PP, 1818, VIII, 297, pp. 60-61.
[192] Ibid, p. 61.
[193] *Report*, PP, 1814-15, IV, 533, p. 195.
[194] Ibid, p. 195.
[195] LCRO QGR/1/27.

'In the printed reports for Kirkdale, the Extras are noticed under the general head of Medicine, Wine and Salt, for the first four Years: – in the two last the items are particularized. After deducting £75.0s.5d. for Salt as not belonging to the Extras, the average annual cost for the six Years amounts to £285.2s.7d.' The surgeon also adds a note: 'No notice is taken of the annual cost of Milk for Preston, for five years, the average is therefore presumed to correspond with the last year's printed report which amounts to £16.6s.0d.'

On the face of it, the cost of medicines at Lancaster and Salford (about 6s per head annually) exceeded the level of salary surgeons could expect to receive for prisons of that size at that time. The obvious conclusion – that most prison surgeons spent more on medicines than they received in salary – is probably incorrect, the reason being that the Lancashire figures are in effect retail costs. There was a high mark-up on prescriptions[196] so the true cost to a medicine-providing surgeon would have been appreciably less, but still represented a significant proportion of his salary – probably as much as half. This is supported by figures from Stafford in 1793 where the surgeon received £15 per annum with a further £15 paid to the general infirmary for the supply of medicines.[197]

This method of funding medicines was still thought satisfactory in 1816 when it was recommended that a prison surgeon: 'should have sufficient Salary to enable him to include all medicines, without making any Bill or separate charges for the same',[198] but twenty-seven years later attitudes were changing:

> We beg however, to express our opinion that it is unwise to include the cost of medicines in the salary of the surgeon, and we think that the salary is not in any instance so large, considering the duties which he has to perform, but that the expenses of the medicines might reasonably form a separate charge.

In the same report it is noted that the surgeon at Gloucester county gaol was reimbursed for leeches, tea, camomile flowers and poppy flowers.[199] Leeches, costing 4d. each, were also paid for at Worcester, Bristol and Stafford.[200]

In general the level of remuneration seems to have been acceptable but there were exceptions. In 1843 the surgeon at Horsley house of correction, Thomas Stokes, evidently considered his salary insufficient: 'The Chairman [of quarter sessions] said he was sorry to intimate that the surgeon, who had discharged his duties in a very satisfactory manner, had intimated his

---

[196] Mr Box at Newgate, speaking of the time when he charged for medicines, stated: 'it was considered I was to charge a reasonable profit on medicines'. *Report*, PP, 1818, VIII, 297, p. 62.

[197] Standley, p. 37.

[198] *Report from the Committee of Aldermen appointed to visit several Gaols in England*, (London: Nichols, Son and Bentley, 1816), p. 11.

[199] *The Report to the Rt. Hon. Sir James Graham on the Case of Charles Beale*, PP, 1843, XLIII, 375, p. 21 and p. 30.

[200] *Fourth Report of Inspector, Southern and Western Districts*, PP, 1839, XXII, 215, p. 179.

intention of resigning, as he considered his salary [£20] too low by one half'.[201] Presumably no increase was forthcoming because the last entry in the surgeon's journal by Stokes is his quarterly report dated 14 April 1843, after that entries are made by James Henry Wells. There is evidence of real hardship on one occasion. William Vann Hadwen, surgeon to Northleach house of correction from October 1825 to October 1835 had, to judge by the increasing frequency of his absences and deteriorating handwriting, been ill for some months. Cover was provided during these absences and after Hadwen's death by Thomas Cheatle of Burford, some nine miles distant. For a month or two afterwards, before a new surgeon was appointed, Cheatle continued to cover and asked that payment be continued to Hadwen's widow: '... seeing the destitute situation in which [Hadwen's] widow and young family were left' (27 October 1835 & 3 January 1836).

Whatever motivated prison surgeons it was not the lure of financial gain so why did they carry out this work? It has been suggested that an established practitioner might well accept a poorly paid publicly funded post purely as a way of preventing a newcomer gaining a foothold in the district.[202] Also, in an era when bills were often left unpaid for long periods, the security of even a small reliable income from a public post was probably welcome.[203] It may even be that to some extent they were working on a *pro bono publico* basis – emulating the great men they had followed in the wards of voluntary hospitals.[204] These men provided their services *gratis* to patients in the wards knowing that the prestige conferred by holding an honorary post would benefit their private practices. Equally, many prisons were able to avail themselves of the services of a physician *gratis* (see references to Gloucester and Norwich in chapters four, five and six). Perhaps surgeons felt that a public post enhanced their status among the local worthies – all potential private patients – but evidence is lacking so this aspect of their motivation can only remain a matter of speculation.

WORKING PRACTICES

Howard's 1774 bill outlined the duties of prison surgeon's, recommending that they should attend the prison regularly, that they should keep an account of their activities, and that regular reports should be made to the justices. This, and subsequent bills on prison regulation were permissive. Until much later

---

[201] *Wilts and Gloucestershire Standard*, 22 April 1843.

[202] Digby, *Making*, p. 50.

[203] Other public posts would be at the workhouse or, as at King's Lynn borough gaol where the surgeon was also employed at a public dispensary and received £130 for the two positions. *First Report of Inspector, Northern and Eastern Districts*, PP, 1836 (117), XXXV, 161, p. 74.

[204] There were no publicly funded hospitals at this time. A rapid move towards the building of infirmaries as adjuncts to workhouses – but for the use of the general public – began in 1867. Driver, p. 89.

there were no standardised national rules: details were a matter of negotiation between the surgeon and the magistrates who appointed him; even then much was left to the individual. Inspectors, arriving on the scene after 1835, had no executive powers but 'by the act of inspection and by public and private exhortation the inspectorate became a potent instrument for changing the local administration of prisons', although their recommendations were sometimes resisted.[205] In 1843 the prison inspectors, as part of a general report on prison discipline, listed twenty-three rules governing the conduct of medical officers.[206] These detail the surgeon's responsibilities: checking the prison environment; prisoners' diet, cleanliness, clothing, and need for exercise; supervising any punishment; and writing up full details 'in the English language' of every sick patient. Treatment was to be described and 'no medicines shall be issued except by the immediate direction of the medical officer in each particular case'. He must give a full account of any death; and 'no capital operation shall be performed without a previous consultation being held with another medical practitioner, except under very urgent circumstances not admitting of delay'.

Some descriptions of a surgeon's *modus operandi* suggest a rough and ready approach. At Ilchester county gaol Mr Bryer describes his routine:

> I generally go round from ward to ward,[207] and the man who attends me bellows out "Who wants the doctor." If there is any body, they generally make their appearance, and I hear what they have to say, and treat them accordingly. After that I go to the surgery, and put up the medicine, and send it to those whom I think are in want of it.[208]

A more sophisticated variation of this approach was used at Newgate in 1814 where: 'A man ... is chosen by the Surgeon from the best educated of the Prisoners, and employed to go round the Prison, and to examine and report all the Sick, who are immediately removed to the Infirmary', where the surgeon would see them later.[209] It was fortunate that at Newgate 'we have had men who have been brought up to the medical profession for years; he is generally a transport'.[210] If a letter from David Benfield, written (in a less literate manner, it must be admitted, than surgeons usually contrived) from Maryland in 1772 is anything to go by, the fate of a transported medical

---

[205] McConville, p. 170 and pp. 251-254.

[206] *Report relative to the system of Prison Discipline, by the Inspectors of Prisons*, PP, 1843, XXV and XXVI, 1, pp. 23-24.

[207] Ilchester still had an open ward plan for most of its inmates.

[208] *Reports from the Commissioners appointed to inquire into the state of Ilchester Gaol*, PP, 1822, XI, 313, p. 130.

[209] *Report from the Committee on the State of the Gaols of the City of London etc.* PP, 1813-14, IV, 249, p. 8.

[210] Ibid, p. 53.

man could be enviable: '... since I have been in a merika I have had very Great Success in My undertakings I have folloed nothing but physick and Surgeorey ... I have Dun many Good and famus Cures ... this yeare I Shall yearn upwards of a hundred pounds...'.[211]

In 1835 the routine at Newgate varied with the time of year: in the six months of winter the surgeon visited the prison between 12 and 1 o'clock but in summer he called in before breakfast ('being an early Man') and returned home a little after 8 o'clock. His first duty of the day was to see any newly committed prisoner: 'for the express Purpose of ascertaining whether he has the Itch, which is a most infectious Complaint'. There had been 110 cases of Itch in the previous year, these from rather fewer than 2,000 committals.[212]

Such working practices were unusual. In most prisons, those wishing to report sick made their complaint known to the turnkey or the governor who reported to the surgeon at his next visit or, if the case was urgent, sending for him. There are suggestions that, at least occasionally, the governor or the turnkeys "filtered" complaints, disregarding those not considered serious. Criticisms of failures to pass prisoners' complaints on to the surgeon at Knutsford were upheld at an enquiry in 1843,[213] and a rather enigmatic entry at Northleach indicates a similar problem: 'Visited the prison and was informed, no sick, and no complaint, apart from Mr Lord, one of the Magistrates, who informed me by letter, that there were complaints, which I attended to' (16 September 1817).

INFIRMARY FACILITIES

When Howard produced his first report in 1777, infirmary provision was patchy. By 1812 when Neild reported, most of the county gaols and many of the newer bridewells had infirmaries. Some were very good, as at Hereford county gaol: 'Here are four excellent Infirmary-rooms, and the sick appear to be as well attended as in an hospital. The humane Surgeon having a discretionary power to order all things necessary, every page of the Prison book bears ample witness to his great attention'.[214] Dorchester county gaol (an 'excellent prison') had two infirmaries with water closets and washing troughs, a dispensary, warm and cold baths and facilities for convalescent prisoners to take the air on the roof.[215] Ipswich town and borough gaol had:

---

[211] Mark Davies, *Stories of Oxford Castle: From Dungeon to Dunghill*, (Oxford: Towpath Press, 2005), p. 66.

[212] *Second Report from the Select Committee of the House of Lords appointed to Inquire into the Present State of the several Gaols etc.*, PP. 1835, XI, 495, p. 382.

[213] *Report of the Inspector of Prisons for the Northern District in the Inquiry into the Treatment of Prisoners in the House of Correction at Knutsford*, PP, 1843, XLIII, 325, pp. 4-5.

[214] Neild, p. 266.

[215] Ibid., pp. 163-169.

four neat Infirmary Rooms, 19 feet square, with fire-places, sash windows iron grated, water closets etc., and above them is the lead flat of the building, appropriated to the use of convalescents, for the benefits of air and exercise. The Infirmaries have iron-framed and latticed wooden bedsteads, with a mattress to each, two blankets, two sheets, and a coverlet; and the sick are well supplied with suitable food, and wine, if necessary, at the discretion of the surgeon.[216]

Equally praiseworthy were Wakefield, York, Southwark and Newgate, mostly with good bedding, water closets and warm and cold baths.[217] Of Newgate, the redoubtable Mrs Elizabeth Fry commented favourably: 'The women's infirmary is kept very clean, they have nice beds, at least what I think sufficiently so; they are well attended to; they have all necessary medical aid and great attention from the surgeon, as far as I can see; and all the nourishment they require'.[218] By 1836 an infirmary had been built at the new Worcester county gaol where there were 'abundant means of ventilation, water closet, bath room, a room for operations, coroner's room, and every suitable convenience'.[219]

**Bath (approx 4 x 3 x 1.5 metres) at Northleach house of correction.
It was fed by a conduit from an adjacent stream.**

In addition all the better-run prisons had a room set aside as a "foul ward" for patients with the itch, also used at times for other contagious diseases. Whether such provision would be adequate for a serious outbreak of contagious disease

---

[216] Ibid., p. 297.

[217] Ibid., pp. 566, 613, 547 & 423-424.

[218] *Report*, PP, 1818, VIII, 297, p. 43. Mrs Fry first visited Newgate in 1813 and regularly inspected the prison after Christmas 1816. Among her principal aims were provision of work and education for female prisoners.

[219] *First Report of Inspector, Southern and Western District*, PP, 1836, XXXV, 269, p. 81.

was queried by Thomas Chalmers, surgeon at Kirkdale (Liverpool). Showing commendable prescience in his 1831 annual report: 'he begs most respectfully to point out to the Magistrates the inconveniences suffered at present from the want of a separate Building for Patients afflicted with infectious disease and how much these inconveniences would be increased should the Continental Epidemic [Asiatic cholera] visit this country'.[220] Asiatic cholera did indeed visit the country shortly afterwards (see chapter four). A sensible arrangement is described at Preston county house of correction: 'When a case of fever occurs, an order is procured from the magistrates, and the patient is removed to the Fever Hospital, a parochial establishment in Preston. A fixed sum is paid by the county, and the prisoner returns when in a state of convalescence'.[221]

Not all infirmaries were top quality. Unsurprisingly there were teething problems at the newly built Gloucester county gaol, the surgeon writes: 'The Hospital wards not being in condition to receive the sick, they are all kept in their respective apartments' (6 July 1791). Eighteen months later conditions were not perfect: 'Mary Hicks, who I found in Labour, orderd her to the Hospital ward, but was Obliged to remove her to the Convalescent, on acct of the Smoak [sic] in the felons' (21 December 1792). Neild noted that Chelmsford county gaol had male and female infirmaries for felons but both were poorly ventilated and damp.[222] Inspectors were occasionally critical of conditions. At Bath city gaol: 'In the itch-room, however, I found three sleeping under the same bed-clothes, on an inclined plane. Four others in the same place were sleeping separately'; at Warwick county gaol: 'a water closet would be a wholesome addition to the male infirmary'; at Plymouth borough gaol there were no infirmaries 'nor any night stools or water closets for the sick, except the closets in the sleeping or day-rooms'; at Bodmin county gaol: 'A night-stool should be provided, both in the male and female infirmaries, instead of one being borrowed, when it happens to be wanted from the debtor's side, which is the situation at present'; at Aylesbury county gaol the infirmary was dirty and neglected – rarely visited by turnkeys or the governor; and at Stafford county gaol: 'a water-closet would be a valuable addition to the male infirmary [and] the privies of the male infirmary are very offensive, and particularly the lower one, which is unwholesome and damp'.[223]

Many prisons were actually over-provided with facilities – infirmaries were built for a worst-case-scenario of large numbers of sick prisoners and there were not always sufficient numbers of seriously ill patients (see chapter four)

[220] LCRO, QGR/3/37.

[221] *Second Report of Inspector, Northern and Eastern District*, PP, 1837, XXXII, 499, p. 53.

[222] Neild, p. 120.

[223] *Sixth Report of Inspector, Southern and Western District*, 1841 Sess. 2, V, 177, pp. 124, 44, 167, 186, 65, 219 and 516.

to keep them full. Available space might then be utilised by prison governors for other purposes such as for workspace, for vagrants, or the storage of lumber.[224] In other instances, under-utilised infirmaries were occupied by prisoners who were in some way troublesome or difficult to classify.[225]

The surgeon at Lancaster took up some slack by making extensive use of the hospital for cases not strictly medical: 'Beattie has returned to the hospital, he does not like to sleep in the dark, yesterday he told me the cell was cold' (8 December 1848); and: 'I have sent a broken down woman called Jackson into the penitentiary hospital. She has looked most miserable ever since she came into the prison, and to my mind cannot bear up long but we must see what good nursing will do. She has a child at the breast' (13 April 1844). Another instance of hospital usage for compassionate reasons occurred at Norwich:

> J. G. – Age 71; committed 24th August 1831, convicted of bestiality, sentence of death recorded. Health perfectly good, the only reason not sent to the hulks was his old age; he was kept nearly two years alone, but his health and spirits breaking down it was found necessary to class him, and he is placed in the hospital. He passes his time knitting stockings.[226]

Over-provision of beds meant prolonged stays were acceptable: 'Poor Stewart is gone home after nearly two years in our hospital' (4 December 1847, Lancaster).[227] On another occasion a patient received hospital care for purely social reasons: 'Captn Hansbrow [the governor] has transmitted a debtors' petition for the removal of John Bibley (on the grounds of a disease of an infectious kind) to hospital. This man has sore throat, he says from the use of mercury, he is free from sore on the genitals' (30 January 1846, Lancaster). There can be little doubt that the 'disease of an infectious kind' worrying the debtors was syphilis.

From a disciplinary point of view, a downside to this generally good provision of infirmaries was that they were notoriously attractive to prisoners because of the relaxed discipline, the freedom from work and the better quality of food: 'The infirmary of a prison is always that part which is most opposed to, and subversive of, its discipline, and has hitherto rendered the association of prisoners almost inevitable'.[228] When Captain Chesterton was appointed

---

[224] Neild, pp. 492, 272 and 516.

[225] *Second Report of Inspector, Home District*, PP, 1837, XXXII, 1, p. 106; *Ninth Report of Inspector, Northern and Eastern District*, PP, 1844, XXIX, 227, p. 46; Ibid., pp 53-56; and *First Report of Inspector, Home District*, PP, 1836, XXXV, 1, p. 88.

[226] *Fifth Report of Inspector, Northern and Eastern District*, PP, 1840, XXV, 565, p. 92.

[227] This patient first features in the journal on 19 December 1845: 'We have got an ailing man with incontinence of urine from Liverpool, he is gone into hospital, name Stewart'; then on 12 February 1847, 'Stewart wets his bed nearly every night, I think he has a disordered brain'; on 1 March 'Stewart walks badly altogether, he appears to fail but there is no home for him'; and on 21 March, 'Stewart is not so well again, threatened with palsy'.

[228] *First Report of Inspector, Home District*, PP, 1836, XXXV, 1, p. 81.

governor in 1829 at Coldbath-fields with the object of raising the extremely low moral tone, he made an unannounced infirmary inspection one night and 'found the mattresses stuffed with [contraband] merchandise, while the beds were occupied by able-bodied prisoners who paid half-a-crown a night for this extra comfort'.[229] Later, when Chesterton introduced the silent system to Coldbath-fields, conversation in the infirmaries was 'strictly forbidden' but this rule must have been impossible to enforce, particularly since nursing staff were recruited from the prisoners.[230] The impossibility of enforcing the silent system in the infirmary was also noted at Bedford county gaol:

> The most numerous class by far, especially at certain periods of the year, is that of the poacher; and if a prisoner made no other proficiency in acquiring knowledge from his opportunities of association within the prison, he might, at least in theory, become an expert poacher by association in the infirmary alone.[231]

It seems that at the Eastern Penitentiary, Philadelphia, this problem had been overcome by keeping sick prisoners in their cells. 'A few cells have been set apart for the sick ... when the patients are confined to their beds, the cell doors are left open and the infirmary officers go from cell to cell'.[232] A slavish adherence to the separate system led to neglect at Leicester county gaol and house of correction, which had been extensively rebuilt and enlarged in 1846. No infirmary was provided – patients were "nursed" in their cells. The commissioners inquiring into a variety of abuses at the prison included in their conclusions: '[there is] no want of proper care and humanity ... but ... even in cases of pulmonary consumption, except in its last stage, the prisoners have been left under the full depressing influence of separate imprisonment: and this we regard as a serious and lamentable error'.[233]

Despite these occasional abuses by prisoners and administrators alike, it seems clear that prison surgeons were provided with – and used – infirmary facilities which on the whole were good, verging on the lavish. I think it can safely be said that the situation encountered at King's Lynn borough gaol was exceptional:

> The surgeon who has only held the post for five months ... says that he was never made acquainted, until questioned by the Inspector in the presence of the Keeper, of there being an infirmary, or he would most certainly have removed

---

[229] Collins, p. 55.

[230] *Second Report of Inspector, Home District*, PP, 1837, XXXII, 1, p. 81.

[231] Ibid, p. 229.

[232] *Third Report of Inspector, Home District*, PP, 1837-38, XXX, 1, p. 57.

[233] *Report of the Commissioners Appointed to Inquire into the Condition and Treatment of the Prisoners confined in Leicester County Gaol and House of Correction*, PP, 1854, XXXIV, 197, p. x.

there a patient suffering under the most violent diarrhoea.[234]

NURSING CARE

In this pre-Nightingale era, skilled nursing care was exiguous in prisons as it was in the community at large. The set-up reported in 1777 by Howard at Bridewell was most unusual: 'to the women's ward there is a Matron, Sarah Lyon, Salary £60. She takes care of the sick, both men and women, and is allowed a shilling a day for those that are put on the sick diet'.[235] More often, (although still infrequently) payment was made on an *ad hoc* basis to a nurse from outside. At Salisbury county gaol: 'Sometimes a female nurse has been engaged from the town';[236] at Lancaster county gaol: 'A female nurse, a paid servant, attends the sick';[237] at Beccles county house of correction a female prisoner confined 'for a considerable time for want of sureties' and 'labouring under mental irritation to an extent approaching insanity [who] had attempted to set the prison on fire and other outrageous acts [was] placed under the care of a hired nurse, and had improved materially under the careful treatment she received';[238] and at Gloucester city gaol, Sarah Harris underwent prolonged labour ('during which she was constantly attended by my brother and occasionally by myself') and '… she has a dead child. I have directed Mr Turner [the governor] to procure a person to attend upon her, as there is no other female prisoner to do so' (23 October 1825). At Norwich on 20 June 1848 a payment of £3 was authorised to 'Mary Reeve, a nurse attending of Benjamin Elsey, 4 weeks at 15*s*.'.[239] This was a rather special case in that Elsey had suffered an injury on the treadmill (q.v.) and was probably receiving unusually favourable treatment.

Midwives were sometimes employed. Normally the surgeon presided over childbirth but at Bodmin county gaol the inspector reports that there had been 'two lyings-in, both attended by midwifes, as well as by the surgeon';[240] and at Penzance town gaol:[241] 'One woman lay-in here, June 1840. The child lived only ten minutes: the mother is now healthy. She was attended by a

---

[234] *First Report of Inspector, Northern and Eastern District*, PP, 1836, XXXV, 161, p. 73.

[235] Howard, *The State* (1ˢᵗ edn.) pp. 178-179. As will be seen in chapter seven, nurses were employed in the women's infirmary at Millbank penitentiary.

[236] *Second Report of Inspector, Southern and Western District*, PP, 1837, XXXII, 659, p. 4.

[237] *Second Report of Inspector, Northern and Eastern District*, PP, 1837, XXXII, 499, p. 42. Entries in the Lancaster surgeon's journal indicate this was not the norm.

[238] *Ninth Report of Inspector, Northern and Eastern District*, PP, 1844, XXIX, 227, p. 59.

[239] *Visiting Justices Minute Book*, NCRO, MF 880.

[240] *Sixth Report of Inspector Southern and Western District*, PP, 1841 Sess. 2, V, 177, p. 179.

[241] Where there was no surgeon, but when one was needed: 'The keeper has sent once to the Union work-house surgeon for assistance, who came immediately'.

midwife, by permission of the magistrates'.[242] Outside assistance was also obtained for *accouchements* at Ipswich borough gaol where £4 18s.6d. was paid for two deliveries: 'they were treated and attended in a manner quite superior to what they would have been in their own homes'.[243] This statement is quite credible; similar claims will be encountered regularly.

Nursing as practised at this time did not necessitate great skill and could be provided by turnkeys or other inmates. Thus at Bath city gaol: 'one woman in bed with the dropsy, aged 59, untried, who came in unwell, who sleeps in a separate bed and is attended by a female prisoner'.[244] And at Lichfield borough gaol, what could be regarded as an example of "suicide watch": 'On the night preceding my visit all the prisoners were sleeping in separate cells, except one, who was put in the same bed with a debtor, who was melancholy and likely to commit suicide'.[245] Using other prisoners in this way was not unusual: 'I was summoned to see Francis Linford. He appears in a very excited condition and talks very much, principally on the matter of his commitment having an idea that he would be hanged. I ordered two men to sleep in his cell' (21 August 1848, Norwich).

Inmates providing nursing care were usually rewarded for what could be unpleasant or tiring work with extra diet and ale. At Newgate, the helpers in the female infirmaries (prisoners) '... are not exactly paid; they have a trifling allowance from the Court of Aldermen; and they have an allowance of victuals, and a pint of porter and a pint of milk each, per day'[246]; at Clerkenwell: 'The patients, at the discretion of the Surgeon, are supplied with better diet, etc., and a Woman Prisoner attends as Nurse, who is allowed a double dole of bread, with half a pound of meat, and a pint of porter a day';[247] at Gloucester city gaol: 'In the Female division all were healthy, Eliz. Scull is taking a meat dinner daily with a pint of beer which I order'd her some time since on account of her employment as a nurse' (9 March 1825); also at Gloucester city gaol:

> I have ordered the Woman who waits upon her and has a most disagreeable office to be supplied in addition to her ale with a small allowance of meat every second day, perhaps a pound of meat a week would be a fair allowance. There is a second attendant during the night to whom the Matron has given a pint of ale every night (4 September 1833).

---

242 *Sixth Report of Inspector, Southern and Western District*, PP, 1841 Sess. 2, V, 177, p. 193.

243 *First Report of Inspector, Northern and Eastern District*, PP, 1836, XXXV, 161, p. 90.

244 *Sixth Report of Inspector, Southern and Western District*, PP, 1841 Sess. 2, V, 177, p. 125

245 Ibid., p. 210.

246 *Report from the Committee on the State of the Gaols of the City of London etc.* PP, 1813-14, IV, 249, p. 55.

247 Neild, p. 137.

The patient in question (Mary Daunton) had been ill for about three weeks with typhus, (she died after another three weeks) and had developed 'a large slough on her back' (a bedsore). The smell would have been very unpleasant and doubtless in consideration of this, ten days later: 'I have requested the Governor to provide Harriet Hulbert with a pair of Shoes, as at present she has none to her feet, and constant attendance on Daunton is such, that an indulgence of this kind is what she deserves'. At Gloucester county gaol the allowance of the attendant on Comley (who was dying of typhus) was increased from a pint to a quart of ale daily (2 May 1819) and two days later: 'I have given directions for the Attendant to be allowed Tobacco to smoak [sic] considering it in some measure a preventative of infection'. Attitudes to smoking varied. Paul had opined 'Smoking or chewing tobacco is an admirable preservative' but, 'they should be attentive not to swallow their spittle'.[248] In 1832, 68 (male) prisoners at Lancaster castle signed a petition to 'The Magistrates, Governor, and Medical Gentlemen visiting and acting for the Gaol the Castle of Lancaster' begging to be allowed the use of tobacco. The reason they gave was the outbreak of Asiatic cholera in the immediate neighbourhood: 'many persons have died of the Cholera in the Asylum near this Prison'. They promised not to spit on the floor if their request were granted, suggesting that they may have wanted the tobacco to chew rather than to smoke.[249] The extent of the desire for tobacco can be inferred from the 1826 surgeon's report at Kirkdale: 'The great attention which has been paid to prevent the introduction of Tobacco has done away with the cases of Starvation which used frequently to occur from the Prisoners selling their food for it'.[250] A similar comment was made by the inspector after his visit to Norwich city gaol: 'Tobacco smoking seems to occupy the greater proportion of their [the debtors] time. The turnkey states 'I have heard several of them say they would rather go without their meal than a pipe'.[251] The debtors were the most difficult to police: 'There was a strong smell of tobacco both in a privy and in one of the day-rooms. The keeper believes that it comes from the debtors'.[252] The surgeon at Newgate was against smoking in prison although he accepted that some cases of asthma might be helped and that in some 'chronic complaints it appears to assuage their sufferings'.[253]

To return to the subject of nursing – it is clear that sometimes the 'hospital nurse' was given a measure of responsibility well beyond prudence. 'R.W.R'., serving two years imprisonment at Kirkdale, gives a detailed description of

[248] Paul, *Thoughts*, p. 27.

[249] LCRO, QGV 1/5..

[250] LCRO, QGR/3/18.

[251] *Third Report of Inspector, Northern and Eastern District*, PP, 1837-38, XXXI, 1, p. 156.

[252] *Seventh Report of Inspector, Southern and Western District*, PP, 1842, XXI, 193, p. 119.

[253] *First Report of Inspector, Home District*, PP. 1836, XXXV, 1, appendix p. 379.

his duties:

> "I have been in the situation of hospital nurse since last September. The medicines kept in the hospital are ready made up, and I take the directions from the surgeon verbally, for the prisoners in the hospital. I am allowed a pint of ale daily. The officers come to me for medicines, which I suppose are to administer to the prisoners in their wards. They bring no regular direction, but say they want sweating powder, purging powder; pills such as calomel, or what we have ready made up in hospital. When a prisoner is sent into the hospital of a night, complaining of being ill, I sometimes give him a dose of salts or castor-oil, as the case may require, or a sweating powder, and put him to bed. ... There is always another prisoner besides myself, who assists in hospital. I never received any directions from the medical officer to give medicines to the prisoners when sent to hospital, but I followed the practice of the prisoner who was hospital nurse before me".[254]

A similar set-up existed at Knutsford where the "nurse" (by trade a shoemaker) was paid 12*s*. weekly.[255] These examples occurred in the early 1840s and the inspector makes it clear that prisoners, however competent, should not be so heavily involved in the preparation and delivery of medication. The rules drawn up in 1843 were designed to prevent this and other abuses. Nonetheless, there is no indication that those on the receiving end of these unorthodox systems came to any harm.

Nursing posts in the hospital were no sinecure, carrying occupational hazards. At Northleach, Cox had been attending a fellow-prisoner named Spittal suffering from pleurisy and delirium: 'Edmund Cox complains of pain in his shoulders and back which in all probability proceeds from cold, having been much disturbed o'nights in waiting on Spittal' (29 October 1825); and at Gloucester city gaol a second attendant was supplied for Henry Williams (who probably had typhus – he survived) and: 'as [Williams] is sometimes violent, Ale should be allowed to [the attendant]' (28 September 1836). At Lancaster castle: 'Doyle[256] has given the hospital cleaner two black eyes. This Doyle has long been troublesome in hospital' (11 July 1847).

Although this method of providing nursing care worked well in general there were occasional problems. At Lancaster Castle the surgeon sometimes had to search for the right person to carry out these duties: 'I have for some time wanted a better man as nurse in the debtors' hospital. John Ainsworth was appointed to this place on the 5th of this month' (12 December 1843); 'I have one or two ailing debtors that would be better in hospital if we can find a good nurse' 14 January 1846); and, 'There is some difficulty in getting a

---

[254] *Eighth Report of Inspector, Northern and Eastern District*, PP, 1843, XXV and XXVI, 249, p. 11.

[255] Ibid, pp. 133-134.

[256] Previously noted: 'Matthew Doyle for trial was admitted to hospital yesterday, he has a bad head' (30 December 1846).

suitable nurse for the debtors hospital, I think it will be best to take Neald again' (29 July 1847).

Particularly in the smaller prisons, where infirmaries were little used, the lack of skilled nursing care and means of communication caused concern:

> In cases of confluent smallpox the patient frequently dies suddenly in the night and without any apparent cause, and such appears to have been the case in this instance, for the person who was appointed to wait upon him was not aware of his Decease until he awoke this morning (Northleach, 16 January 1835).

And at Littledean: 'I wish to record to the Visiting Magistrates noting the great want of bells in the Hospital especially in the present case where immediate want of aid and assistance might arise during the night' (25 January 1847). Even worse was the situation described by the governor of York city prison:

> If a prisoner were taken ill in the night I should not be able to hear him, nor would any other officer, unless he succeeded in awakening several other prisoners and they all shouted together. About seven years ago a boy in the prison was one morning found dead in his bed, and the jury at the inquest found great fault with the want of the means of communication in the prison; but nothing has been done to remedy the evil.[257]

An example of the problems facing a medical officer trying to ensure that turnkeys carried out their nursing and other duties took place at Gloucester county gaol in 1796. Mr Parker (the surgeon) had previously criticised a turnkey for failing to provide a prisoner with a clean shirt, despite having been told to do so, and then two months later:

> ... think Meek and Poulson [both subsequently died] rather better, but strangely neglected by the Turnkeys, whose business, I presume, it is to be attentive to directions. No one has seen the sick this morning till I visited, altho I left particular orders last night, for them to have rice and oatmeal early in the morning, also fire for other purposes. I acquainted the Govr of the above neglect (26 January 1796).

Three days later Parker was called in late at night, he ordered medicines which were prepared, but the apprentice taking them back found everybody asleep. Since the turnkey on the gate refused to be roused, Parker himself went along and woke another staff member 'who was exceedingly impertinent ... I have reported the shameful conduct of Edward Green and Corbett to the Govr in this as well as in many other instances of neglect to the sick' (29 January 1796). Parker continued to make critical comments regarding

---

257 *Sixteenth Report of Inspector, Northern and Eastern District*, PP, 1851, XXVII, 461, p. 71.

both bedding and turnkeys: 'Jno Sheppard has been purged much during last night, he has been much neglected by the turnkeys, mutton and rice (his dietary) was orderd to be continued last Monday, which he did not get till this day. Mills and Crook have in like manner been neglected' (19 February 1796).

Criticism of turnkeys' nursing skills was also voiced by a coroner's juryman at Bridewell in 1818: 'Two persons ... left, for a period of time ... unattended by any person but the common turnkeys; and certainly it was impossible for a man so situated to give a person in a sick and dying condition the attention that we thought requisite for the unhappy persons who had died'.[258]

As an alternative to prisoners or turnkeys – sometimes as extra help – relatives would be used: 'It is desirable that Mrs Peers should be allowed to remain in the hospital to nurse her husband' (Lancaster, 3 January 1849). At Exeter county prison for debtors: 'An old man, aged 83, died here during the last two years: he was seen by the surgeon. His daughter slept in the prison and nursed him'.[259] A variety of nurses were used in the case of Jones (suffering from typhus – he subsequently died) at Gloucester city gaol. On 30 January 1830, the surgeon 'directed the Governor to get some woman to apply them [12 leeches to the head] and nurse him whilst he is in so much danger and requiring so much attention'. On the following day: 'The man who attends him should be allowed a pint of ale daily. His mother is now with him and with the assistance of the fellow prisoner (Kirk) gives him such nursing as is necessary'.

In general the system worked satisfactorily and occasionally the surgeon lavished praise: 'I beg to observe that I have derived much satisfaction and assistance from the kind and humane attendance of the Keeper and Turnkey who have paid the poor man [a fever patient] every attention' (Littledean, 3 November 1824). Despite the apparently haphazard nature of the provision of nursing care it is clear that surgeons generally managed to ensure that their patients were adequately looked after.

PRISONERS' HYGIENE

Howard had intended that surgeons should take a keen interest in prison hygiene and cleanliness and the journals of Thomas Parker, surgeon at Gloucester county gaol from 1791 to 1799 demonstrate his enthusiasm in this respect. His quarterly report (10 January 1792) reads: 'Think it highly necessary and essential to health that clean sheets be given and the beds

---

[258] *Report*, PP, 1818, VIII, 297, pp. 192-193.
[259] *Sixth Report of Inspector, Southern and Western District*, PP, 1841 Sess. 2, V, 177, p. 165.

changd at least once in six weeks in winter and four in the summer months.
Observe that some beds have not had clean sheets for nine or ten weeks
together – is this not a Great neglect?' Debtors were a particular problem:
'Inspected the Prisoners Persons, find them clean and decent, the Debtors in
the Sheriffs ward[260] excepted, whose Morals seem to be as Corrupt as their
Persons; room, and cells are filthy' (2 December 1792); and on 12 February
1793 the residents of the Sheriffs ward again attracted adverse comment:
'The beds of Partloe and Ellis were in so filthy a condition and made up
with Stinking rags etc. I orderd them to be Burnt'. He liked the prisoners to
be clean. On his second visit: 'Orderd several that were dirty to the Bath' (2
July 1791); and: 'Carter who was swarmg with Lice to have his head shavd
and to be washed in the warm Bath, and to have clean bedg etc.' (19 January
1792). Also:

> Visited Phillips [who had been treated the previous day for cold and a pain in
> the head] who I found rather better, perceiving last night a noisome vapour in
> the cell, which I judged proceeded from his feet, I orderd them to be washd
> twice a day, which has been done, a general heat now appears on the whole
> surface of the skin unaccompanied by a fever (17 May 1795).

This episode led to a complaint against the surgeon: 'I find that one of the
Debtors has reported (by a written paper) that Phillips has a <u>putrid fever,</u>
and that he will be fast away for want of necessaries. This report is an utter
falsehood' (18 May 1795). In fact Phillips recovered uneventfully.

Parker showed a practical eye: 'NB The Iron seats of the water closets rust
very much, should be now and then look too [sic], and the rust taken off, or
much damage will be done to the Prisoners' cloathes [sic]. Query, if a good
coat of paint wd not prevent the rust in great measure?' (19 June 1792).

The emphasis placed on cleanliness varied. Those committed at Newgate
and Giltspur Street prisons were not washed routinely on admission 'except
in very extreme Cases where Vermin and Dirt are excessive'.[261] At Coldbath-
fields: 'it is proper to remark that the surgeon very strongly recommends
(and apparently with good reason) that means should be provided to enable
the whole of the prisoners occasionally to take a bath, at least during the
summer months for the promotion of cleanliness and health'.[262]

The near-universal chorus of praise for personal hygiene was offset by the
lone voice of the surgeon at Warwick county gaol, extolling the protective
value of a good healthy coating of dirt. He was averse to prisoners' feet

---

[260] The Sheriff's ward seems to have been a place of punishment for debtors.

[261] *Second Report from the Select Committee* , PP, 1835, VII, 495, p. 387. (Whereas at Coldbath Fields and
Clerkenwell all prisoners were washed on entry, p. 385)

[262] *Second Report of Inspector, Home District*, PP, 1837, XXXII, 1, p. 81.

being washed 'as he had traced colds and other illnesses to that source'.[263] By the time of the 1852 report, this surgeon had retired and a satisfied inspector commented: 'It is probable that so unusual an opinion will not be held by the present medical officer and that cleanliness will no longer be regarded as at variance with health'.[264] Nonetheless, the fear of washing lingered elsewhere. In 1853 the surgeon at Walsingham house of correction wrote: 'The employment of the bath during the winter months I consider fraught with many evils, and therefore strongly advise its discontinuance from November until March'.[265]

SANITARY CONDITIONS

Although surgeons might hope to improve prisoners' personal hygiene, their control over the prison environment was limited. Neild's 1812 report showed that many prisons had improved since Howard's visits some forty years earlier, but not uncommonly there was a failure to use parts of the prisons as their designers intended, particularly in the smaller prisons where medical and magisterial attendance was infrequent. Prison governors converted exercise yards to gardens, a bathing room housed the keeper's horse, and even worse, in several prisons what was doubtless a lucrative sideline in poultry-breeding was conducted.[266] At Nottingham house of correction a small crumb of comfort was provided for Neild, to whom poultry were obviously *bêtes noires*: '[this] very offensive practice has now been discontinued'.[267]

Prison medical staff also had to contend with water supply and plumbing problems. Answering criticism of the prison's water supply, the surgeon at Marshalsea in 1814 took a robust stance, denying any problems – the water was the same as that supplied by the London Bridge Company to his own house. He considered, doubtless with good reason, that the prevailing 'noisome smell' was no worse than that in 'many of our London houses, having a privy near the kitchen or in the cellar, which on the water rising will scent the whole house'.[268] At Wakefield county house of correction the water supply was unsatisfactory beyond doubt. On 1 June 1839 the surgeon noted: 'The water has latterly been very impure, and disagreeable to the taste and smell, and loaded with animalcula and vegetable matter'. A year later the inspector was able to report that the prison water supply now came from the

[263] *Fourteenth Report of Inspector, Midland and Eastern District*, PP, 1849, XXVI, 167, p. 67.
[264] *Seventeenth Report of Inspector, Southern and Western District*, PP, 1852, XXIV, 1, p. 20.
[265] *Nineteenth Report of Inspector, Northern and Eastern District*, PP, 1856, XXXIII, 385, pp. 52-53.
[266] Neild, pp. 561, 458, 332 and 339-344.
[267] Ibid., p. 458.
[268] *Report*, PP, 1814-15 (152), IV, 249, pp 196.

water-works rather than from the beck as formerly. This change, he thought, had resulted in a tendency to constipation rather than the reverse.[269]

The proximity of Gloucester county gaol to the river Severn regularly led to flooding of the prison[270] and of the well. After an episode in 1794 the surgeon noted that the water in the well was 'not affected in taste, colour or in any other respect whatsoever' (16 April 1794) but there was sufficient concern later that a sample was sent to a Dr Babbington for analysis (11 March 1799). On 24 May 1816: 'Several prisoners very unwell in their Bowells arising from the water of the large well which at this time must imbibe some foul properties from the flood'. In 1817 a builder was called in: 'Mr Collingwood has discovered the well and examined it. He finds the bricks as well as some beavers that were in it thickly coated with mud which has every appearance of having come from the Severn'.[271] It is to be hoped that Mr Collingwood was a better builder than a natural historian – beavers had been extinct in England for several hundred years. Perhaps they were otters – then still quite common. Northleach was another prison built close to running water, in this case only a stream, but enough to cause trouble: 'There has been an irruption of water into the prison which has caused the cells to be very damp. The General health of the Prisoners has certainly not been so good this quarter: perhaps the excessive severity of the weather and the dampness of the cells has been the cause of it' (5 April 1838). At the same time, a clergyman diarist living a few miles away noted: 'Very heavy rain and a rapid thaw led to a more decided flood for some hours that I have ever observed in this valley. The bridges over the brook were nearly submerged, the direct access to the lower part of the village was impeded, and many cottages, gardens and yards were under water'.[272]

Sewage disposal was often unsatisfactory and conditions which might adversely affect the health of prisoners were reported from some smaller prisons. The four court-yards of Cambridge town bridewell were: 'rendered offensive by the sewer in each. Within the cells a tub is made to serve the purpose'; Doncaster town gaol (only one debtor and one felon) was 'most intolerably offensive'; and Northampton town gaol had no infirmary and the 'cells extremely offensive, for want of proper drains'.[273]

[269] *Seventh Report of Inspector, Northern and Eastern District*, PP, 1842, XXI, 1, p. 53, & *Eighth Report of Inspector, Northern and Eastern District*, PP, 1843, XXV and XXVI, 249, p. 152.

[270] Surgeon's journal entries 10 January 1809, 1 March 1814, and 10 January 1815.

[271] *Justices' Journal*, GRO, Gc1/2.

[272] David Verey, *The Diary of a Cotswold Parson: Reverend F.E. Witts 1783-1854* (Gloucester: Alan Sutton, 1978), pp. 146-147.

[273] Neild, p. 14, p. 162 and p. 434. Unusually, Cambridge town bridewell had two surgeons, Mr Tinney for university prisoners and Mr Bond for those from the town. Each 'sent a bill' when his services were needed.

Dr William Babington giving evidence on conditions at Newgate 'could not help remarking of what moment it must be to the cleanliness and health of the prisoners, if it were possible that the privies be furnished with pans, and a proper supply of water'.[274] Plumbing at the ancient prison of Lancaster castle often attracted comments in the surgeon's journal: '[there is] an odious smell in the first backyard – the prisoners were moved to another cell' (24 May 1844); 'The closet or drain going down the steps into the backyard is particularly offensive this morning' (24 June 1848); 'The convenience in B ward going down the steps is most offensive this morning' (4 November 1848); 'I have spoken to Beech about the closet in no. 2 which is most offensive this morning' (16 January 1849); 'The yard is smelling bad again' (6 August 1849); followed by: 'The latrine in the backyard has again become offensive.' (6 September 1849) and a despairing: 'The only remark I have to make this morning is as to the bad smell infesting the Back Yard and it is as bad now I think, tho so much has been done' (15 September 1849). Similar problems were noted at Norwich castle. On 28 December 1824 a magistrate wrote: 'Visited, a dreadful stench upon entering the old castle, the pipe defective';[275] and on 2 June 1843 the surgeon notes: 'I have inspected the Prison, and all the Drains have been carefully cleared out, and the air of the buildings is very much improved as they were in a very bad state'. A very over-crowded Liverpool borough gaol (built for a maximum 339 prisoners but holding 1,047 at the end of 1848) attracted adverse comments from Hepworth Dixon:

> The stench that arises in consequence [of there being no water-closets] is unbearable, especially in the morning. To keep down putrid fevers – indeed to render the corridors at all passable – it is found necessary to burn chloride of lime in them incessantly, as well as in the day rooms and eating rooms.[276]

Clearly Dixon held the still-prevalent belief in the miasmic origin of diseases – as did the prison inspectors – making the matter of foul smells a matter a particular concern. At Warwick county gaol: 'the tread-wheel privies have an offensive smell; and this is the case with some other privies: in a crowded prison, like the present, this is an object to be constantly attended to, with a view to the prevention of disease'. He also suggested that hinged lids should be fitted to the 'pots employed in the sleeping cells'.[277]

---

[274] *Report*, PP, 1818, VIII, 297, p. 206.

[275] NCRO, MF 879.

[276] Hepworth Dixon, *The London Prisons with an account of the More Distinguished Persons who have been confined in them to which is added a description of the Chief Provincial Prisons* (London: Jackson & Wilford, 1850), p. 333.

[277] *Sixth Report of Inspector, Southern and Western District*, PP, 1841 Sess. 2, V, 177, p. 44.

ENVIRONMENTAL AND OTHER PROBLEMS

As well as concerning himself with problems caused by what he saw as inadequate nursing and intermittent flooding, Mr Parker at Gloucester county gaol took a keen interest in the impact of other environmental changes on the prisoners' welfare. In July 1793 there was a warm spell causing him to note that the temperature in the prison was 71.2 (76.8 outside); later in the day the respective readings were 80 and 84.5. He wrote: 'The Prison altogether feels comfortably cool to what it is in the difft Houses I have visited this day' (10 July 1793). He was no doubt pleased to read Sir George Paul's comment (made in the surgeon's journal on the same day) on these measurements: 'A very proper Experiment and Observation. The like should be made in extreme cold'. Six months later he had cause to take Paul at his word:

> I think it necessary to observe that during the last year I have not met with one Prisoner where I have found health to be affected, either by discipline or diet. The Constitution of some, requires a little extra Cloathing [sic], and with regard to warmth, I find that when the Thermometer sink to 34 or 5, fire necessary, it also facilitates their Industrious employ (14 January 1794).

The winter of 1795 was particularly cold: 'Altho several had been absent from Chappel [sic], I could not discover they had any real Complaints (except cold). The Thermometer this morning was 12 degrees under the freezg point' (4 January 1795). The extreme cold persisted and had two effects: there was no supply of water for the inmates[278] and, perhaps in sympathy with their plight: 'His Royal Highness Prince William of Gloucester, I find has sent a ten Pound note for the use of the Prisoners' (27 January 1795). Heavy snow-falls and a thaw produced more problems: 'I found the water had rose [sic] so much in the night, as to surround the entire Building above the height of the first step into the Lodge. I therefore returned and put on my boots to enter the Prison' (12 February 1795). After the subsidence of the flood the opportunity was taken to carry out some spring-cleaning: 'Mrs Pearce very properly with my approbation, has set several of the prisoners to wash and Cleanse the Debtors' division [because] the late severe weather has rendered the whole of the Prison rather dirty' (26 February 1795). Not surprisingly, adverse weather conditions affected health: 'Such sudden and fluctuating changes in the air are severely felt by every human being, and generally productive of many complaints, nor shall I wonder at seeing them here' (1 March 1795). The early part of the winter of 1796 was unusually mild: 'Observe (on going round) the walls and Flagstones of the

---

[278] Later there was another episode of water shortage: 'The Prisoners complain of shortage of water, the engine (the prisoner-driven water-raising pump) being out of order' (25 June 1798). That problem persisted for over two weeks.

prison are exceedingly damp and chilling from the Humidity and uncommon warmth of the atmosphere at this season. The Thermometer up to 56 degrees' (12 January 1796). On the following day he noted that since November 25 1795 the temperature had not once fallen to freezing point and had generally been between 40 and 50, but the following autumn was colder: 'The Thermometer having fallen to 36, it was necessary to allow Fire' (26 October 1796).

Lancaster castle had a hilltop position: 'after Windsor Castle, perhaps the most imposing baronial edifice in England'; but its splendid aspect and the magnificent views it commanded were of little comfort to the prisoners: it was 'a very miserable sort of prison' and 'the buildings are very irregular and utterly unfit for gaol purposes'.[279] Although protected from flooding the summer heat could be oppressive. The surgeon responded to the challenge: 'It is so warm I shall further reduce the clothing on the Crown side and penitentiary. I will speak to the debtors on the same subject' (12 June 1845). On the other hand it was so cold in November 1848 that extra blankets were ordered. And, despite its lofty site: 'It is so damp fires will be put into the stairs of the towers' (4 October 1848).

This concern with the general environment extended to individual prisoners: at Gloucester county gaol. 'Wm Thompson Penitentiary has been accustomed to Hot Climates and is now suffering from the Cold. He shd consequently be placed in the Warmest Cell and be allowed an extra covering to his Bed' (14 October 1817).

DISCHARGE FROM PRISON

Another aspect of prisoner welfare to which surgeons often attended was the need to authorise transport home on discharge. Normally, prisoners were expected to make their own way home but compassion was shown to those unable to make the journey unaided or too ill to leave at all. Typical are entries at Northleach: 'find Thomas Saffron [who had recovered from a 'weak and debilitated state'] strong enough to be moved on the 18th in a Chaise' (17 March 1815); at Gloucester county gaol: 'recommended that [Priscilla Neale] be allowed sufficient money to bear her expenses home on the Coach, as she is at present totally unable to walk such a distance as sixteen miles' (9 September 1811); at Norwich (29 June 1844) regarding Samuel Browne (who had been confined for eighteen months and had, on health grounds, received two meat dinners per week for the last eleven months): 'his health has declined, I have now directed that he should be sent home this day in the Carrier Van as his term has expired'; Charles Lesley

---

[279] Dixon, pp. 345-346.

(who had recovered from smallpox): 'sent to Pulham Union Work House in a covered carriage by my recommendation to the Governor of the Gaol as the weather is very severe' (16 March 1845); and 'Robert Sparks with a Malignant Tumour on his leg, has received a free pardon, and is returned to his home, by the Rail Road, having refused to go to the Norfolk and Norwich Hospital' (11 September 1845). At Lancaster: 'Holdcroft leaves the hospital and prison this morning, he must be conveyed to the train in a fly' (24 August 1848). At Littledean: 'Richard Baldwin is too ill to walk home, requires a conveyance for the purpose of taking him to Dymock [a village about 10 miles from the prison]. His disease arising from organic disease of the heart it would be dangerous not to convey him' (11 March 1849).

At times it was thought better not to discharge sick prisoners, as is shown by an inspector's reference to Devizes house of correction: 'There is a notice board hung up in the infirmary offering to sick prisoners permission to remain after their imprisonment has expired, until their recovery; this was first introduced at Michaelmas 1837'.[280] Two female prisoners who died at Kirkdale house of correction had been 'allowed to remain after their period of imprisonment had expired, owing to their having no Friends to receive them, and being too unwell to be removed without a home to go to'.[281] An even sadder occurrence is recorded at Wakefield where it proved impossible to discharge a prisoner who subsequently died. This was a girl whose parents were reluctant to take her home on conclusion of her sentence – even though the chaplain said 'I firmly believe her quite penitent'. This refusal was despite their being offered 3s. 6d. weekly for ten weeks and 2s. 6d. weekly 'for a considerable time thereafter', together with 10s. for a bed. The surgeon wrote: 'The poor girl had set her heart on going home, that this harsh refusal from her relations had a most depressing effect and undoubtedly accelerated her death, which happened shortly afterwards'.[282] At Lancaster there was an instance of a patient's apparent reluctance to move too far from the sheltered environment of prison. Reid, who had been in and out of hospital for over a year for reasons such as: 'he says he parts with blood ... he is delicate', features on 23 October 1849: 'Reid's time will end tomorrow and he will, if in a fit state, be removed to a lodging near the prison, by his own wish'.

---

[280] *Fourth Report of Inspector, Southern and Western District*, PP, 1839, XXII, 215, p.103.
[281] LCRO, QGR/3/30.
[282] *Tenth Report of Inspector, Northern and Eastern District*, PP, 1845, XXIV, 1, p. 30.

CONCLUSION

In this chapter it has emerged that prison surgeons were, on the whole and by the standards of the time, well-educated and thus capable of provided a good standard of care; and that the facilities provided, although of variable quality, were in general adequate and used in a sensible way. Indeed, prisoners lucky enough to be admitted to infirmaries with the luxuries of water closets, washing troughs, warm and cold baths, bedsteads with mattresses, pillows, blankets, sheets and a coverlet must have wondered just what sort of punishment they were enduring. Inevitably, in a system almost completely lacking central control, conditions varied greatly but the providers of medical care in prisons did their best to ensure that the environment was as healthy as possible and that some sort of nursing care was available. They spared their patients the worst rigours of confinement, and showed concern for their welfare.

4

CLINICAL MEDICINE IN PRISONS

In this chapter I will examine those activities of prison surgeons that were of most direct concern to patients – the management of their complaints. I will give a detailed description of the diseases encountered and the treatments employed. It will become clear that the prime concern of prison medical surgeons was not with the subjection and control of patients but with their health. Clinical details show that the care administered was first class by the standards of the time. *Pace* Porter, the regime <u>did</u> focus on 'preventative and curative medicine'.[283] There is ample evidence that patients appreciated the efforts of prison surgeons.

GAOL FEVER[284]

In 1750 John Pringle wrote on the subject of "Hospital and Jayl Fevers".[285] His use of the plural suggests recognition that there might be more than one disease involved and although typhus probably was the commonest form of gaol fever the word *typhoid* (meaning *typhus-like*) was also in use. It wasn't until 1849 that Sir William Jenner, on the basis of post-mortem

---

[283] Porter, 'Howard's', p. 16.
[284] Also known as camp fever (armies), road fever (beggars) and ship fever – all situations associated with squalor and close proximity.
[285] John Pringle, *Observations on the Nature and Cure of Hospital and Jayl Fevers* (London: Millor and Wilson, 1750).

examinations, differentiated the two diseases and until then the term gaol fever (or putrid fever) was used for both – and probably for other conditions which would now warrant individual diagnoses.[286]

Typhus is one of a group of infections caused by the *Rickettsias*: small micro-organisms occupying a position between viruses and bacteria and spread by the bite or attachment of lice, fleas, ticks or mites. Significantly, lice cannot fly and die quickly once infected so the disease was – and still is – most likely to spread where humans are crowded together in conditions where cleanliness is difficult to maintain. Unsurprisingly, the disease is most virulent in those with lowered resistance. Pringle confidently asserted: 'The cause seems plainly to arise from a corruption of the air, pent up and deprived of its elastic parts by the respiration of a multitude', associated with overcrowding and 'confined' air.[287] It is clear that he adhered to the miasmic theory of disease – a belief held for many centuries that fevers were attributable to 'poisons in the air, exuded from rotting animal and vegetable material, the soil, and standing water'.[288] This belief was widely held well into the second half of the nineteenth century although even in the early-eighteenth century, there were those who supported the rival theory of contagion.[289] Although the reformers were wrong on aetiology, their emphases on cleanliness and separation in prisons were exactly those best calculated to reduce the risk of typhus transmission.

Characteristics described by Pringle were: 'petechial spots, blotches, parotids[290], frequent mortification [gangrene], and its great mortality, [which] characterised a pestilential malignancy'.[291] Death could ensue in fourteen to twenty-eight days with longer lasting cases prone to abscesses in the parotids or axillary glands. Post-mortem examination sometimes showed brain abscesses or intestinal gangrene.[292]

Typhoid fever and the less severe paratyphoid are caused by bacteria of the *Salmonella* group, and this of course accounts for the differing modes of spread – by infected water or food rather than by lice. Its symptoms and signs differ from those of typhus but insufficiently so to allow a confident differential diagnosis without laboratory tests.[293]

---

[286] And also applied to other 'low fevers' particularly those of the 'putrid kind' (associated with suppuration or gangrene).

[287] Pringle, p. 4.

[288] Porter, *The Greatest*, p. 10.

[289] Richard Mead, *A Short Discourse Concerning Pestilential Contagion and the Methods to be Used to Prevent it* (London, 1720), pp. 47-48.

[290] "Parotids" in this context probably means a general enlargement of the lymph nodes in the neck.

[291] Pringle, p. 11.

[292] Ibid., pp. 26 & 30.

[293] L.P.S. Davidson, *The Principles and Practice of Medicine* (Edinburgh: Livingstone, 1954), pp. 22-23.

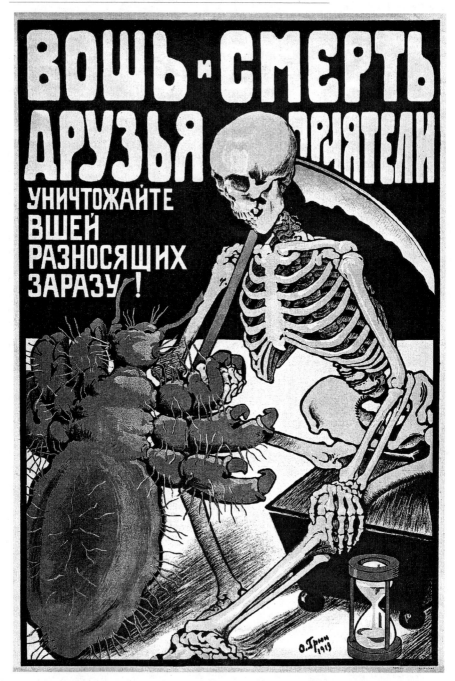

'The louse and death are friends and comrades. Kill all lice carrying
infection!' The typhus-carrying louse is shaking hands with death.
Lithograph, Moscow, 1919.

Paul also wrote on gaol fever, quoting widely from Lind[294]. He concludes: 'The preservation of health in *them* [the prisons] must depend on the possibility of introducing air and separating the prisoners'. Paul estimated the mortality rate at about 20%[295] – a figure probably on the high side of reality; Charles Creighton reported death rates varying from 2% to 50% or more and concludes that a reasonable average would be 10%.[296]

INCIDENCE OF GAOL FEVER

Howard wrote: 'From my own observations in 1773 and 1774, I was fully convinced that many more were destroyed by [gaol fever], than were put to death by all the public executions in the kingdom'. This sounds dramatic, but the only evidence he gives is that the average number of executions in London for the previous twenty-three years was 29-30 so it is likely that he was guessing. [297]

Typhus was not peculiar to prisons, being endemic in Britain throughout the period under study. Outbreaks of 'putrid fever' were quite common during the eighteenth century, becoming less common in the early-nineteenth century but increasing after 1815. Between mid-1837 and the end of 1838 there were 6,011 typhus deaths in London and 18,775 nation wide. It was not until the second half of the nineteenth century that the mortality rate began to fall.[298] Therefore it is not surprising that cases of typhus, with some deaths, cropped up among the prison population. Mostly the outbreaks were isolated with low mortality but early on there were serious episodes at Ilchester and Maidstone (see chapter two). However, lack of information on prison mortality rates in the 1780s makes it difficult to know just how frequently such episodes occurred.

None of the thirteen deaths at Gloucester county gaol between July 1791 and March 1799 were attributed to this cause – and we can safely assume that surgeons of this time were able to recognise typhus/typhoid. That is not to say that Gloucestershire prisons were completely spared. At Gloucester county gaol, Comley (no first name given) had been ill since 25 April 1819 and, in consultation with Dr Shute, the diagnosis was made: 'tho with more that usual affection of the Brain' on 1 May. Despite ale and port wine he died on 10 May – his room was fumigated with saltpetre and oil of vitriol.

[294] Sir G.O. Paul, *Thoughts on the Alarming Progress of the Gaol Fever with Rules for the Treatment of the Disease and Means to Prevent Its Further Communication* (Gloucester: Raikes, 1784); and James Lind, *Essays on Preserving the Health of Seamen, with Considerations of the Gaol Distemper* (London: Wilson & Nicol, 1774).

[295] Paul, *Thoughts*, pp. 14-15.

[296] Creighton, p. 100.

[297] Howard, *The State*, (1st edn.), p. 16-17.

[298] Creighton, pp. 133-212.

Perhaps because of these measures there were no other cases in the prison. At Littledean house of correction there was one case of 'typhoid' in October 1824 and two cases of typhus in January 1825. In 1847 two prisoners were committed who had recently suffered from typhus but no cases followed within the prison.[299] There were no typhus deaths at Littledean and just one (in 1841) at Northleach – the patient in question (Sarah Norris) probably contracted the disease before committal. Gloucester city gaol had a typhus death and several non-fatal cases but these were all isolated instances. A famous victim of gaol fever was Lord George Gordon, whose death in Newgate in 1793 is described in detail by Dr Lettsom.[300]

Remarkably, at Lancaster during the six years for which journals are available there were no outbreaks but the risk was ever-present and there are several examples of precautionary measures: 'Captain Hansbrow consulted me as to the propriety of taking back some bedsteads that had been borrowed for typhus fever cases at Hatton' (20 February 1844), and: 'As I find there have been many deaths from fever at Pilling it will be better to prevent Sandam's wife from visiting her husband at present' (31 October 1846).

Some prisons were more seriously affected. At Preston in 1817 at least twenty prisoners were affected with three deaths and in 1822 there were 67 cases in one week.[301] An outbreak of probable typhus is recorded at Wakefield house of correction:

> A very serious epidemic prevailed in the prison in the early part of 1838. About one-fifth of the number of prisoners were attacked by it in one or other of its forms, 11 died therefrom making the number of deaths in the year 24. The disease prevailed at the same time in the town, but in a much milder form.[302]

At Worcester county gaol (and in the town of Worcester) there was an outbreak of typhus in January-February 1839. The prison was very crowded at the time but of the thirteen cases (all female) only one was fatal.[303] Ipswich county prison suffered several cases of typhus in 1849 with three deaths.[304]

Sometimes the origin of the disease was obvious, as at Louth house of correction: 'Typhus broke out in the prison about six years ago, it was

---

[299] Of one these the surgeon wrote: 'I wish this person to be kept separate from the other prisoners and from chapel and school because I find she is but recently recovered from an attack of Typhus fever' (17 September 1847).

[300] J.C. Lettsom, *Hints Respecting the Prison of Newgate* (London: Darton & Harvey, 1794), p. 3. Lettsom, a forward thinking physician was an early supporter of Jenner's vaccination and founded the Royal Sea Bathing Hospital for Scrofula at Margate, Thomas Dormandy, *The White Death: A History of Tuberculosis* (London: Hambledon, 1999), pp. 147-148. Sadly for Lettsom's posthumous reputation his name lent itself to doggerel: "When any sick to me apply,/ I physics, bleeds and sweats 'em./ If after that they choose to die, / Why verily I Lettsom."

[301] DeLacy, p. 188.

[302] *Fourth Report of Inspector, Northern and Eastern District*, PP, 1839, XXII, 1, p. 121.

[303] *Fourth Report of Inspector, Southern and Western District*, PP, 1839, XXII, 215, p. 179.

[304] *Sixteenth Report of Inspector, Northern and Eastern District*, PP, 1851, XXVII, 2, p. 168

communicated by a vagrant, and in spite of every care spread itself through the prison; a turnkey died of it'.[305] The mortality amongst prison staff seems to have been quite high. At Westminster bridewell: 'There was typhus fever in the prison soon after the severe weather broke up: all the prisoners who had it did well; the only two officers who were attacked by it both died'.[306] During the Irish famine in the late 1840s, immigrants often brought the disease with them to prisons in Lancashire and Yorkshire – the comment of the surgeon at Kirkdale is typical: 'The typhus fever was brought in chiefly by destitute Irish. Two cases were fatal, but in neither instance had the patient been more than a few days in prison'.[307] Also, at Warwick county gaol: 'The fever ... was upon the prisoners when they were admitted, or appeared soon after, and was the accompaniment of extreme poverty'. Two died: 'they were represented as being in great wretchedness, and were charged with the offence of stealing bread'.[308]

On one occasion typhus – and other diseases – were attributed to conditions in the prison. This was at Northallerton county gaol where the surgeon stated:

> The general health of the prisoners since Captain Williams' last visit in November 1844, has been very bad. Typhus fever, dysentery, and diarrhoea have generally prevailed in a very alarming degree. Most of the disease is brought into the prison, but owing to the badness of the drainage, the want of better ventilation, and to the frequently crowded state of the prison of late, when illness once gets in it is very difficult to get it out again. There were seven deaths last year in an average of 122 prisoners. Of these six died of typhus fever.[309]

A year later conditions had not improved and gastro-intestinal ailments were still rampant.[310] Happily, by 1851 a new wing had been built with improved drainage and ventilation, and in 1852 the inspector was able to report: '... there has been no return of the diarrhoea or fever so prevalent before the prisoners were removed into the new buildings.'[311]

Despite these occasional episodes it is clear that, in terms of a relatively low incidence of typhus, the hopes of the reformers had been realised – to a degree beyond their reasonable expectations. It is equally clear (and will become clearer still in the next section) that prison medical staff were closely involved in the prevention and treatment of the disease.

[305] *Third Report of Inspector, Northern and Eastern District, PP, 1837-38, XXXI, 1, p. 53.*

[306] *Third Report of Inspector, Home District, 1838, PP, XXX, 1, p. 51.*

[307] *Thirteenth Report of Inspector, Northern and Eastern District, PP, 1847-48, XXXVI, 361, p. 2*

[308] *Fourteenth Report of Inspector, Midland and Eastern District, PP, 1849, XXVI, 167, p. 67.*

[309] *Fourteenth Report of Inspector, Northern District, 1849, PP, XXVI, 167, p. 21.*

[310] *Fifteenth Report of Inspector, Northern and Eastern District, PP, 1850, XXVIII, 291, p. 48.*

[311] *Sixteenth Report of Inspector, Northern and Eastern District, PP, 1851, XXVII, 461, pp. 88-89. Eighteenth Report of Inspector, Northern and Eastern District, PP, 1856, XXXIII, 1, p. 67.*

THE MANAGEMENT OF AN OUTBREAK

I will now describe the management of a fairly severe but probably not entirely atypical outbreak at Ilchester county gaol in 1817.[312] The fever had already raged nation wide ('almost universally in England, Scotland and Ireland, especially Ireland'); and 'the epidemic fever of 1817 ... appeared in the adjacent towns and villages many months before it discovered itself in the jail, and must therefore be considered as an imported disease'.[313]

On its appearance in the gaol, the magistrates wasted little time and, perhaps aware of the shortcomings of Mr Bryer, the surgeon (see chapter seven), summoned Dr Woodford. On the day he took charge, twelve prisoners were affected, and there had already been one death.[314] Dr Woodford was greatly helped by 'a medical gentleman then a prisoner for debt, who assisted for Mr Bryer almost hourly in some cases'.[315] This 'medical gentleman' was Mr John Palfreyman, surgeon and apothecary, who lived about eighty miles away and was in gaol from October 1817 to April 1818.[316] Palfreyman thought there were about 250 inmates at the time and, according to Dr Woodford, there were 'sixty marked and confirmed cases of the disease.' Of this number only two died compared to an 'average number of deaths in typhus fever [of] one in fifteen [or] twenty'.[317]

Sufferers were placed in 'wards appropriated for their reception' which were 'carefully whitewashed, ventilated, fumigated and otherwise properly aired'.[318] The healthy prisoners were 'washed every morning with salt and water; they were not all washed every morning, some one morning and some another'. The sick prisoners 'were sponged every morning with vinegar, and sometimes in the course of the day besides'. Their rooms were sprinkled every morning with vinegar and 'they had clean linen every other day; the bedding was washed once a week and sometimes oftener'.[319] They were well supplied with tea, coffee, meat, gruel, broth, beer and tobacco: 'inasmuch as their friends when they came to see them have frequently said they are better supplied here than they could have been at home'.[320] Anticipating trouble, Dr Woodford acted decisively: '... finding the disease make great progress in the prison, I deemed it advisable to obtain a house of recovery detached from the prison [at Lymington, about two miles away], to which every first

---

[312] *Appendix to Report from the Commissioners Appointed to inquire into the state of Ilchester Gaol,* PP, 1822, XI, 313, pp. 242-247
[313] Ibid., pp. 243 and 33.
[314] Ibid., p. 242.
[315] Ibid., p. 243. I suspect the term "assisted for" is to be interpreted as "deputised for".
[316] Ibid., p. 244.
[317] Ibid., p. 243.
[318] Ibid., p. 243.
[319] Ibid., p. 244.
[320] Ibid., p. 245.

DOCTOR WOODFORD.

Published by T.Dolby, 299, Strand, Sept.1821.

Dr Woodford. Engraving, 1821, from Henry Hunt,
***Investigation at Ilchester Gaol*, (London: Dolby, 1821).**

case could be removed'; and this had the desired effect of preventing extension of the disease.[321] For his sterling efforts during the outbreak Mr Palfreyman was presented with a gratuity of £20 when he left the prison.[322]

The measures taken seem sensible and were undoubtedly effective. The statement: 'they are better supplied here than they could have been at home' rings true. The medical men concerned showed ample competence in this – probably typical – instance.

---

[321] Ibid., p. 243.
[322] Ibid., p. 246.

SMALLPOX

The other disease highlighted by reformers was smallpox, but again so far as prisons were concerned, its impact was relatively small. The first case of smallpox at Gloucester county gaol was recorded a few months after it opened: on 1 December 1793. Nelmer, a debtor, became ill and since the foul ward was 'not in a proper state' he was moved to the hospital. On 2 December the surgeon noted that Nelmer was 'destitute of any allowances' and after consultation with the Governor and the Chaplain a daily allowance of two pints of ale and a loaf was made. By 12 December Nelmer was back in 'his proper apartments'. George Barnes was diagnosed with smallpox on 4 February 1794, and on 5 February: 'is likely to have a great Burden of the Confluent kind'. His passage was stormy, but with extra food, ale, milk, tea and sugar, and 'a pint of good wine whey'[323] (15 February) he recovered and was discharged from the foul ward on 28 March (although needing an additional waistcoat for cold on 30 March). On 9 February five penitentiary prisoners who had not had smallpox were inoculated[324] immediately 'as they have no objection.' By 16 February: 'Find those that were inoculated, are all of them sick' but none suffered serious problems. On another occasion: 'Recollecting that I had (inadvertently) just come from a small Pox patient, and finding that she [Hannah Smith] has not had it, I thought prudent to inoculate her, to prevent further progress of that disease' (12 February 1797). And a few days later: '[Hannah Smith] – a favourable irruption of small Pox'. On 6 March: 'Hannah Smith perfectly recovered from the small Pox etc. Directed for her to be washed in the warm Bath and discharged the Foul ward'. Mary Birch had an attack of smallpox but recovered quickly (28 March & 9 April 1798).

There were outbreaks of smallpox at Northleach in 1835 and 1838 (with one death in each). These were contained by the surgeon's efforts. He went to considerable lengths in obtaining vaccine ('lymph' or 'matter') for other prisoners. On 11 November 1838: 'I have vaccinated all the prisoners who have never had Cow Pox and as many more as I had matter for, amounting in all to 16 Men and 7 Women'. On 28 November: 'I can procure no vaccine lymph here and I shall write to London tonight for some. When I obtain it I will vaccinate all the Prisoners, who have not been done since their admission'; and on 29 November: 'I have written to London, Cheltenham, and Burford for Lymph'. He made sure the sufferers were isolated and that

---

[323] Whey: the watery part of curdled milk.

[324] Inoculation – popularised in Britain in the early-eighteenth century by Lady Mary Wortley Montagu. Involved giving a small dose of live smallpox virus intravenously in the hope that the resultant infection would be mild but would confer immunity. Vaccination, relying on cross-immunity between the harmless cowpox and smallpox, introduced in 1796 by Edward Jenner, was much safer.

affected areas of the prison were fumigated, limed, and whitewashed. At Littledean there were three cases (one fatal) of smallpox in 1821.

At Gloucester city gaol, with Jane Porter's child: 'sickening for small pox' (7 September 1837), enquiries among the female prisoners revealed two who had never had either smallpox or cowpox. They were offered vaccination or inoculation (by this date, vaccination had largely – but evidently not completely – replaced inoculation) both refused but one changed her mind on the following day and went ahead with vaccination when the patient's condition worsened. Jane Porter's child died a week later but no other cases followed. At Ipswich county gaol there were 12 cases of smallpox and 'several of the cases were very severe but none died'. All prisoners were re-vaccinated.[325] Then – as now – some patients viewed immunisation with suspicion; at Norwich county gaol in 1839 there were three smallpox cases, one fatal, and the surgeon wrote:

> It was impossible to trace how it originated, the man on whom it first broke out had been in for months. It was raging in the town and county, and I might have brought it in myself. Many of the prisoners had been previously vaccinated, others refused to have it done. There appears to be a want of confidence in its efficacy among the humbler classes.[326]

Only one serious outbreak is recorded in the surgeon's journal at Norwich, beginning on 15 February 1845 when the disease was diagnosed in William Mitchell. He became very ill: 'being so very full of the Small pox, which is confluent and attended with great danger'. A few days later Charles Lesley ('[who] has never been vaccinated') also became ill but both recovered. Less fortunate was Dennis King who became ill on March 16, the disease was confluent on 20 March, he became delirious on the following day and died on 24 March. The outbreak continued and on 23 March John King became very ill, to be followed by two more cases in the next few days. These last recovered but King became progressively worse and by 7 April he was '... rapidly sinking. The Brandy and Cordial Medicines to be continued, and the Solution of Chloride of Lime must be freely used, as he is become so very offensive that no one can go near him despite its use'. At one stage: 'contrary to all expectations, [King] is still alive' but on 12 April he had a relapse and died. There was yet one more case, Charles Cater, but no doubt helped by the oranges, lemons, and the two glasses of port wine he received daily, recovery followed. Perhaps rather belatedly, on 27 April eighty-five prisoners were vaccinated and there were no more cases. On 18 July 1846

---

[325] *Fourth Report of Inspector, Northern and Eastern District*, PP, 1839, XXII, 1, p. 158.

[326] *Fifth Report of Inspector, Northern and Eastern District*, PP, 1840, XXV, 565, p. 92.

John Mayre was brought into the prison with mild smallpox but he soon recovered and no other prisoners were affected.

At Wakefield county house of correction there was an outbreak of smallpox affecting two officers and a child – the child and one of the officers died but 'In consequence of the precautions used, and the cutting off of all communication with the person infected, the further spread of the disease was arrested'.[327] At Walsingham county house of correction a prisoner brought the disease into prison (and died) but only two other cases followed – including the son of the surgeon (his assistant) – and as a result of vaccination both experienced the disease in a mitigated form.[328] At Taunton county gaol there were ten cases of smallpox with one death.[329] In a London epidemic beginning in the spring of 1847 and lasting through 1848 there were thirteen cases at Millbank in 1848, one of which was fatal.[330]

This is an impressively low tally of problems with smallpox in an era when the disease was common and again, it is clear that the efforts of prison medical officers were of vital importance in its control. It is also clear that they went to considerable lengths to use the same control methods (inoculation – and later vaccination) as were used on other patients. Equally important, it is clear that despite the supposed over-arching control exerted by medical staff, prisoners were allowed to refuse vaccination if they saw fit.

CHOLERA

Unfortunately, separation and cleanliness, which must have lessened the spread of typhus – and to a lesser extent of smallpox – proved no safeguard against cholera. The disease was unknown in Britain until October 1831 when there was an outbreak at Sunderland – imported from India where it had been present in epidemic form since 1817.[331] This was <u>Asiatic</u> cholera, caused by the bacterium *Vibrio cholerae*. Having gained a foothold, it soon spread to the rest of the country, the midlands being particularly affected. There were further outbreaks in 1834 and 1837, followed by a major epidemic in 1848.[332]

The term cholera had long been in use, appearing in Chaucer's *The Nun's Tale*, and the diagnosis cholera morbus (morbus = disease) was in use by the <u>end of the sixteenth</u> century to describe a bilious disorder characterised by

---

[327] *Tenth Report of Inspector, Northern and Eastern District*, PP, 1845, XXIV, 1, p. 20.
[328] *Fifteenth Report of Inspector, Northern and Eastern District*, PP, 1850, XXVIII, 291, p. 37
[329] *Fifteenth Report of Inspector, Southern and Western District*, PP, 1850, XXVIII, 579, p. 15.
[330] *Sixth Report of Inspectors into Millbank Prison for the year 1848 and part of 1849*, 1850, XXIX, 55, p. 5.
[331] Creighton, p. 793.
[332] Robert McRorie Higgins, 'The 1832 Cholera Epidemic in East London', *East London Record*, 2 (1979), p. 13.

John Bull puts aside his attention to the Reform Bill and defends Britain against the cholera invasion. Coloured lithograph, 1831. Such bravado proved of little avail against *V. cholerae*, the result all too often being that shown overleaf.

A corpse is lifted onto the back of a wagon. Coloured lithograph, c. 1832.

Jenner and two colleagues seeing off three anti-vaccination opponents, the dead littered at their feet. Coloured etching by I Cruickshank, 1808.

diarrhoea, vomiting, abdominal pains and cramps[333] – what we would now call gastro-enteritis. This was known as English cholera, and as late as 1852 the diagnosis was still used as at Derby county and borough gaol: 'English cholera had been prevalent in the neighbourhood, but not in the prison'.[334] It was rarely fatal to adults – whereas Asiatic cholera carried (and unless adequately treated still carries) a high mortality.

The arrival of Asiatic cholera had devastating effects both in the country at large and in some prisons. In 1832 there were nine deaths from cholera (out of a total of fourteen deaths in the year) at Aylesbury county gaol; six deaths (from eleven cases) at Carlisle county gaol; one at Exeter house of correction;[335] three at Exeter county gaol; nineteen at Salford county gaol, twenty at Wakefield (from 78 cases), nine at Bristol city gaol (from fourteen cases), but only two each at Newgate, Giltspur Street compter and Borough compter.[336] There were 64 deaths that year at Coldbath-fields house of correction and although no cause is given, probably most of these were due to cholera since the usual death rate was much lower (17 in 1840 and 24 in 1841).[337] There was a bad outbreak at Northallerton county gaol in 1832.[338] At Oxford county gaol: 'Three deaths occurred here from the epidemic cholera, during its prevalence'.[339] At Shrewsbury county gaol and house of correction: 'There were 18 confirmed cases of epidemic cholera during its prevalence formerly, and many bowel complaints at the same time. Two cases were fatal, both in old people'.[340]

A later epidemic was equally serious. Perhaps worst affected was Millbank (now a prison rather than a penitentiary). Cholera, having manifested itself in London on 28 September 1848, appeared in the prison on 15 October. Between then and 6 September 1849 (there was a spell of freedom from the disease between March and June 1849) 48 prisoners, one male infirmary nurse, and the wife of a staff member succumbed – almost doubling the already high prison mortality rate.[341] This outbreak was sufficiently serious that a considerable number of prisoners were evacuated to Shorncliff barracks – an expedient also resorted to in another outbreak in 1854 when

---

[333] OED.

[334] *Eighteenth Report of Inspector, Northern and Eastern District*, PP, 1856, XXXIII, 1, p. 14.

[335] Where the surgeon thought that the cases in the bridewell were the result of its being downwind of the town's cholera burying ground – the corpses were often left unburied.

[336] *Reports and Schedules Pursuant to the Gaol Acts*, PP, 1831-1832, XXXIII, 1, pp. 22, 31,127, 300, 303, & 319.

[337] *Reports and Schedules Pursuant to the Gaol Acts*, PP, 1833, XXVIII, 1, p. 168, and *Sixth Report of Inspector, Home District*, PP, 1841 Sess. 2, IV, 1, p. 250.

[338] *Sixteenth Report of Inspector, Northern and Eastern District*, PP, 1851, XXVII, 461, p. 90.

[339] *First Report of Inspector, Southern and Western District*, PP, 1836 , XXXV, 1, p. 50.

[340] *Fourth Report of Inspector, Southern and Western District*, PP, 1839, XXII, 215, p. 203.

[341] *Report of the Inspectors of Millbank Prison for the year 1949*, PP, 1850, XXIX, 73, pp. 9-10.

most of the inmates were removed to Dorchester barracks.[342]

In 1849, prison inspector Frederic Hill wrote (of his Northern District):

> Since the close of the year however, cholera has appeared in three of the prisons,
> namely, those at Wakefield, Carlisle, and Leeds; the chief attack having been at
> Wakefield Prison. The whole number of cases in the district has been 33, and
> the number of deaths 19; and of these, 28 cases and 16 deaths were at the prison
> at Wakefield. ... At Carlisle Prison there were four cases of cholera, three of
> which were fatal; but at the prison at Leeds there was only one case, and the
> prisoner was cured.[343]

At Shrewsbury county gaol and house of correction, at a time when the
disease was very prevalent in the town, there were 14 cholera deaths.[344]
Elsewhere, there were outbreaks at Gloucester county gaol, Gloucester
city gaol,[345] Hertford county gaol,[346] and Oxford county gaol; Oxford city
gaol was spared.[347] In his 1850 report for the Home District, William J.
Williams noted that of 341 prison deaths, no fewer than 99 were the result of
cholera.[348] Of the same year, Hill noted that the Northern District had fared
better: 'The cholera found an entrance into few of the prisons, and the whole
number of deaths caused by that disease was small, being not more than 29
in a prison population of above 6,000'.[349]

Some were lucky. In the 1832 epidemic there was no cholera in the gaols
at Chester, Bodmin, Dorset, nor at Durham.[350] The 1839 report notes that
in Gloucester county gaol: 'There was no epidemic cholera here, though
there were numerous cases in the town'; and at Lichfield city gaol: 'The
cholera did not show itself here at the time of the epidemic visitation'.[351]
Lawford's Gate house of correction had been free from cases both in 1832
and in the late 1840s outbreak, despite cases in the surrounding districts of
Bristol.[352] In 1848 there were no cholera deaths at Pentonville 'although it
raged so fearfully in the metropolis'.[353] In 1850, at Lancaster there was only
one cholera death – a prisoner who had been received a few days previously,
and: 'when diarrhoea and cholera were prevalent in Lancaster, [the acting
surgeon] was struck with the immunity from sickness in the prison'. In his

---

[342] *Report on the Discipline of the Convict Prisons*, PP, 1854-1855, XXV, 435, pp. 44-45.

[343] *Fourteenth Report of Inspector, Northern District*, 1849, XXVI, 167, pp. xii-xiii.

[344] *Sixteenth Report of Inspector, Southern and Western District*, PP, 1852, XXIV, 1, pp. 47-48.

[345] *Fifteenth Report of Inspector, Southern and Western District*, PP, 1850, XXVIII, 579, pp. 100 and 104.

[346] *Fourteenth Report of Inspector, Home District*, PP, 1850, XXVIII, 1, p. 91.

[347] *Sixteenth Report of Inspector, Northern and Eastern District*, PP, 1851, XXVII, 461, pp. 45-47 and 54.

[348] *Fourteenth Report of Inspector, Home District, Part 2*, PP, 1850, XXVIII, 1, p. xi.

[349] *Fifteenth Report of Inspector, Northern District and Eastern District*, PP, 1850, XXVIII, 291, p. xix.

[350] *Reports*, PP, 1833, XXVIII, 1, p. 38.

[351] *Fourth Report of Inspector, Southern and Western District*, PP, 1839, XXII, 215, pp. 66 and 142.

[352] *Fifteenth Report of Inspector, Southern and Western District*, PP, 1850, XXVIII, 579, p. 119.

[353] *Eighth Report of the Commissioners for the Government of the Pentonville Prison*, PP, 1850, XXIX, 125, p. 5.

1851 report the inspector notes that at Peterborough liberty gaol and house of correction: 'Asiatic cholera, although prevalent in the neighbourhood, did not visit the prison'.[354] Surgeons at some of these gaols attributed their freedom from disease variously to a pint of new milk daily, smoking two pipes of tobacco daily and astringent medicine. Clearly, whether or not a particular prison was affected in an epidemic had nothing to do with milk nor tobacco, nor even with the impurity of the prison atmosphere. The spread of the disease was entirely a function of the water supply: contamination with faecal material from infected patients meant that infection was inevitable but if by some happy chance the prison water supply was free from such contamination, its occupants were spared.

Perhaps the remarkable fact is that cholera mortality was not much higher in these places of confinement – this relative escape due in some measure to the efforts of prison medical staff.

THE INCIDENCE OF ILLNESS IN PRISONS

Although prison sickness rates were apparently high, most of the "illness" was of a minor nature. This was probably true throughout the period under discussion and although detailed accounts of medical care in prisons before Howard's efforts bore fruit are rare, we have the description of William Smith, a physician, who was given 'a sum of money' by the Westminster Charity to visit various gaols in 1776.[355] He was highly critical of conditions. At Poultry Compter: 'When I first visited this gaol, the prisoners were very sickly, and a putrid fever seemed to threaten great destruction. Few were free from itch, scurvy, venereal complaints and vermin'.[356] Nevertheless, and despite random provision of medical care and widespread prevalence of minor disease, the death rate in the prisons he attended was not as high as might have been supposed. He visited twice weekly over a six-month period and modestly felt able to state:

> as much attention has been paid to the sick in the different gaols under my care as could have been bestowed upon any private patient ... Since the end of March, when I first began to visit the gaols, to the fourteenth of September, three hundred and eighty persons have been cured of various complaints, mostly of the putrid kind; six are now under cure; seven dead, three of whom died of the small-pox.[357]

---

[354] *Sixteenth Report of Inspector, Southern and Western District*, PP, 1851, XXVII, 669, p. 155.

[355] William Smith, *State of the Gaols in London, Westminster and Borough of Southwark* (London: Bew, 1776).

[356] Ibid., p. 32.

[357] Ibid., pp. 6 &7.

Smith's account suggests that even in pre-reform London prisons, provision of even a modicum of medical attention resulted in improved health standards amongst prisoners.

The information provided by Smith, although interesting, is of no more than anecdotal value. More significant is a report on the incidence of sickness in Newgate 1815 to 1818.[358] The prison (rebuilt in 1783 after being burnt down in The Gordon riots of 1780) was constructed in the traditional fashion with a ward system and thus potentially unhealthy but, as has already been described, it had a surgeon (Mr Box), and infirmaries. The prisoners were mostly awaiting trial or transportation.[359] Showing a remarkable degree of enthusiasm for the collection of statistics, Box lists the weekly return of those reporting sick for the period 17 January 1815 to 16 September 1817. Prisoner numbers varied between 386 and 645 and of these between 18 and 61 (between 4.0% and 9.5%) reported sick each day. [360] Many complaints were of a trivial nature but a significant proportion were more serious (table 4:1). The proportion of serious diseases seems high (from a total of 1,400 committals[361]) and, allowing for the element of double counting (with regard to the relapses) equates to 385 infirmary cases – about 9.3% of all patients seen required hospital care.

Table 4.1 More Serious Diseases in Newgate Gaol, 16 May 1817 – 1 January 1818

Total cases of fever admitted to the male infirmary	284
Number relapsed	126
Fractures, severe ulcers, venereal disease, and cutaneous eruptions taken to convalescent wards	41
Cases of fever taken to female infirmary	32
Various diseases taken to male infirmary	28
Total	511

This apparently alarming sickness rate is put into perspective by the fact that only seven deaths occurred. There were '12-14' deaths in the previous year and only 3 in the year before that.[362] 24 deaths in 2½ years from an average of about 500 inmates (1.9% per annum) is to be expected for this

[358] *Report*, PP, 1818, VIII, 297, passim.
[359] Ibid., p. 46.
[360] Ibid., p. 173.
[361] Ibid., p. 205.
[362] Ibid., p. 61.

type of prison and it can safely be concluded that most of the infirmary cases were not seriously ill.

Box made a regularly recurring lament – one which goes a long way to explain the problems involved in prison health care – 'those people, from the dreadful state of illness when they come in, are not able to withstand the rigours of confinement'. Apart from fever, the common diseases at Newgate were 'the venereal disease [which] is always very prevalent there; the itch, ulcerated legs, and very often dropsies'.[363]

The point that most complaints were minor can be confirmed by diagnoses compiled from surgeons' journals at Gloucestershire prisons (Table 4:2). Listed are new complaints. Two ailments probably relating to the same disease, e.g. 'disordered habit of the bowels and general debility of the whole system' are counted as one. If different systems were affected, for instance the not uncommon combination of 'The Itch and Venereal Disease'[364] these are itemised separately.

Table 4:2 Analysis of 6,905 Complaints of Illness at Gloucester county gaol (2,081 complaints); and at Northleach (3,460 complaints) and Littledean houses of correction (1,364 complaints) (expressed as a percentage of the total number of complaints at that prison)[365]

Prison	Ulcers Boils Wounds	The Itch	Venereal Skin	Rheumatic	Gastro-intestinal	Respiratory	Fever	Miscell-aneous	Unspecified
Gloucester 1809-1818	6.2	9.1	3.3	4.5	16.6	10.7	5.2	9.9	34.5
Northleach 1801-41*	9.6	11.6	14 .8	9.7	22.2	8.4	2.2	17.2	4.3
Littledean 1807-48**	10	5.7	11.2	7.2	26.3	12.2	4.5	21.8	1.1

*Excluding 1816 (records inadequate) and the second half of 1841 (no journals extant after June 1841).
**Excluding the years 1838 – 1842 (journals missing).

The rather unsatisfactory category of "unspecified" largely comprises vague entries in the journals such as those reading: 'complains of illness, sent medicines'. Such entries were particularly common at Gloucester after 1816 when the workload had tripled and the surgeon had time to make detailed

---

[363] Ibid., p. 64. Dropsy: an unnatural accumulation of fluid in any part of the body, most notably in the ankles. From the Greek, Hudrops (water). Now known as oedema.

[364] The same happened elsewhere: 'William Smith a Vagrant who was brought to the Castle last night in a most abject state of Poverty, covered with Vermin, has the Itch very bad, and the Venereal Disease in a most aggravated form.' (1 February 1845, Norwich).

[365] Peter McRorie Higgins, 'Medical Care in Three Gloucestershire Prisons in the Early 19th Century', *Transactions of the Bristol and Gloucestershire Archaeological Society*, 120 (2002), 213-228, (p. 215).

notes only for seriously ill patients. Also included in this category are those cases for which no diagnosis was entered and simply merit the comment 'sent aperient'. Prescribing an aperient might suggest that constipation was the problem, but aperients were used then (and until quite recently) for a wide variety of minor complaints. This is borne out by figures from Pentonville where the surgeon classified his 2,202 patients seen in the year as 16 'severe cases', 1,365 'slighter cases' and in a category he clearly regarded as trivial, 821 'requiring a purgative'.[366] Compared with figures given by Mary Fissell for admissions to Bristol Infirmary at about the same period (fever 16.6%, respiratory diseases 15.1%, trauma 13.9%, abscess or ulcer 13.2%) the preponderance of relatively minor ailments treated in these prisons is clear.[367] Information from other prisons shows differences so far as the ratios of the various minor complaints were concerned, but always a relative sparseness of serious disease.[368]

A survey carried out by inspector D. O'Brien reaches a similar conclusion. The thirty-one prisons in his Midland and Eastern District contained a total of 1,778 males and 255 females (omitting debtors). Excluding itch cases, there were 73 males (4.1%) and 14 females (5.4%) on the sick list. Of these, 26 males and 3 females had slight indisposition: 'as might entitle the patient to be entitled to out-door tickets for medical treatment at a metropolitan hospital'. 48 males and 12 females had diseases contracted out of gaol and only 25 males and 2 females had 'indispositions, mostly slight, [which] could be referred, directly or indirectly to the particular circumstances of their confinement'.[369] There was one anomaly. The surgeon at Shrewsbury county gaol made a diagnosis of typhus in over 10% of 1,339 prisoners reporting sick. Almost certainly he exaggerated the frequency of this condition – there were only 62 infirmary cases in all and but two deaths from 'fever'.[370]

Why so much sickness, trivial or not, in prisons? At the very least, reporting sick offered the chance of a welcome break from the dull routine of prison life. Additionally, the lure of the infirmary was ever-present: 'In the large wards [of the infirmaries] they lounge away their time enjoying plenty of good eating and drinking, with no lack of idle corrupting talk'.[371] But quite apart from this was the attraction of free medical attention. As the

[366] *Report of the Directors of Convict Prisons*, PP, 1852, XXIV, 197, p. 36.

[367] Fissell, pp. 106-107.

[368] Horsley house of correction, GRO, Q/Gh 12; Winchester house of correction, *Sixth Report of Inspector, Southern and Western District*, PP, 1841 Sess. 2, V, 177, p. 108; Shepton Mallet house of correction, *Fifth Report of Inspector, Southern and Western District*, PP, 1840, XXV, 721,, p. 114; Gloucester county gaol (*Seventh Report of Inspector, Southern and Western District*, PP, 1842, XXI, 193, p. 114; and Pentonville, *Return of Health of Convicts in Pentonville Prison*, 1842-1843, PP, 1843, XXIX, 377, p. 45.

[369] *Fourteenth Report of Inspector, Midland and Eastern District*, PP, 1849, XXVI, 1, p. vi.

[370] *Tenth Report of Inspector, Southern and Western District*, PP, 1845, XXIV, 207, p. 20.

[371] Arthur Griffiths, *Memorials of Millbank and Chapters in Prison History* (London: King, 1875), p. 299.

surgeon at Wakefield count house of correction pointed out: 'The number of complaints of slight ailments is greatly increased since they [the prisoners] have the right to see the medical officer'.[372] A similar point was made by Holford:

> I believe that a great majority of the cases, for which medicine may have been properly given in the Penitentiary would never have been brought under the observation of a Physician or Apothecary, if they had occurred out of the prison, or have been known to any but the parties affected, who would (to use a common phrase) have allowed the disorder to carry itself off, or perhaps have varied their food ... if a medical man were to tour the streets of a particular district giving medicine to any who chose to apply for it, at the end of a year the consumption of medicine in that district would be much greater than in those adjoining.[373]

ULCERS AND WOUNDS

Prisoners were often committed with ulcers already present: 'Philip Lancet – found him a weak old man 70 years of age with a very bad ulcerated sore leg' (3 December 1809, Northleach). They were perhaps more common in the early years when the use of leg irons was widespread, indeed the journal's opening sentence at Gloucester county gaol reads: 'My first Visit, find several prisoners with very bad ulcers of long standing, dress'd them' (1 July 1791). 'Long standing' could be very long standing indeed: the surgeon at Norwich had been dressing J. Nicol's leg ulcer every day: '[it] is healing rapidly but it has been constantly breaking out again for the last 45 years.' (7 September 1845). Treatment was with various balms, local dressings (usually of saline) and general supportive treatment – the latter nearly always including wine.

Some had injuries inflicted in the course of arrest: 'John Hill brought into custody from the Hospital with a severe wound from a Spring Gun [a man trap]' (28 December 1824, Norwich}[374]; at Derby county gaol: '29th September:– J.M., well, except seven cuts on his scalp and bruises on his right knee and arms from blows given him by the gamekeeper whilst taking him last Saturday night near Ashford';[375] and at Bridgnorth borough gaol: 'Some poachers who came in wounded have had their wounds dressed'.[376] A prisoner arrived at Norwich castle with a fractured jaw 'from a severe kick' (6 October 1843). His condition necessitated the removal of five teeth and he was prescribed two pints of milk daily as he could not eat bread.

[372] *Eighth Report of Inspector, Northern and Eastern District*, PP, 1843, XXV and XXVI, 249, p. 152.

[373] George Holford, *Third Vindication of the General Penitentiary* (London: Rivington, 1825), p. 71.

[374] *Keeper's daily journal 1822-1835*, NRO, MF/RO 576/1.

[375] *Eleventh Report of Inspector, Northern and Eastern District*, PP, 1846, XXI, 483, p. 37.

[376] *Seventh Report of Inspector, Southern and Western District*, PP, 1842, XXI, 193, p. 167.

Some wounds tested the surgeon's skill (and luck) to the limit. When committed to Gloucester county gaol on 23 February 1818 George Harter was noted to have a cut throat, already sutured. On 28 February the wound developed a very offensive discharge and on 1 March this became worse and he was taken into the hospital. The stitches fell out and the surgeon observed that the trachea and oesophagus were exposed, the former intact but the latter leaking ingested food. This (an oesophago-cutaneous fistula) can be very difficult to heal, but, with 'sick diet', cordial medicine and broth, and regular dressings, it did. Two weeks later, although the patient was 'very weak and nervous', the wound was 'remarkably healthy and healing very rapidly' (17 March 1818). There were other, notable, recoveries from self-inflicted cut throats. The inspector quotes from the surgeon's journal at Lancaster: 'I was sent for between 5 and 6 o'clock this morning to see [name not given], who had cut his throat. I found him insensible and nearly pulseless, with an extensive wound of his throat, completely dividing the windpipe'. Amazingly, with little more than dressings and a diet of warm milk he recovered.[377] Equally fortunate were two similar cases at Walsingham house of correction. The first was stated to have 'divided the windpipe on its anterior surface' – this was sutured – and the second had '[a] very severe wound to the right side of the throat, dividing the principal arteries, muscles etc. in that part ... the loss of blood was very great ... bleeding vessels were with difficulty secured'.[378]

Truly heroic surgery was performed by the surgeon at Portsmouth borough gaol:

I was sent for a ½ past 10 o'clock in the morning of the 22nd of July to visit John Blower, who had just been convicted of felony, and who, on coming from the court and placed in the yard, had made a violent attempt on his life, by cutting his throat with a razor, which he took from a shelf in the room immediately after sentence of transportation for 7 years had been passed on him. I attended instantly, and found him standing between two prisoners, who were supporting him, bleeding profusely, and to every appearance lifeless, with an immense pool of blood before him. He was immediately placed in a recumbent position, and I found a wound in his throat extending almost from ear to ear. Seeing instantly that the carotids had not been wounded, I immediately secured by ligature the larger branches of the lingual and thyroideal arteries, and united the external wound with five sutures, and placed the head in such a position as would facilitate the reunion of the trachea, which was completely divided. On removing him to hospital he was pulseless; the trachea was widely separated from the larynx, immediately below which it was cut through. I instantly determined to remove the threads (three of them), and placing the trachea in

[377] *Fourth Report of Inspector, Northern and Eastern District*, PP, 1839, XXII, 1, p. 33.
[378] *Fifth Report of Inspector, Northern and Eastern District*, PP, 1840, XXV, 565, p. 116.

close apposition with the larynx, I applied a suture through it (avoiding the lining membrane as far as was possible) and the cricoid cartilage or lower part of the larynx. The external wound was then closed by sutures and adhesive plaster; and cold-water dressings constantly applied. From that moment he had not a bad symptom ... .[379]

This episode is impressive in that the surgeon (displaying an enviable knowledge of anatomy) refused to take the easy option of letting the prisoner die and then embarked on another operation when the first failed.

Some injuries were acquired as a result of fights in the prisons, the most serious a fatal instance at Preston county house of correction: 'The only death that has occurred was occasioned by an insane prisoner kicking a boy [aged 15] in the day-room who died in 24 hours of rupture of the intestines'.[380] At Norwich on 12 May 1843 the surgeon attended to a debtor whose hand was burnt: 'during a Dispute in the Prison'. Fights within the gaol were a particular problem at Lancaster: '[I] was sent for last night to see Henry Robinson, a debtor, the poor man had his leg broken in a fight I find, (2 January 1845); 'Two women have been fighting but with the exception of a black eye and a bruise on the head I do not think they are injured' (21 July 1845); 'I was sent for early to see Parkinson who has been kicked with a clog by another prisoner, I find the upper lip and lining of the nose nearly cut through on the left side. The boy has lost a great deal of blood' (24 July 1846); and on 16 June 1847 the surgeon dressed a cut lip resulting from a kick, a tooth had also been knocked out. Knutsford saw a fatal case of tetanus following a penetrating wound in the thigh inflicted by a pair of scissors wielded by one of the other prisoners – supposedly as a joke.[381] An indication of the generally lax supervision at Newgate is the surgeon's complaint of the number of injuries he had to treat – although treat them he did, and with care and compassion:

> [the surgeon] says he has no doubt that the severe accidents amongst the prisoners, which are mentioned in the Surgeon's Journal as of frequent occurrence, are caused by the prisoners fighting and larking with one another; these accidents cause him to be called in at uncertain and irregular hours and occupy a great deal of his time, and were one of the principal grounds of his application to the Court of Aldermen for an increased salary.[382] The accidents are caused by want of control and insubordination amongst the prisoners; they would never occur if there was proper discipline.

The report enlarges on the laxity of discipline: food was brought in for the

[379] *Fifteenth Report of Inspector, Home District*, PP, 1851, XXVII, 1, p.36.

[380] *Eighth Report of Inspector, Northern and Eastern District*, PP, 1843, XXV and XXVI, 249, p. 66.

[381] *Tenth Report of Inspector, Northern and Eastern District*, PP, 1845, XXIV, 1, p. 149.

[382] This request for an increase in salary seems to have been met: in 1840 he received £450 (from £250 in 1835), including Giltspur Street and £100 to the assistant. *Sixth Report of Inspector, Home District*, PP, 1841 Sess. 2, IV, 1, p. 282.

prisoners by their friends and visitors ('altogether a bad set') including: 'persons of notoriously bad character … many of the prostitutes are very young girls, sometimes not more than twelve of thirteen years of age'. There was drunkenness – and – to the disgust of the surgeon, tobacco was widely available. The wards were not entered at night except by the surgeon or in cases of extreme disorder.[383] The prison was 'a great school of crime'.[384]

General indiscipline among male inmates in a dormitory at Newgate gaol. Etching, George Cruikshank, 1845.

Escape attempts provided work for the surgeon. At Norwich castle two men used knotted blankets which broke. One fell: 'his thigh dreadfully broke' (5 March 1830).[385] Less serious injuries acquired during escape attempts are noted at Gloucester county gaol: 'Attended to find no particular complaints, except Jno Williams much bruised about the Hips by an attempt to get through his cell window, after sawing the Bar out' (24 February 1792); and at Northleach: 'Joseph Painter strained [sic] his ankle in attempting to get out of prison' (27 October 1807). More mundanely: 'Cornetti has broken his

[383] *First Report of Inspector, Home District*, PP, 1836, XXXV, 1, p. 37. p.5, p.39, p.6, p. 76.

[384] *Seventh Report of Inspector, Home District*, PP, 1842, XX, 1, pp. 185-186.

[385] MF/RO 576/1.

Collar bone, he fell in the Yard' (10 January 1848, Lancaster).

The introduction of hard labour brought a new dimension to the problem of injuries. Between 1820 and 1827 at Northleach, when the handmill was in operation, there were six injuries: all blows to various parts of the body from the handle – none serious. Perhaps surprisingly at the same prison, between October 1827 and 1841 when the treadmill was in use, only three injuries are recorded, all to the feet and all minor. Much worse treadmill injuries were reported from other prisons, many of which were beyond the surgeons' healing powers. At Leicester house of correction:

> The Wheel was originally one of 20 feet diameter, and the parties were principally worked on the inside of it. At that time, two fatal accidents occurred from the perverseness and wilful misconduct of the men. Joseph Sumner was killed in 1821, and Thomas Saunders in July 1823, and three other persons were slightly bruised. The Wheel has been recently altered to one of five feet diameter, and of the usual construction, and we trust, that all chance of further accidents is removed.[386]

Other fatal or serious injuries are recorded from time to time in the inspectors' reports. Some sufferers might have been spared had they been imprisoned at Exeter city gaol and house of correction where 'The surgeon never allows any man above 63 years of age to be placed on the wheel, and always reduces the labour, when it appears to him to be excessive'.[387]

Members of the prison medical service could hardly be blamed for the presence of the treadmill in prisons and they tried to ensure that those working on the mill were adequately fed and, if injured, cared for. The deaths and injuries associated with the wheel were largely the results of unfamiliarity with machinery – in an age when most of its users were unlikely to be accustomed to technology any more advanced than the spade and the farm cart. Quarrying was even more dangerous than the treadmill: five fatal accidents occurred at Portland in the year it opened.[388] Presumably lessons were learnt there for in later years there was only about one trauma death annually, although serious accidents were not uncommon and the surgeon regularly reports the need to carry out amputations.

There were other occupational hazards: 'Thomas Fletcher, Penitentiary Prisoner, has severe ophthalmy, I have ordered him proper Medicines and Application and directed his abstinence from his employment as <u>White Washer</u>' (19 August 1819, Gloucester county gaol); 'Williams is admitted

---

[386] *Copies*, PP, 1824, XIX, 165, p. 7. Strangely, this first incident is not mentioned in the 1823 report.

[387] *Sixth Report of Inspector, Southern and Western District*, PP, 1841 Sess 2, V, 177, p. 134.

[388] *Reports of the Directors of Convict Prisons on the Discipline and Management of Pentonville, Parkhurst, and Millbank Prison, and of Portland Prison and the Hulks, for the year 1850*, PP, 1851, XXVIII, 1, (Portland Prison), p. 8.

for Colic brought on by painting' (25 July 1844, Lancaster);[389] and: 'There are nearly 30 reports [of sickness] on the crown side chiefly on account of the dust (as they say) in picking the ropes' (9 May 1849, Lancaster).

THE ITCH

'The Itch' was common amongst those committed to prison. Now known as scabies, this highly contagious parasitic skin disease is caused by the itch mite; the impregnated female lays her eggs in the skin and her offspring live in hair follicles. Itching results from sensitisation of host to parasite. In general, all prisoners were examined for the disease on arrival. At Lancaster, itch does not crop up in the journals as often as at other prisons but the entry: 'we have had itch cases as usual from Manchester' (23 April 1844) suggests that the condition was too common to be worth mentioning.[390] The ideal – that all cases of itch were diagnosed and cured as soon as they entered prison, and that no new cases arose – was not always achieved. Despairingly Mr Wilton at Gloucester city gaol writes:

> Several of the Women (who are now <u>many</u> in number) have slight complaints, it is impossible on the frequent introduction of dirty girls and others to the Prison to prevent a frequent recurrence of the Itch which has lately been recorded in many instances, there are now one or two with the disease (27 July 1833).

The itch might be combined with other diseases – but could still be successfully treated:

> This day, discharged from the foul ward Isaac Gillam, he having perfectly recoverd of a most inveterate foul disease of the scrophula kind with Itch, and scald Head [ringworm] of several years standing, he has been discharged from the [Gloucester] Infirmary without receiving any material benefit in many months. His situation upon being brought into Gaol, was truly deplorable, the foul stench arising from his disease was intolerably offensive (22 November 1796, Gloucester county gaol).

Although the treatment is not usually specified, sulphur ointment seems to have been the usual remedy and most cases were probably managed in a manner similar to that described in 1836 by Mr Macmurdo, surgeon at Newgate: 'Their clothes are taken away, and their skin saturated with sulphur, and in two or three days they are well'.[391] Similarly at Devizes

---

[389] Intestinal colic is a prominent symptom of lead poisoning.

[390] It was not uncommon for prisoners to arrive in a poor state: 'There is hardly a single clean head of hair of the men for trial' (14 February 1845); and 'The three boys just come in for trial are in such a filthy state and one with itch, they had better remain in the lock-up at present' (13 February 1849).

[391] *Copy of a Report made on 2ⁿᵈ July 1836, by a Committee of the Court of Aldermen to that Court upon the Report of the Inspectors of Prisons in relation to the Gaol of Newgate*, PP, 1836, XLII, 231, p. 37.

house of correction: 'When a prisoner comes in with the itch he is retained in the reception cell for three days; during that time the compound sulphur ointment is rubbed three times, in the quantity of a quarter of a pound once a-day. At the end of this time he is bathed, and is invariably cured'.[392] The close relationship in the public mind between the itch and sulphur can be inferred from a court case in 1767 when the author of the doggerel "Old Villers, so strong of brimstone you smell / as if not long since you had got out of hell" lost a suit of libel brought against him on the grounds of the clear imputation in the verse that Villers had the itch – then regarded as an antisocial disease.[393] A high-tech version of the treatment was in use at Shrewsbury county gaol in the 1840s: '[The surgeon] treats itch here by fumigation from a pan in which sulphur and coals are burnt. By this means the itch is usually cured in ten minutes (according to the statement of the surgeon), so they have no itch-cells at present'.[394] This may have been the same machine used at Knutsford: essentially an airtight box in which the patient stood – the level of the floor could be adjusted to suit his or her height – with the head protruding through a linen or woollen collar. The lower part of the box had a drawer where sulphur and hot coals were placed – the drawer was inserted when the patient was ready. No technological advance is without its problems as this episode recorded in the surgeon's journal shows:

> March 20, 1841. I take the liberty of troubling the visiting magistrates with a few remarks in reference to the death of John Entwistle, on whose body an inquest was held in the gaol on Wednesday last. Entwistle applied on Monday last for permission to go into the sulphur bath, which was granted to him, and he went in on the afternoon of that day with a man named Brown.

He goes on to describe how both complained of heat, particularly Entwistle, so they were allowed out after only twenty minutes – less than half the usual time. Brown had no problems but Entwistle complained of feeling unwell and within fifteen minutes or so was dead. At autopsy there was no abnormality other than congested lungs and it was concluded that the unfortunate Entwistle was 'in a state peculiarly liable to suffer from [the treatment's] influence'. In reality, he probably died from heat stroke – a condition in which the body's thermo-regulatory mechanism catastrophically fails. He was unlucky, apparently 'upwards of 1,200 men had been in it in about eight months'.[395] Later, the prison inspector John G Perry was to recommend

---

[392] *Second Report of Inspector, Southern and Western District*, PP, 1837, XXXII, 659, p. 11.
[393] *Villers v. Mosley, The English Reports, King's Bench Division*, (London 1909), Vol. XCV, pp. 886-887.
[394] *Sixth Report of Inspector, Southern and Western District*, PP, 1841 Sess. 2, V, 177, p. 227.
[395] *Sixth Report of Inspector, Northern and Eastern District*, PP, 1841 Sess. 2 , V, 1, p. 9.

the general adoption of the fumigator in all prisons[396] but George Shaw, surgeon to the county prison at Durham had invented his own technique – a treatment that at the very least must have left the prisoner with a warm, comforting glow:

> The method … is simple and effective. The patient is first put into a warm or hot bath, where he is washed perfectly clean with plenty of soap. On leaving the bath he is slightly dried, and then with a flannel, on which a little fine sand been sprinkled, every part of his body is well rubbed until not a spot is to be seen. The scouring is carried out to the extent of making the skin tender and sensitive but *not* painful. The patient is then *well* rubbed before a hot fire with the compound sulphur ointment for thirty or forty minutes, he is then well washed, when he is perfectly cured of his itch.[397]

In general it is clear that in most prisons the itch was treated efficiently and promptly but Wisbeach was a lamentable exception: 'If the prisoners come in with the itch for a week, they are not treated for it in consequence of the expense and the shortness of the stay. This has the tendency to spread the disease through the prison'.[398]

VENEREAL AND SKIN DISEASES

The incidence of venereal disease fluctuated, but it was rarely absent from the annual tally of disease in any prison and features regularly in the inspectors' reports. As regards the Gloucestershire prisons, when its nature is specified, gonorrhoea was the most common (this diagnosis probably included cases of non-specific urethritis, not then recognised as a disease entity), followed by primary syphilis (sometimes the two together), with an occasional case of secondary syphilis, venereal warts or even venereal ophthalmia (22 June 1835 Gloucester city gaol). A condition not recognised as such until much later (1889) but which must have occurred, was chancroid, a disease with similar manifestations to primary syphilis but much less dangerous.

Comments in the journals reflect the extent of the problem. At Northleach: 'Venereal cases … more common this quarter' (16 October 1826); and: 'a large increase in venereal cases in the past three months, the chief part of them committed from Cheltenham' (28 November 1833). The sufferers were often regular cases. 'Elizabeth Stevens is again in the Bridewell and is diseased as usual. It is not more than four and a half months since she left this place completely cured of Syphilis and is now as bad as ever. Ordered Medicines' (21 March 1832); and: 'Elizabeth Stevens, an incorrigible old prostitute is again in the Bridewell and as usual has Syphilis' (8

---

[396] *Eighteenth Report of Inspector, Southern and Western District*, PP, 1852-53, LII, 113, p 88.

[397] *Twenty-First Report of Inspector, Scotland*, PP, 1856, XXXIII, 659, p. 71.

[398] *First Report of Inspector, Northern and Eastern District*, PP, 1836, XXV, 161, p. 27.

November 1834). Sometimes there is a note of sadness. 'Eliza Jones has Gonorrhoea. This girl is now only seventeen years of age and this is the third time she has been here with the same Disease in rather more than two years' (2 December 1833). Perhaps naively, on one occasion the surgeon seems to have taken at face value an explanation any modern-day medical student would recognise as bogus: 'Fereby has Gonorrhoea caught by inoculation from matter left on the seat of the privy' (10 November 1827). A particularly nasty case is mentioned at Norwich '[name illegible] has the Venereal in the most malignant form and is in great danger from Mortification of the Penis' (27 September 1845).

The treatment (where specified) of syphilis was with mercury, probably in the form of mercurous chloride (calomel), which was also sometimes used in small amounts for worms, skin disease and other ailments, particularly for diarrhoea.[399] Calomel was extensively used at Horsley and Norwich in the form of 'Blue Pills'. However the surgeon always watched for excessive salivation, the first indication of overdosage, and then discontinued the treatment. When the surgeon at Northleach stated: 'The Venereal cases (as usual) have been very numerous but I have much pleasure in stating that they all (I believe without exception) left the prison cured' (8 January 1827) he was unduly optimistic, given the available therapeutic armamentarium. Doubtless symptoms were relieved and as we will see later, patients were sufficiently content with the treatment they were given that it was common to engineer commitment to prison purely for this purpose.

Skin disease was often described as an 'eruption' and was usually treated with simple ointments. Included in this group are ringworm, scrofula,[400] oral thrush and infestation by vermin. Simon Jackson probably had ringworm: '... bad head, and as the complaint is of a most contagious nature, I have removed him from his Class, and he is in a room in the Hospital and not allowed to mix with any of the Prisoners' (1 April 1843, Norwich) – he recovered. There was the occasional *rara avis*: at Littledean a diagnoses of 'Severe Leprosy' was made – treatment was felt to be contraindicated: 'From the nature of his case and necessary Medicines requisit [sic] for his relief being attended with risk in his present confinement and which being for so short a time, I do not think it safe to have him under such treatment' (30 July 1821).[401] At Kirton (Lincolnshire) house of correction a 25 year old male was diagnosed as being 'leprous' on admission to prison and when he died ten months later the cause

---

[399] Mercury had been used medicinally since the 16th century. Porter, *The Greatest Benefit*, p. 175. It was still recommended (in the form of calomel) in medical textbooks of the 1920s. Ibid., p. 674. Although often used in gonorrhoea, its lack of value in this condition was known. David Innes Williams, *The London Lock: A Charitable Hospital for Venereal Disease 1746-1952* (London: R.S.M. Press, 1997), pp. 5-6 & 57.

[400] Scrofula: tuberculous lymph node infection ulcerating through the skin. It seems likely that the term was also used for a variety of purulent skin conditions.

[401] Leprosy, like syphilis, would probably have been treated with mercury.

of death was given as: 'leprous and general breaking up of constitution.[402] A single case of leprosy is listed among the diagnoses at Shepton Mallet county gaol and house of correction in 1838-1839.[403]

RHEUMATIC COMPLAINTS

Rheumatic complaints, usually aches in the joints or limbs and 'pain in the side' were fairly common; liniments were usually prescribed. Serious episodes were less frequent:

> visited James Browning (debtor) who was just brought in. I found him exceedingly Ill with a Rheumatic Gout in his limbs ... he having little or nothing to subsist on, and requiring a more generous diet (than he can find himself) as essentially necessary to his recovery, I have directed him to be sent to the Hospital ward and to have a meat and milk dietary in aid of medicine. (14 March 1798, Gloucester county gaol)

It might have been thought that hard labour on the treadwheel would have resulted in rheumatic problems but these were unusual. The experience at Northleach was probably fairly typical. Two weeks after its installation the surgeon noted an immediate impact on prisoners' health: 'Several of the men complain of pain in their limbs all of which with one exception are unworthy of notice. The Mill is new to most of them and they will have pain in their lower extremities until they get accustomed to it'. (27 September 1827). And get accustomed to it they did:

> Since the treadwheel has been erected the men have many of them had cold and have complained of the work being too hard for them but they appear now to be pretty well reconciled to it. Those men who have been confined the greatest length of time are in much better health since the allowance of meat ... and express themselves grateful for it (14 October 1827).

Indeed some found it of positive benefit, at Brixton Hill house of correction: '[I asked] a woman who had been at the Wheel for a month awhile ago, and who went to work with a rheumatic complaint, how she felt when she went away; and she replied, that her rheumatism was completely cured'.[404] And at Bedford house of correction:

> [one of the prisoners reports that] he has enjoyed perfect health during the whole of the period of his year's hard labour at the Tread Mill: that he has never felt any pain in the loins or shoulders, or in the tendons near the heel; that he has experienced no numbness of hands or arms; that he has never heard any

---

[402] *Seventh Report of Inspector, Northern and Eastern District*, PP, 1842, XXI,1, p. 107.

[403] *Fifth Report of Inspector, Southern and Western District*, PP, 1840, XXV, 721, p. 114

[404] *Copies*, PP, 1824, XIX, 165, p. 14.

complaint from his fellow convicts, except, that when some of them first began to labour on the Wheel in their high shoes, the stepping galled their ancles [sic]; but that after they put on proper shoes, no inconvenience was experienced by them.[405]

As will become apparent later, the treadwheel produced problems for medical officers but complaints of persisting muscular aches and pains were not unduly common.

GASTRO-INTESTINAL PROBLEMS

Table 4:2 demonstrates that in Gloucestershire prisons gastro-intestinal complaints comprised the largest single category. This was equally true of other prisons – a typical journal entry (from Lancaster) reads: 'There are many cases of disordered bowels amongst the debtors, but none as yet serious' (18 April 1848). Other outbreaks were more dangerous. At Norwich on 6 December 1845 there were two cases of diarrhoea one, Samuel Balls, ill enough to be admitted to hospital. A few days later another case, John Baker, was also put in hospital and both continued very ill. Of Balls, the surgeon wrote on 27 December: '[he] has been so bad, that I despaired of his life and he continues in a most dangerous state. He has Brandy, Broth often allowed to him, and anything he can take. If he should live, his time for being in the Castle expires next Thursday'. He was seen daily by the visiting physician but did not live to achieve his discharge and died on 31 December; Baker was luckier and survived. Also at Norwich Francis Cushion was seen on 28 August 1848 with a 'severe attack of spasmodic cholera'. His diarrhoea and vomiting eased but then he experienced acute spasms of the limbs and his body was very cold. He recovered with the aid of calomel, a vapour bath, tincture of opium and brandy and, although another six cases of diarrhoea and vomiting followed, none was serious. A more alarming outbreak started on 9 October 1849 when the surgeon (Mr Master) was called to see ten men: 'seized with purging this evening accompanied by pain in their legs and bodyes [sic].' One of the warders was also affected and, significantly, all had been in 'No 2' (presumably one of the workrooms) and so Master ordered: 'The water closet attached to No 2 to have chloride of Lime in the cistern and the Day Room to be whitewashed'. All were given Dover's powder and mercury and chalk but on the following day were still ill, as were three others. They were transferred to 'No 8, in which I had a sufficiency of mats laid on forms to form temporary beds'. A measure of Master's concern is that he visited the prison five times on 10 October, but by 17 October all his

---

[405] *Copies*, PP, 1823, XV, 307, p. 5.

patients were better.

The summer months could be particularly unhealthy. At Kirkdale in his October 1824 report the surgeon wrote:

> [the prison had been] tolerably healthy and free from infectious diseases except during the months of August and September, at which period the dysentery and bowel complaints made their appearance to rather an alarming extent namely one hundred and fifty cases occurred but none of them proved fatal, the treatment adopted was to exhibit with Calomel and Opium or Ipecacuanha[406] on the first appearance and a mild purgative afterwards, which seldom failed.[407]

The following year: 'the males have suffered from it ['dysentery'] and Cholera but no case has proved fatal although there has been a necessity for pouring in brandy in three or four hours after the attack in several cases'. He attributed 'the escape of the females to be owing the superior warmth of their accommodations'.[408] There was an unpleasant episode at Wakefield county house of correction:

> June 27 1841. This evening, soon after the prisoners had retired to bed, several of them were seized with violent griping pains of the bowels, diarrhoea, vomiting, and cramp of the extremities. It soon became general, and before 11 o'clock most of the prisoners, male and female, were attacked. Many of the cases consisted of diarrhoea alone, without fever, in others the purging was incessant and uncontrollable; but there was no morbid quality in the evacuations, except that they were watery. The tongue was generally clean and moist, and of its natural colour, the pulse feeble, and the strength much prostrated. Those most debilitated by long confinement, and the boys, were most seriously affected.

No deaths were recorded and the surgeon blamed 'the *bad quality* of the *bread*, which, from some cause, for a few days previous had been *acid, heavy*, conjoined with a *peculiar fusty smell*. The potatoes also had begun to vegetate, and no doubt fermented in the stomach'.[409] In contrast, at Devizes house of correction the inspector notes the tendency to diarrhoea 'seems to have prevailed most in the months of November and December, and also at all seasons after sudden changes of the temperature. During April and May (1838) almost every prisoner seems to have more less been subject to it'. Nobody had died as a result of diarrhoea and, discarding the theory that the problem was the consequence of 'a *malaria* when the air ascends from the drains', recommended – with good results – a pint of warm gruel for supper each day. Well ahead of his time he notes that the water in the gruel was well

---

[406] Ipecacuanha: root of a South American plant, used as an emetic or purgative.

[407] LCRO, QGR/3/10.

[408] LCRO, QGR/3/15.

[409] *Seventh Report of Inspector, Northern and Eastern District*, PP, 1842, XXI, 1, pp. 53 and 55.

boiled 'which is no unimportant point'. For treatment the surgeon had moved from: *'Cretaceous Mixtures* with *Dover's Powders*, and *rice puddings'* to the much more dangerous-sounding but evidently more effective: '1 *grain doses of acetate of lead* combined with one-third of a grain of *opium* every six or eight hours ... combined with *warmth* and rice pudding'.[410]

The town of Northallerton was particularly unhealthy as a result of its poor sewage disposal system. Unsurprisingly the prison was affected – as the deputy-governor reported:

> Last spring, when the prison was very full, and when there was a great deal of diarrhoea, the place was in such an offensive state, that after making my morning round, I frequently vomited. I believe it was the same with the other officers. Every spring there is a good deal of diarrhoea and dysentery in the prison. This has been especially the case the last two years, when our number of prisoners has been much larger than heretofore. Last winter every officer, I believe, without exception, was attacked either with diarrhoea or fever. Those prisoners who are sent in for short periods generally improve in health, if they do not die from the debilitated state in which most of them come; but most of those who remain more than about three months, fall off in health, whatever be their condition of health on admission.[411]

This was an unhealthy prison due to sanitary conditions beyond the surgeon's control although as already noted, the situation was alleviated when eventually a new wing was built.

The favoured prophylactics against infectious disease were limewashing or chloride of lime. A doubtless equally effective approach was adopted by the surgeon at Kirton-in-Lindsey house of correction: 'When fever takes place, I always fumigate, using saltpetre and salt in equal parts; a table spoonful of each, and a couple of teaspoonfuls of oil of vitriol. I have noticed the most beneficial effects from it in cases of typhus and cholera'.[412]

Such fairly serious outbreaks of gastro-intestinal complaints were relatively rare but were obviously taken seriously by the surgeons who did all they could both in treatment and preventive measures and, despite adhering to the general (and as we know mistaken) belief in the miasmic theory of spread, were successful in controlling these potentially serious episodes.

Much more common complaints relating to the intestinal tract were constipation, less often mild (non-infective) diarrhoea, followed by abdominal pain, piles, hernia, jaundice, 'obstruction of the bowel', sickness, an occasional 'prolapsus ani' (perhaps a more severe case of piles but sometimes the result of debility), and worms. A spectacular example of the

---

[410] *Fourth Report of Inspector, Southern and Western District*, PP, 1839, XXII, 215, p. 103.

[411] *Fourteenth Report of Inspector, Northern District*, PP, 1849, XXVI, 167, p. 21.

[412] *Third Report of Inspector, Northern and Eastern District*, PP, 1837-38, XXXI, 1, p. 47.

last occurred at Norwich: 'William Porter who was for several days very ill, and a long worm was voided from his throat, which nearly suffocated him' (3 May 1845). Constipation was treated with aperients, their nature usually unspecified but at Littledean sometimes elaborated as a 'soothing aperient' or a 'cooling aperient' and salts were used in huge quantities at Northleach in the early 1820s. Sufferers from diarrhoea generally were given mixtures of chalk and opium, sometimes with mercury. Oddly, Charles L. Bradley at Pentonville successfully treated his many cases of diarrhoea with dilute sulphuric acid, sometimes leavened with ether or opium.[413]

Hernias were always noted carefully, more so in the later period, perhaps as a result of a communication received on 5 March 1825 from the Secretary of State requesting the surgeon 'to make a particular report, whether any Prisoner upon entering the Gaol has a tendency to Rupture and the Gaoler is directed not to place upon the Tread-wheel any Prisoner who has such tendency to Rupture'.[414] This arose because Robert Peel[415] had been informed of several cases of rupture at Shepton Mallet in 1825. The seriousness with which such matters were taken is shown by the fact that a visit was made by no less a personage than the president of the Royal College of Surgeons (W. Norris) accompanied by two council members (Sir William Blizard[416] and Henry Cline). These luminaries examined six of the eight prisoners concerned, had a spell on the wheel (Blizard was 82 years of age) themselves and concluded:

> We are unanimously of the opinion, that the labour of the Tread Wheel, at its velocity of 48 steps in a minute, cannot be prejudicial to the health of any person who is equal to common labour. That of the nine persons stated to have been afflicted with rupture, two only of such ruptures appear to us to be in any degree attributable to the labour of the Tread Wheel ... and that the labour of the Tread Wheel ... is not more likely to cause rupture or other injury, than the ordinary exertions of laborious life.[417]

Hernias are of course prone to complications and three obstructed hernias occurring at Norwich illustrate how far surgeons were prepared to go to alleviate suffering. The first on 20 January 1844 occurred in a debtor named

[413] *Reports of the Directors of Convict Prisons*, PP, 1854-55, XXV, 33, p. 31.
[414] NCRO, MF/RO 576/1.
[415] Sir Robert Peel: Home Secretary 1822-1827.
[416] Blizard, a redoubtable character, was surgeon to the London Hospital. In his time as President of the Royal College of Surgeons, one of his duties was to take over the bodies of executed criminals at Newgate in a shed near the prison where they were dissected. In the performance of this duty he would wear his robes of office over court dress, his appearance '...contrasting strangely with the surly shabbiness of the hangman ...' He retired from his post at The London (reluctantly one senses) at the age of 90. A.E. Clark-Kennedy, *The London: A Study in the Voluntary System, Vol. 1, 1740-1840* (London: Pitman, 1962), pp. 227 and 239
[417] *Copies*, PP, 1825 (34), XXIII, 567, pp. 15-18.

Wright, it was reduced with difficulty. On 17 February 1845 John Bunn (alias Grant) became very ill, with vomiting, and it took Mr Scott four hours, a warm bath and the help of Mr Master and Mr Johnson (another surgeon) to effect a reduction. Each patient was then supplied with a truss. More dramatically: 'At 3 o'clock this morning I visited Elizabeth Mason who was in a state of great suffering for an increase in size of a Rupture, which she has had all her life' (8 May 1845). This was 'a case of great danger', she was placed in the hospital and Messrs Master and Frith were consulted. However, by afternoon: 'her bowels have been opened and the great danger of this case removed'. At Lancaster on 20 February 1846 there is an entry: 'I was called this afternoon to reduce a hernia for James Wright, there was some trouble in doing so from the swollen state of the abdomen. Ordered a truss and an injection' (probably a suppository). And later the same day: 'Wright has not parted with the injection, he has pains like colic, he will take some castor oil and laudanum'.

RESPIRATORY DISORDERS

Respiratory tract complaints were mostly colds. An entry at Norwich is typical: 'Several prisoners have Colds from the severity of the weather, for which they are supplied with medicines in their cells' (20 January 1844). More serious cases were diagnosed as bronchitis, pleurisy, haemoptysis ('spitting of blood') or even pneumonia – some of which resulted in death. In the 1830s and 1840s there were influenza outbreaks: 'The Influenza has been very severe, but at present we are free from it and the prisoners are uncommonly healthy' (26 December 1843, Horsley). At Lewes county house of correction: 'February 25, 1841. The influenza is now raging with considerable violence throughout the prison. The vitiation of the atmosphere by the necessary trebling the cells occasioning it to be much more severe than would probably be the case could each prisoner be placed in a separate cell'. No deaths are recorded.[418] There were twelve cases at Littledean in the first half of 1848; two developed fever sufficient to need admission to the infirmary, but there were no deaths. Other outbreaks – a total of some 300 cases with two deaths – were recorded at Coldbath Fields, Bedford, Gloucester, Hereford, Worcester and Oxford.[419]

A notable absentee from the state of medical knowledge at that time was the disease entity of tuberculosis. "Consumption" had been recognised since the sixteenth century as a wasting disease, often accompanied by pulmonary

[418] *Fifth Report of Inspector, Southern and Western District*, PP, 1840 , XXV, 721, p. 377.
[419] *First Report of Inspector, Home District*, PP, 1836, XXCV, 1, pp. 94 and 214. *Fourth Report of Inspector, Southern and Western District*, PP 1839, XXII, 215, pp. 66, 166, 178 and 194.

symptoms, and usually fatal. Other manifestations of tuberculosis such as lymph node infection (often leading to scrofula), bone and joint infection, intestinal infection, urinary tract infection, and skin infection (lupus vulgaris) were recognised diseases but it was not until the similarity of the microscopic lesions (tubercles) in these apparently unrelated conditions was noted, that suspicion of a common aetiology arose.[420] Consequently most cases (and there must have been many) appeared under other labels. In prisons where stays were generally short diagnoses of what we can now safely say was tuberculosis was made – but infrequently. In the Northleach journals there was just one definite case: 'Robert Lock is affected with some of the early symptoms of consumption' (24 October 1834) and another at Lancaster: 'Iram Fay, a delicate man will go into the Debtor's Hospital, he is Consumptive I fancy' (12 November 1848). A case described at Northleach: 'distortion of the spine and psoas abscess therefrom' (27 February 1835) can confidently be ascribed to spinal tuberculosis. Myers, seen repeatedly at Lancaster in the second half of 1848 with 'a large collection of matter in this thigh' and who was 'failing' may have had bone tuberculosis. Probably tuberculous were the many cases of haemoptysis, persistent coughing, scrofula, and almost certainly many instances of "debility". However, even allowing for these, tuberculosis was not as common as might have been expected in the town and county gaols, in marked contrast to the situation described by William Baly in prisons such as Millbank, where confinement was longer and tuberculosis was rampant.[421] Most cases were treated with rest, improved diet and general supportive measures such as wine.

FEVERS

The fever category includes many relatively mild cases of undiagnosed febrile complaints as well as the serious infectious diseases already dealt with; the overall incidence of the latter was low. At Littledean in the 1820s there was a surge in cases mostly labelled 'cold and fever' or 'low fever of the typhoid kind'; they recovered quickly as did occasional cases of measles or hooping (sic) cough. More serious was an outbreak of measles at Norwich in July 1844. Two patients were very ill and needed a week or so in hospital before recovering. Less fortunate was Henry Rumsbye ('a boy') who became ill on 13 July and the following day was 'in a state of Delirium'. He was seen by Dr Hall and Dr Tawke, given meat, tea and port wine (in escalating

---

[420] Not confirmed until 1882 when Robert Koch isolated *Mycobacterium tuberculosis*.

[421] William Baly, 'On the Mortality in Prisons and the Diseases most frequently fatal to prisoners', *Medico-Chirurgical Transactions*' XXVIII (1845), p. 198. This matter will be covered in detail in a later chapter.

doses) reaching a pint daily ('the Port Wine has been of great use') but died a week later. The surgeon writes: 'since the disease is of a contagious nature, I have directed the Disinfecting Solution of Chloride of Lime to be used freely in the room'.

Erysipelas[422] occasionally assumed epidemic form – although hardly enough to warrant Porter's description of it 'decimating the population of gaols'.[423] The surgeon at Walsingham diagnosed an 'epidemical disease … in the form of erysipelas and typhus'. There were forty cases with five deaths.[424] At Wakefield, at a time when the prison was very overcrowded, there was an epidemic of erysipelas with three fatal cases – although 'little severe illness has been observed among the females, and they appear generally to bear the discomfort of the prison much better than the males'.[425] More serious outbreaks occurred at Millbank penitentiary, as reported by William Baly, physician to the prison:

> Erysipelas was more fatal than fever during the last year. Cases of this disease had become frequent in the prison in the previous year; but the mortality from it in London generally was then unusually high. In 1848 the number of deaths in the metropolis was 573; in 1849 the number had fallen to 459; but the frequency of cases of the disease in the prison still increased, and eight prisoners died of it; the ratio of mortality per 1,000 prisoners being 8.92 while in the previous year it was only 2.43. The disease manifested, in fact, its well-known tendency to become fixed in a particular building or part of a building. A large proportion of the cases, and all but one of the fatal cases, commenced in the infirmary. At length, it being found, that in spite of the ordinary methods of prevention, patients admitted to the infirmary for other complaints continued to be attacked with erysipelas, all the patients were temporarily removed from it; and it was thoroughly cleansed, and the walls and ceilings lime-washed. Since then no case of the disease has appeared.'[426]

Here Baly has made scientific observations and applied the conclusion for the benefit of the prisoners.

Some conditions are notable for their complete or relative absence. Few diagnoses of scarlet fever were made. A non-fatal case occurred at Gloucester city gaol on 19 February 1826 and the prison inspector reported a case at Southampton gaol – the keeper and two of his children also caught it probably because the keeper's bedroom adjoined the infirmary'.[427] No

---

[422] An acute, local, haemolytic streptococcal infection of the skin. Now rare and easily treatable with antibiotics.

[423] Porter, *The Greatest*, p. 259.

[424] *First Report of Inspector, Northern and Eastern District*, PP, 1836, XXXV, 161, p. 55.

[425] *Seventh Report of Inspector, Northern and Eastern District*, PP, 1842, XXI, 1, p. 51.

[426] *Report of the Inspectors of the Millbank Prison for the year 1849*, 1850, XXIX, 73, p. 14.

[427] *Sixth Report of Inspector Southern and Western District*, PP, 1841 Sess. 2, V, 177 , p. 91.

diagnoses of diphtheria were made.[428]

MISCELLANEOUS DISEASES

The miscellaneous category in table 3:2 includes such ailments as headaches ('a fullness in the head'), fits, sore eyes, chilblains (unsurprisingly, of 665 diseases among boy prisoners at Parkhurst gaol in 1843, 121 were ulcerated chilblains[429]), teething problems, menstrual irregularities, bedwetting (particularly at Lancaster), problems with micturition such as retention of urine, dysuria, slowing of the urinary stream or 'gravel', testicular problems, delirium tremens (again particularly at Lancaster), debility (where unaccompanied with any localising symptom), and toothache. The surgeon at Bristol city gaol had his own theory as to the cause of some of the testicular disease: '[he] thinks he has occasionally seen affections of the testicles, arising from masturbation, which he believes is not uncommon'.[430]

Ophthalmic disease could be serious. At Northleach Mary Chat with her infant were committed on 21 April 1821, the latter with purulent eyes. Despite washes with warm milk and water, the child developed corneal ulceration and then an aqueous discharge with protrusion of the iris. Two days later: 'sight irretrievably lost'.[431] And at Lancaster a corneal ulcer gave trouble: 'Blower has an ulcer on his cornea, I fancy produced by lime or other caustic' (2 April 1846) and: 'Blower wishes Mr Gaskell to see his eyes (having known him in Manchester), there can be no objection, indeed it may be as well as he will be blind' (25 August 1846). This is one of several examples of the prison surgeon happily acquiescing in a prisoner's request for a second opinion – something that could not happen in a despotic system.

There were few records of diabetes: 'Kearton has diabetes, she will go into the Penitentiary Hospital that she may have more animal food' (3 November 1848, Lancaster); although it is highly likely that other patients – perhaps some of the cases of debility – were sufferers. A detailed and accurate description is given by the surgeon at Wakefield house of correction of the case of a thirteen year old boy committed already suffering from diabetes. Despite the surgeon's best efforts the boy gradually lapsed into diabetic coma and died. A full autopsy was performed.[432]

---

[428] Although a clinical description of diphtheria had been published in 1748, major pandemics of the disease occurred only after 1850. Porter, *The Greatest*, pp. 158 & 438.

[429] *Reports relating to Parkhurst prison*, PP, 1844 , XXVII, 17, p. 17.

[430] *Sixth Report of Inspector, Southern and Western District*, PP, 1841 Sess. 2, V. 177, p. 134.

[431] This could well have been gonococcal. Williams, *London*, pp. 100-101.

[432] *Eleventh Report of Inspector, Northern and Eastern District*, PP, 1846, XXI, 483, p. 45.

A few cases of cancer were diagnosed.[433] At Kirkdale one of the deaths was: 'Catherine Kelly who was recommended to the mercy of the magistrates as labouring under cancer of the womb which is an incurable disease. She survived the period of her imprisonment about ten days then died in the hospital whence she had never been removed'.[434] At Spilsby house of correction John Pickering, who was serving one year, died from cancer of the face – rather poignantly his pardon was signed on the day of his death.[435]

Heart disease does not seem to have been common in these prison populations and was rarely diagnosed as such, except at Lancaster where it is mentioned under various labels: 'disease of the heart with dropsy', 'disturbed circulation of blood through the heart', 'irregularity of heart action', and plain: 'disease of the heart'. In most prisons there were instances of dropsy, almost certainly the result of heart failure, as well as the occasional: 'weakness of the heart'. Also at Lancaster a case of rheumatic fever was diagnosed: 'Kynan's case is one of rheumatic fever which will run its course' (7 July 1847). A much more detailed description of the management of a case of rheumatic fever was given by the surgeon at Salford house of correction. William H., aged 19, on 6 June 1844 was admitted to the infirmary:

> Has all the symptoms of this complaint, viz., intense fever, pain and swelling in the larger joints, especially the wrists, etc. He is ordered to bed. To apply warm fomentations, and to take a saline mixture with two grains of tartar emetic, one ounce every four hours; also to take at bed-time a powder with five grains each of calomel and James's powder. To have 'hospital diet'. June 7. Somewhat relieved, but the knees are now extremely swollen and painful. To continue the means ordered yesterday. June 8. Still increasing as regards the spreading of the rheumatic affection, but the pulse and other general symptoms are improved. To take a calomel and opium pill (two grains of the former with one-fourth of a grain of the latter) every four hours, alternately with the mixture. To continue the saline mixture simply, without the tartar emetic.

From then William H. improved steadily. Compound tincture of gentian was added to the medication and later, powdered bark; by 3 July he was discharged cured – perhaps lucky enough to escape valvular disease of the heart which was such a common sequel of this now virtually extinct disease.[436] At that time the relationship between the two conditions was not recognised.

An interesting complication of childbirth was noted at Gloucester city gaol and house of correction: 'Eleanor Jones ['safely delivered of a female child' three weeks earlier] has a swelling of her left leg which is peculiar to

[433] The word 'tumour' crops up in the Gloucestershire journals but in most of these the swelling (tumour means swelling) turned out to be inflammatory in origin.

[434] LCRO, QGR/3/22.

[435] *Reports and Schedules Pursuant to Gaol Acts*, PP, 1833, XXVIII, 1, p.153.

[436] *Tenth Report of Inspector, Northern and Eastern District*, PP, 1845, XXIV, 1, p. 121.

women lately confined' (14 January 1831). The leg was poulticed but did not improve: 'the disease is usually slow to be settled' – but after some bed rest she recovered. The surgeon is describing deep venous thrombosis which, although not peculiar to women 'lately confined', in the early-nineteenth century was probably most commonly seen as a post-partum complication. Unusual diagnoses were made at Kirton-in-Lindsey house of correction where there was a case of 'boulimia'[sic][437] and at Lancaster castle gaol, where the prisoners in one ward were 'affected by a most singular kind of swine-pock'. They had pustules on the face and chest lasting a few days.[438]

Major psychiatric problems will be covered in chapter five but there were a few relatively minor cases. The problem of reactive depression was understood: 'Clarice Powell seems to be much affected by her sentence and is become thin and depressed in her spirits, she also has chronic Pains in her joints etc., disorders common in girls of her past habits' (2 March 1832, Gloucester city gaol). Anxiety-induced illness was also recognised: 'Thos Blake, a debtor, much indisposed in his head, which I find arise from a derangement in his private affairs at home' (11 August 1795, Gloucester county gaol). Blake caused concern, needing visits several times daily and warranting the opinion of Dr Cheston ('who approves of his medical treatment' 13 August 1795), but he recovered. Another example of what he felt was anxiety-induced illness occurred in the case of Kid Wake, a political prisoner[439], who took up a good deal of the surgeon's time complaining of stomach trouble and weakness. A rather exasperated Parker wrote: 'Having observd his wife with him for several days passd, I cannot but remark that her frequent visits will not contribute to his case. Therefore have asked the Govr that it wd be right to dispense with her attention' (18 September 1797).

Since opium in various forms was freely available it is not surprising that some prisoners had usage problems. The surgeons dealt with these cases sympathetically. At Northleach: 'Visited Elizabeth Goodhead who complained very much of not having Opium to take; It being a very dangerous medicine, to be putting in the hands of people not competent to use it, and likewise a very Dear Article, I objected to her having it, without the sanction of the Magistrates' (19 August 1817). The sanction was granted. At Lancaster: 'One of the debtors had a narrow escape from the abuse of opium, he was discovered in the morning in a deep sleep and upon him was found a box of opium pills, marked "strong aperient pills", and he had a strong fit, and required strong efforts and treatment all the day and night to keep him awake'

---

[437] *Fifth Report of Inspector, Northern and Eastern District*, PP, 1840, XXV, 565, p. 26. Bulimia: a morbid hunger chiefly occurring in idiots and maniacs, OED.

[438] *Eighth Report of Inspector, Northern and Eastern District*, PP, 1843, XXV and XXVI, 249, p. 85.

[439] Whiting, *Prison*, p. 68.

(22 June 1844); 'Samples, a delicate woman for trial is admitted to hospital. She is a confirmed opium eater' (2 August 1844); and: '11.45 p.m. I have sent W. Molyneaux into hospital. He has been in the habit of taking opium – says he cannot sleep without it and disturbs the other inmates. I have taken a stack of opium from this man. He promised to aid me in the attempt to help him' (12 September 1849). We cannot know whether the problem was quite as widespread as reported by the surgeon at Wymondham:

> [I have] had occasion to believe the humbler classes are becoming addicted to the taking of opium, and to a much greater extent than supposed. Detected one woman here with half an ounce of opium concealed in her hair. She had been long an opium taker, and used to take a large quantity. She was a tramp, and was very grateful on going out for being taught to do without it. The prisoners frequently ask for opium in the shape of pills. Infants come here quite enervated from the use of opium, and go out in rude health from its discontinuance. In my private practice I have met with instances of the practice, but much more frequently among the poor. [440]

Perhaps the taking of opium was particularly prevalent in East Anglia for in 1853 at Wisbeach house of correction:

> The practice of eating opium is indulged to a great extent in this district. One woman who had been accustomed to take extraordinary quantities before she came to prison, felt the deprivation so keenly that she made an attempt to destroy herself. She had been some time in the prison when I saw her, and expressed herself very thankful for having been broken of the habit. [441]

His belief in the permanence of relief was shared by the surgeons at Wakefield house of correction and at Great Yarmouth borough gaol, both of whom give lengthy accounts of remarkable cures of opium addicts. [442] It might reasonably be objected that these surgeons were over-optimistic in their approach to the problem of abuse but at least they showed an impressive (touching even) faith in their patients' veracity.

GENERAL TREATMENT

Perhaps the most valuable help to the sick the surgeon could give was the ordering of extra diet, examples of which have already been given. Often this could be used prophylactically as with Ann Carpenter, delivered of a boy at Northleach on 29 November 1811 and generously treated. She was given oatmeal, beer, candles, and a bottle of gin together with three

---

[440] *Fifth Report of Inspector, Northern and Eastern District*, PP, 1840, XXV, 565, p. 99.

[441] *Nineteenth Report of Inspector, Northern and Eastern District*, PP, 1856, XXXIII, 385, p. 13.

[442] *Seventh Report of Inspector, Northern and Eastern District*, PP, 1842, XXI, 1, pp. 53 and 156.

quarters of a pound of mutton daily. And at Gloucester city gaol: 'Mary Peters who is suckling a young child should be allowed an extra quantity of diet, say ½ as much again as her present allowance' (29 October 1829). Two weeks later the surgeon notes that as Peters was already having enough bread the governor had given her an extra two pence daily: 'to buy sugar and the like for her child, an alteration of which I approve'. On 28 November 1829 Peters took the pitcher to the well once too often: '[she] begs to be allowed a pint of Beer in addition, as she however and her child are both appearing very healthy I have not considered it necessary to order it for her'. At Lancaster and at other gaols, milk was often given to those considered weak or in need of extra nourishment.[443] Writing of his orders for extra milk and vegetables the surgeon at Walsingham states: 'If I did not interfere in this general way and order extra diet, I should have nothing but disease; the numerous orders for extra diet in my journal are cases of prevention, not of actual disease'.[444] A different prophylactic was adopted at Worcester city gaol and house of correction: 'Daily attention is paid to the bowels of each prisoner, and if necessary, house medicine is administered, by which any threatened complaints are arrested'.[445]

Sometimes no more than robust common sense was needed:

> I was sent for late last night to see Higgin, this man was wet with sweat, he had his stockings round his throat, handkerchief round his head, was tied tightly up in his hammock with all his clothes, in short was parboiled. I gave him a dry blanket last night and a dry shirt this morning. (9 May 1844, Lancaster).

Mr Parker at Gloucester believed in the virtues of fresh air: 'observed the Gyptsy [sic] woman and Sara [indecipherable] much indisposed for want of walks out in the fresh air, order'd they air an hour daily' (8 August 1795); and: 'Lt Edward Fitzgerald (Debtor) is very unwell with a consumptive cough, Ordered medicines – as there are three gentlemen debtors they may have one of the Hospital rooms to sit in, as being more airy' (30 October 1798). He too showed common sense in advising that prisoners coming off the wheel[446] should not immediately drink cold water (22 July 1798).

Occasionally the patient's requirements were even more obvious:

> James Seymore was suddenly seized and fell to the ground with a fainting

---

[443] See footnote to table 3:1.

[444] *Seventh Report of Inspector, Northern and Eastern District*, PP, 1842, XXI, 1, p. 137.

[445] *First Report of Inspector, Southern and Western District*, PP, 1836, XXXV, 269, p. 84.

[446] This was a wheel in the prison yard for raising water. Prisoners worked on it for relatively short spells.

fit. On his recovery: I found he had eaten little that day, as he had nothing to subsist on, being out of work, and when employ'd his earnings amounted to only fourpence per day. I think the cause of this sudden attack arose from a want of a sufft Quantity of food to supply the natural craving of his appetite. Mr Cunningham (Govr) very humanely sent him a mess of good caudle (20 August 1794, Gloucester county gaol).[447]

Honora Witcroft aged 29 had an unpleasant problem: 'This woman has a sucking child, which has not been admitted into the Prison, the consequence is, one of her breasts is much distended and very painful'. She was given opening medicines and the breast was to be drawn and suffed[448] three times with brandy, resulting in recovery (29 July 1843, Horsley). Similarly at Northleach: 'I have also seen Elizabeth Patway who is suffering from her breasts in consequence of having left her child, I have directed her to have them drawn' (7 January 1838).

Where more active treatment was needed, wounds were dressed, poultices applied, ointments, embrocation, and liniments rubbed in, and medicines given. As Mary Fissell point out: 'All evidence from Bristol, and Britain more generally, points to the consumption of heroic quantities of medicine in the eighteenth century'.[449] Prisoner patients expected medication and they got it – usually in the shape of herbal remedies which were mostly harmless. Bearing in mind that the cost of medication was usually borne by the surgeon, its provision was remarkably liberal. Useful information is given in the journals from the Gloucestershire bridewells where prisoners received sudorific draughts, anodyne draughts, magnesia, camomile flowers, electuaries, fever medicine, rhubarb draughts (particularly for the infants), jalop, tincture cantharidum, tincture of cardamon (for disordered stomach at Horsley), colchicum mixture, bark (quinine), oil of turpentine, opium draughts, camphorated mixture, henbane, valerian, tragacanth, and castor oil.[450] At Norwich, compound ipecacuanha pills were given for asthma, vinegar lotion for an inflamed testicle, arsenical pills for cutaneous psoriasis, a mustard poultice and a warm bath for gravel (renal colic), castor oil and turpentine for worms, quinine pills or powder for ague, and iodide of potassium for secondary syphilis. What must have been a highly foot-

---

447 Caudle: a hot, sweetened drink for invalids.

448 Suffed: probably a version of suffused, to spread or cover with liquid.

449 Fissell, p. 56.

450 Anodyne draught: a medicine which relieves pain and which is quite harmless or perhaps does good in a more general sense; c.f. 'he drank the air as though it held / some healthful anodyne', Oscar Wilde, *The Ballad of Reading Gaol*, lines 117 & 118; and: 'When Rosamund was quiet, and Lydgate had left her, hoping that she might soon sleep under the effect of an anodyne ...', Eliot, *Middlemarch*, p. 839; electuary: medicine compounded with honey or syrup; jalop: root of a Mexican plant used as a laxative; cantharidum: preparation of dried Spanish Fly, used as a diuretic (to increase the renal output of urine); tragacanth: a kind of Asiatic gum.

tingling treatment for chilblains was ordered: 'Horseradish to be mixed with two ounces of Mustard and a gallon of water poured boiling on them to soke [sic] his feet in night and morning' (30 May 1817, Littledean). The use of digitalis had been popularised by William Withering in the 1780s. Although highly effective when administered correctly in appropriate cases, a failure to give the correct dose could result in death. Its use is mentioned only twice: at Northleach in 1838 when it was prescribed to William Atkins (27 December) along with antimony, camphorated mixture and hyoscyamus (he died five days later, apparently from pneumonia); and at Horsley for William Upton, aged 15, who was unwell with: 'scrofulous inflammation of the eyes, an inflamed eruption upon the body etc.' – he was given 'a Mixture with Sweet Spirits of Nitre, Tincture of Digitalis, Sulphate of Magnesia and Mint Water (8 November 1843).

When a patient was ailing, surgeons were as prone as any modern practitioner to use the scattergun approach to therapy. Thus, 22 year old Joseph Purser, complaining of cough and headache, was prescribed: 'Mixture with Ipepacuanha and Antimonal wine, Compound powder of Tragacanth, Compound Tincture of Camphor, Nitrate of Potash and Aniseed water' (Horsley, 28 August 1843) – three days later he was very much better. When an immediate result was not achieved there was no reluctance to change medication. Charles Richards, a thirty-three year old carpenter serving his fifth term at Littledean presented on 11 April 1844 complaining of diarrhoea. He was given aromatic powder, chalk and opium, with two ounces of tea and one pound of sugar per week. No better on the following day, his medication was changed to chalk and mercury, rhubarb and saline mixture, with paregoric and sal volatile added.[451] Two days later boiled rice and a little butter and sugar were substituted for his meat ration, and after another two days, cocoa for tea. On 18 April he was prescribed castor oil and calomel, followed by aromatic mint. Later he had a blister to his side; jalop and calomel; his hair cut close with vinegar and water applied as long as his head was hot; a tartar plaster to his stomach; extra mutton boiled and well seasoned with stale bread and mashed potatoes; four leeches to his head and finally, as a rather anticlimactic conclusion to this extended exercise in polypharmacy:

> Having been applied to certify as to the state of this man's health by the Board of Stamps and Taxes I made the following reply. "I herebye certify that Charles Richards has been under my care from April 11th to the present time, he was for a short period of that time unwell but in my opinion the latter and longer

---

[451] Paregoric: a soothing medicine containing opium. Sal volatile: pungent alcoholic solution of ammonium carbonate.

portion of that illness has been assumed on purpose to procure his liberation."
(8 June 1844).

Although a purist would criticise this therapeutic roller-coaster, the surgeon's enthusiasm and concern for his patient's well-being is beyond reproach.

SURGICAL INTERVENTION

The most commonly performed interventional procedure in Gloucestershire county prisons was bleeding, and although its efficacy was widely accepted there were risks. In the early-nineteenth century John McCall was bled by a student at the London Hospital and subsequently died. His near-relations accused the hospital of using a "poisoned lancet" – an accusation strenuously denied by the hospital governors.[452] In prisons, not uncommonly it was requested by the patient, as in: 'Bled at his own request for an affection of the head to which he states himself to have been for some time subject' (4 June 1821, Northleach). The amount of blood removed was not always specified; in the Gloucestershire prisons; the largest volume noted was twelve ounces (about 350 millilitres). However, at Great Yarmouth borough gaol and house of correction, patient S.B. who was 'subject to epileptic fits' as well as 'under a high degree of excitement she is said to have attempted to destroy herself' was relieved of '2 lbs. 10 oz. [of] much inflamed' blood (about 1,200 ml) – a significant amount.[453] The removal of such large volumes seems to have been unusual, in most instances bloodletting was not repeated and was seldom used for seriously ill patients. At Lancaster bleeding is mentioned only once, for fits on 18 May 1848, but leeches were often used, being applied to the appropriate part of the body for disorder of the bowels, cramps, heart problems and pain in the head – much the same indications as applied in the Gloucestershire prisons for bleeding. Leeches were popular at Gloucester city gaol – as many as twelve to the head of a patient dying of typhus (30 January 1829) as well as for a variety of other conditions such as fits and an inflamed eye.

Blistering (a treatment with a distinguished pedigree, which seems to have been achieved by the application of a hot mustard poultice) was used regularly, particularly for patients with severe aches or pains or undiagnosed neurological disorders such as fits, 'fullness in the head', and disturbances of consciousness; in the last of which the blister was often applied to the nape of the neck or the temple. At Norwich, in addition to these uses, the blister

---

[452] Clark-Kennedy, pp. 218-219.
[453] *Seventh Report of Inspector, Northern and Eastern District*, PP, 1842, XXI, 1, p. 156.

Publish'd Jan' 28th 1804. by H. Humphrey St James's Street. London.

Breathing a vein.

'Breathing a vein'. Etching, J. Gillray, 1804.

was applied to the chest for coughs. At Horsley a sore throat was treated by a blister to the throat, as was 'rheumatism of the face'. There could be complications: At Horsley James Evans complained of pain in his side on 10 July 1843 and a blister was ordered. Five days later: 'Blistered surface very sore and painful, to go to bed and have it poulticed twice a day' and three days later Evans was still in bed on account of this soreness.

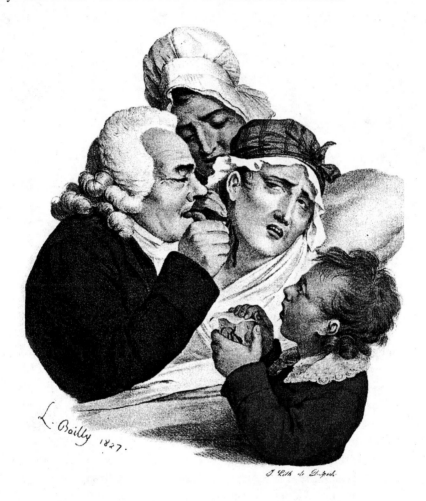

DIE BLUTEGEL
von Louis Boilly (1827).
(Erklärung siehe Rückseite.)

Calcium - Diuretin „Knoll"
(Theobromin.-Calcium-Salicylicum).
Bildserie I, Nr. 3.

Leeches administered to a patient. Lithograph, Boilly, 1827.

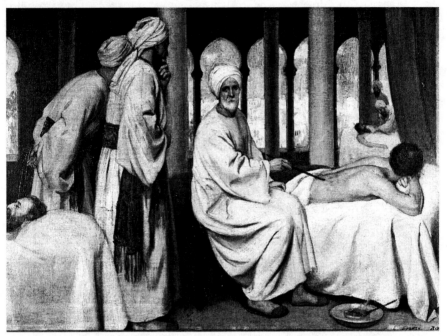

Albucasis blistering a patient in the hospital at Cordova, 1100 AD. Oil painting, Ernest Board, circa. 1912.

Cupping, which had a similar effect to blistering, is mentioned only at Lancaster where it was used for haemoptysis, an inflamed knee, pleurisy, fits, and pain in the chest or side. There, blistering was used for dyspnoea and for enuresis – as in: 'Langton wets the bed again, he will require another blister or two' (5 May 1847). In another instance, despite its being effective, blistering did not gain the patient's approbation: 'Butterworth [a juvenile bed-wetter] is cured, he does not like the blistering system' (3 May 1844).

For prisoners with a hernia the provision of a truss was standard practice, particularly after the introduction of the treadwheel. At Lawford's Gate house of correction the truss had to be handed in on discharge[454] but where such a rule did not exist there was scope for entrepreneurial activity: 'Atkinson who has a large rupture is come in again to us and he has sold the truss that he was given here to him. I shall not supply another without the sanction of the magistrates' (5 April 1848, Lancaster). Perhaps surprisingly, two days later: 'Atkinson is to be supplied with another truss'. These examples indicate that trusses were re-used – a rather unappealing example of re-cycling. On one occasion a hearing aid was recommended: 'Donohoe is deaf, he wants an

---

[454] *Fifth Report of Inspector, Southern and Western District*, PP, 1840, XXV, 721, p. 99.

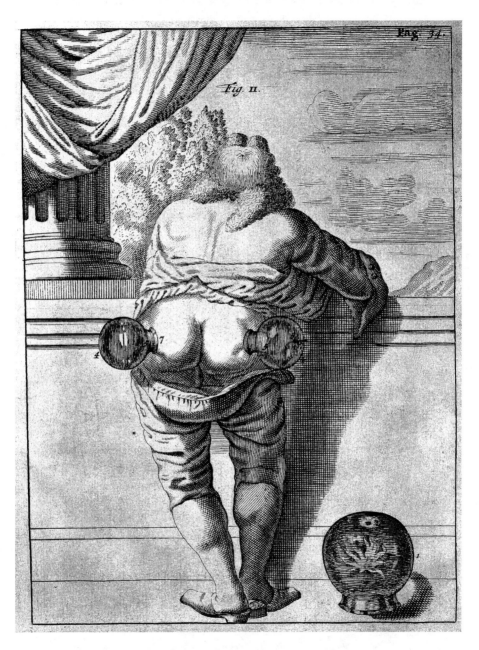

Two cupping glasses on the buttocks of a gentleman. Dutch textbook, 1694.

ear trumpet for use in the chapel' (Lancaster, 10 January 1845). At Portland, the surgeon had an air-bed specially constructed for a patient bedridden with a chronically diseased hip joint.[455] There was even what seems to have been an early example of the practice of intermittent self-catheterisation: 'I have directed Mr Jeffs [the governor] to allow the latter [Thompson, a venereal patient] to receive some catheters he has been in the habit of using' (Gloucester city gaol, 4 April 1832). Medical students are told that a Victorian gentleman unable to empty his bladder in the usual fashion would carry a catheter in the lining of his top hat to use as necessary. With the advent of (comparatively) safe prostatic surgery the practice fell into disuse but was revived in the 1970s (without the top hat) for the management of neurogenic retention of urine.[456]

Operations of an elective nature were rare but minor emergency procedures were regularly carried out. Teeth were pulled, boils lanced, fractures were set and splinted, a seton inserted,[457] urinary catheters passed in cases of retention of urine, hydrocoeles tapped, babies delivered ('delivered Ann Danial of a female Bastard child' (8 May 1792, Gloucester county gaol)), a fistula-in-ano laid open, ears syringed and urethral strictures dilated. This last procedure (as modern surgeons know) is not always easy but prison surgeons were conscientious and persevering in their approach. At Norwich: 'but after considerable difficulty I have passed Bougies [metal rods curved at the tip] into his bladder, the only means that can be employed in such cases' (17 January 1846); and at Gloucester city gaol, Mr Wilton notes that he had to come in at night and 'after a considerable time' passed an instrument into the bladder in a case of retention whilst on the following night: 'I was with him an hour and a half when I succeeded in getting an instrument into his bladder' (30 September and 1 October 1835). The surgeon at Littledean was luckier than he realised to get away with the following intervention:

> Mr Parsons [previously treated for venereal disease] generally better, complaining of difficulty in passing his Water, examined him with a Bougie and found him to be strictured (25 January 1826). Mr Parsons considerably better as to the Venereal disease but labouring under hydrocoele and Dropsy of the Scrotum ... action may be necessary, but at present I do not consider it in a fit Shape (10 February 1826). Mr Parsons being seized with shivering, succeeded by fever in the course of yesterday ... (11 February 1826).

---

[455] *Reports of Directors of Convict Prisons*, PP, 1857-1858, XXIX, 483, p. 322.

[456] H.N. Whitfield, W.F. Hendry, R.S. Kirby, & J.W. Duckett, *Textbook of Genitourinary Surgery* (Oxford: Blackwell, 1998), p. 956.

[457] 2 July 1825, Gloucester city gaol: 'Today I made a Seton in Harris's neck ... it [presumably a chronic abscess in the neck] has been of long standing and its cure or even relief very doubtful'. A seton is a length of non-absorbable suture material inserted to keep a chronic abscess open.

He is, unwittingly, giving a convincing description of the sequence of events following instrumental damage to the urethra, resulting in extravasation of urine and bacteraemia (leakage of urine into the tissues and invasion of the blood stream by bacteria). In the absence of antibiotics, Mr Parson's recovery verged on the miraculous. Less fortunate was a 48 year old at Millbank penitentiary, known to have a stricture, who died on 8 December 1848 from: 'fever and ruptured urethra'.[458] Spontaneous rupture of the urethra is rare so this death probably followed a bouginage. Similarly, in 1832 there was a death at York castle county gaol from 'Spacelus [sic] of the Scrotum, from long continued Stricture. A very old man'.[459]

The surgeon at Devizes house of correction was the most ambitious – and one hopes since we do not have the outcomes, the most competent – of his peers: 'During the last five years the surgeon has performed the operation of castration, of hare lip, hernia humoralis and others'.[460] At Barnstaple borough gaol the inspector notes: 'A woman has been operated on for cancer, she is now doing well'. We are not told what type of cancer but it was probably of the breast as was certainly the case at Oxford county gaol and house of correction where, as already noted in chapter three: '[for] amputation of the breast, he received two guineas'.[461] Mr Macmurdo at Newgate said he had operated 'more frequently than I should have expected to' and 'had a proper Place for those Operations'.[462] A less satisfactory incident is recorded on one of the hulks at Woolwich. Robert Ellis had been subjected to an unsuccessful operation for club-foot at Millbank and was subjected to another – equally unsuccessful – operation on the hulk.[463] The inspector was rightly critical: 'I have always advised medical officers in penal establishments against performing operations other than those rendered indispensable by the condition of the patient'.[464] It would seem that in general this advice was followed and that the vast majority of prison surgeons adopted a cautious approach, avoiding what might have been a temptation to practice their skills on a captive population.

An accident at Norwich on 20 May 1848 was dealt with competently:

[458] *Thirteenth Report of Inspector, Home District*, PP, 1847-48, XXXV, 461, p. xv.

[459] *Second Report of Inspector, Northern and Eastern District*, PP, 1837, XXXII, 499, p. 109. "Sphacelus": inflamed gangrene.

[460] *Second Report of Inspector, Southern and Western District*, PP, 1837, XXXII, 659, p. 11. The meaning of hernia humoralis is unclear. It may have been a hernia filled with fluid.

[461] *Fourth Report of Inspector, Southern and Western Districts*, PP, 1839, XXII, 215, pp. 19 & 195.

[462] *Second Report*, PP, 1835, XI, p. 379.

[463] Shades of Charles Bovary.

[464] *Report of Minutes of Evidence taken upon and Enquiry into the General Treatment and Condition of the Convicts in the Hulks at Woolwich*, PP, 1847, XVIII, 1, p. xxxiii.

> I was summoned shortly after 2 p.m. to see Benjamin Elsey[465] who had met with an accident on the wheel. His right foot had been drawn into the wheel, on examination I found the foot very much lacerated all the toes being fractured and the calcaneo-cuboid joint being opened. I asked Mr Godwin Johnson in to consult on the case and also Mr Cooper; as all agreed that partial amputation of the foot ought to be performed, the operation was immediately performed. Elsey has been watched since the operation by my pupil and an extra nurse and is going on favourably.

Happily he did well and, although three ligatures still remained on 17 June:[466] 'he is now out of danger and I do not see any occasion to keep him longer if he wishes to be discharged'. As well as employing a nurse from outside the prison, an additional indication of the magistrates' concern to "do right" by Elsey is that on 12 August a two guinea subscription to Norfolk and Norwich Hospital was authorised so that he could be transferred there and on 2 December 1848: 'Ordered the Surgeon to provide a Boot for Benjamin Elsey whose foot was mutilated on the Tread Wheel in May last'.[467]

Less successful was the intervention at Wilton county gaol and house of correction, where a 22 year old (sentenced to 15 years) had been admitted in a poor state of health with a diseased knee joint. He died after five months in prison, following an amputation.[468] A better result ensued at Northallerton where a prisoner was discharged after having both feet amputated, the magistrates having 'committed him from motives of charity [with] mortification of the limbs' from lying out in the cold.[469]

Surgeons occasionally showed a willingness to innovate although at Gloucester county gaol in January 1796, application of state-of-the-art science proved unavailing. Mr Parker was particularly worried regarding the progress of two patients with gastro-intestinal infection (possibly typhoid). Dr Roberts (the physician used for consultation) was not available initially, so he asked the advice of another surgeon, Mr Naylor. His help proved to be of no avail and presumably on a "desperate times call for desperate measures" basis he tried an original form of treatment:

> Prior to the Doctor's Visit, I have given each a full spoonful of yeast, on the presumption that the fixable air, generated by that ferment, would operate as a powerful antiseptic. This I communicated to Dr Roberts who in addition whishd [sic] it to be tried by way of Clyster, which has been done. (30 January 1796)

---

[465] Described in the 1850 inspector's report as "a boy", (p. 2).

[466] Ligatures (applied to blood vessels) were made of non-absorbable material and so were left until they fell out.

[467] *Visiting Justices Minute Book*, NCRO, MF 880.

[468] *Ninth Report of Inspector, Southern and Western District*, PP, 1844, XXIX, p. 383.

[469] *Sixteenth Report of Inspector, Northern and Eastern District*, PP, 1851, XXVII, 461, p. 89.

The theory – that fixable air (carbon dioxide) would combat putrid disease – seemed perfectly sound in 1796 but the outcome was unsatisfactory: both died.[470] Even more adventurous and well ahead of his time was a Dr Stevens who offered his help in an outbreak of cholera at Coldbath Fields. The idea was to give intravenous saline but the patient's veins were too collapsed to take a needle. Rather unsportingly, the patient got better anyway.[471]

THE PRISONER/DOCTOR DIALECTIC

One of Sim's contentions is that prisoners developed 'deeply embedded and significant patterns of resistance' to their medical attendants – there was a prisoner/doctor dialectic.[472] If this is to be believed, then there are several ways in which a prisoner could attempt to counter medical hegemony: by violence to the doctor, refusal of treatment, demanding a second opinion, making unnecessary demands on the doctor, or malingering. The last problem, which was common, will be dealt with in the next chapter, but as I will now demonstrate, instances of the other categories were rarities.

Of the most extreme form of violence there are just two examples. Both occurred after the period under study but it would be perverse to ignore them. In February 1856, prisoners on the hulks, seeing themselves deprived of their chance of transportation to Australia by the passage of the Penal Servitude Act, rioted, and one of them murdered Mr Hope, an assistant surgeon. He was described as being: 'most kind, attentive, and humane, clever in his profession and gentle in his treatment of the patients'.[473] The second episode took place at Pentonville in 1857. The offender in this case had been sentenced to four years penal servitude for burglary but proved extremely troublesome. Moved from prison to prison he murdered a warder at Millbank, for which he received a sentence of transportation for life. Moved to Pentonville, he '... *savagely attacked the medical officer, and stabbed him* with a weapon he had previously constructed for the purpose' – claiming his food was being poisoned. The fate of the medical officer is not recorded but presumably the wound was not fatal. The prisoner was judged insane but since at that stage there was no institutional provision for the criminally insane (Broadmoor opened in 1863) he continued his

---

[470] Priestley's work in the 1770s on atmospheric gases led to the idea that 'putrid diseases' could be combated by 'fixable air' released by fermentation. Jenny Uglow, *The Lunar Men: The Friends who Made the Future* (London: Faber and Faber, 2002), p. 233.

[471] Chesterton, pp. 205-214.

[472] Sim, *Medical*, p. x.

[473] Campbell, *The Intolerable*, p. 203. *Reports of the Directors of Convict Prisons*, PP, 1857 Sess. 2, XXIII, 65, p. 370. The offender was tried at Winchester, found guilty, and executed.

perambulation from prison to prison.[474] It seems that both surgeons were attacked as symbols of authority and happened to be available, rather than because they were doctors.

Lesser acts of violence were almost equally rare. At Gloucester county gaol there were two incidents:

> (1) Ann Collett, a Felon, is extremely Riotous and has struck me upon my visit to her. I have recommended the application of the hand Bolts and that shd for the present be confined in a Dark Cell (28 January 1816). (Later): she has begged forgiveness (31 January 1816). (2) This evening visited Mr Franklin Debtor who I was told had been in violent Fits for two hours, during which time he had been very noisy and clamorous. His conduct was so outrageous that on my going to the bed-side he struck me with his fists; as I was immediately convinced of his perfect sanity and that his conduct was the effect of Temper I did not hesitate to return it, and continuing the application of force confined him by strait-waistcoat etc.' (6 February 1820). Upon my expatiating with him upon his impropriety of conduct, after many fruitless attempts to deceive me, [Franklin] at last acknowledged it, and earnestly requested I would not communicate it to the Magistrates (8 February 1820). [Franklin's] conduct is now as it should be (9 February 1820).

Flouting medical authority by refusing treatment or advice was equally rare. From the many thousands of doctor/patient encounters I have examined in surgeons' journals only the following examples emerged. At Gloucester county gaol, Portland, a debtor complained of pain in his face but 'refused the aid of medicine' (27 March 1793); 'Pash, a Debtor has an ulcerated leg, which has been of long standing, he has refused to comply with proper but necessary treatment and regimen. I have therefore left him to his own treatment. He appears to be a very surly fellow' (7 July 1794); and: 'Baldwin has a return of the complaint in his bowells [purging] he, however, refuses to take the rice dietary altho the most proper food for his complaint. Gave him medicines' (30 December 1797). On one occasion the surgeon was willing to let a patient have his own way: 'Glosip, (who thinks himself ill) has again requested I would let him have Dr Lakes Pills to which I have consented' (19 January 1798). At Horsley: 'Daniel King, aged 39, Rheumatism, I sent this man a blister but he refused to put it on' (15 July 1843). At Northleach, Thomas Taynton, on being confronted with the instruments, refused to proceed with a proposed dental extraction (21 February 1826); Thomas Paradine, with chronic inflammation of the lungs, refused to apply a blister (25 August 1827); and Charles Anderson in solitary confinement refused to take medicines: 'I administered a Clyster (an enema) which has considerably relieved him' (14 June 1836). At Littledean, Mary Ann Grant, who had

---

[474] *Report of the Directors of Convict Prisons*, PP, 1857-1858, XXIX, 483, pp. 9-10.

been admitted already having the itch, and 'is otherwise diseased [probably venereal disease] refuses to take part of her medicines' (15 July 1836) but four days later: 'Mary Ann Grant having taken her Medicines since my last visit I find her better'. There were similar occasional problems at Lancaster: 'Mr Hartley is taken to hospital to have a truss for old hernia, he is very obstinate and would gladly avoid the use of one' (20 September 1845), followed by: 'Old Hartley was admitted to hospital, he has left off his truss and got his rupture complication' (1 October 1845); 'The old Italian [Cornetti, who had fallen in the yard and broken his collar bone on 10 January] will not wear a bandage' (11 January 1848); 'Sanderson declined the cupping, the threat cured him' (16 May 1849); and 'McGee, a man lately come in for two years is likely to give some trouble, he wants to write out for remedies and refuses to take the medicines prescribed' (24 June, 1847). The surgeon at Maidstone county gaol and house of correction describes the case of a prisoner who had been advised to have his leg amputated for long-standing disease (probably osteomyelitis) but, even though the operation was to be done in the presence of the senior surgeon from St Thomas's Hospital, he changed his mind at the last minute and asked to have it done at St Thomas's.[475] His release was agreed but in reality his chances of surviving the operation would almost certainly have been better in prison with its lower population of virulent pathogens than those colonising the operating theatre at St Thomas's.

Surgeons occasionally had to put up with irony, at the Ilchester inquiry, Mr Bryer was asked '[question] How with respect to the debtors? – [answer] I go to the window and open it, and ask if any want me, and if they do they come up. They know me very well, and very frequently they tell me facetiously that they want a cook more than a doctor';[476] and at Lancaster: 'Griffiths and McGee want respectively a pint and a gill of turpentine, they say it is a more suitable remedy than any I prescribe for them. Murphy also wants to prescribe for himself. I have never seen the men so out of humour with the surgeon, I think they want more employment' (13 September 1847).[477]

At Norwich, a patient was recalcitrant:

> Henry Stoker, a Debtor, has not eaten any food since Saturday morning. On examining him this morning and asking whether he is sick or not he refuses to give any answer excepting that it is my business to determine that question. In my presence he refused to go to Chapel or to find the Gaoler. I think it improper for him to be left to himself for the present (18 September 1849).

---

[475] *Fifteenth Report of Inspector, Home District,* PP, 1851, XXVII, 1, p. 36.

[476] *Reports (Appendix),* PP, 1822, XI, 313, p. 130.

[477] It was Griffiths who, as described earlier in this chapter, had kicked another prisoner on 16 June 1847, cutting his lip and knocking a tooth out.

The inmates at Lancaster were not disposed to accept what they regarded as second-class service:

> The prisoners are unsettled by the usual allowance on Xmas [sic] day being with-drawn.[478] Bell, the boy who has before been troublesome, injured his shin, and then knocked loudly for the doctor. My assistant would have dressed his leg but he saucily refused. I afterwards went up, dressed his leg, and sent him into a round house cell (25 December 1843).

The assistant was also accused of medical negligence: 'Collins makes a complaint that my young man has taken out the wrong tooth but I think there is some malice behind' (17 February 1846). There could be no criticism of the speed with which the matter was dealt with, for just four days later: 'Mr Bolden [presumably one of the magistrates] has just heard Collins' complaint against my pupil for extracting the wrong tooth and he sees the object'. The language is rather opaque but the assumption must be that Mr Bolden also thought the complaint was motivated by malice.

A technique guaranteed to irritate any doctor is the making of unnecessary calls, particularly at night. Typically at Lancaster: 'Visited Captain Sistain. It seems to me very unreasonable that this man shd send for the medical officers so unnecessarily as he is in the habit of doing' (9 July 1845); 'Bennington and Wilson sent for me late last night. As I had reason to suspect both I made them dress and come to the round house. They made trifling complaints but I believe only excuses for sending for the surgeon' (26 January 1846). There were other similarly unnecessary calls on 4 August 1847 (10.10 p.m.); 8 November 1847; 4 March 1848 (9 p.m.); 13 July 1849 (9.30 p.m.); 20 July 1849 (1 a.m.); and 20 September 1849 (11 p.m.). The journal entry: 'Johnson is complaining about the mill again … he wants to be master, but this we must resist' (13 September 1844) might be seen as an example of resistance to medical hegemony but is more reasonably seen as an example of the generally lax disciplinary regime at Lancaster.[479]

Isolated examples of a prisoner asking to see another doctor took place at Lancaster: 'Bennington is now disposed to be saucy, I forgave him his extra duty in the mill, now he says he cannot do the ordinary time and he will send a doctor out of the town about it' (19 August 1845). There were two such at Gloucester county gaol: 'Mr Yates … complains of the coldness of the Room, he says if he shd find himself ill he shall not apply to me but

---

[478] The governor's journal, (LCRO, MF 1/37) notes, 'Prisoners in wings D and E refused to go to Chapel this afternoon because they were dissatisfied that the Magistrates declined allowing the usual Christmas treat' (25 December 1843). The only explanation forthcoming was that 'they had not deserved it', there were further minor disturbances and on 26 December 'The men appear sullen still'.

[479] DeLacy, pp. 190-208.

to some other Professional Gentleman, to which I informed him he was at perfect liberty to do' (13 February 1810); and:

> Understanding that Champion (Debtor) was in Bed ... learned that he had this morning sent for a Professional Gentleman of the name of Drayton [another Gloucester surgeon, occasionally involved in joint consultations at the gaol] who has not yet visited him. I was inclining to see him but was upon my approach in an insulting tone of voice told that it was not to be wanted ... I very soon left this fellow but directed if he wished me to see him he had only to request it (6 August 1813).

These examples of minor disagreements between surgeon and patient are such as every medical man encounters in routine practice. They cannot seriously be upheld as instances of a dialectic. Noteworthy throughout is the willingness of the surgeon to tolerate the foibles of his charges and the generally good-humoured way with which their complaints were met. As against these few examples of recalcitrance I will now provide ample evidence that prisoners often experienced healthier conditions in gaol than were available to them outside and not infrequently engineered committal in order to take advantage of prison medical care.

PRISON HEALTHIER THAN HOME?

Adulatory remarks made by prison staff on the subject of health care in prisons have to be taken with a certain amount of caution. Nevertheless, it should be remembered that their comments were read by magistrates or made to prison inspectors – men familiar with the events described and therefore well able to detect mendacity. Many surgeons wrote proudly of the healthy state of their charges. At Gloucester county gaol:

> The Surgeon has the Pleasure to report to the justices assembled at the Michaelmas Sessions that the Prisoners (confined) in general enjoy a good state of health. He had the Opportunity of observing in his private practice the almost general prevalence of the Cholera Morbus, and Dysenteric intestinal Flux's. Yet only one instance has occurred within the walls of the Gaol, which he conceives to be owing to the temperance and regular mode of living there observed N.B. those that have been under cure in the foul ward, came in with their diseases (7 October 1794).

Journal entries on 16 April 1795, 26 April 1797, 20 July 1798 and 20 October 1818 are couched in a similar vein, stressing the absence or relative absence of disease in the prison as compared to the town. Similarly, at Littledean house of correction: 'Typhus fever frequently prevails to a great extent in the immediate neighbourhood but no case within these walls' (25 October

1847); at Gloucester city gaol: 'The low fever [another synonym for typhus] so prevalent in the Town is happily not to be found within the walls of the Prison at this time (23 December 1829); 'Scarlet Fever, at this time and for the last fourteen months has been very general throughout the city [Gloucester], to such an extent that three or four persons have died in the same family, but there have not been more than three or four cases in the prison, although several young persons have been confined there';[480] and at Salford house of correction: 'Although there has been much sickness prevailing in the town and district, no particular increase of disease has been observed among the Prisoners confined in this gaol during the last quarter; and this circumstance must be attributed to the excellent regulation by which it is governed with regard to diet, cleanliness and ventilation (quarterly report, 24 October 1824).[481]

Such comments were echoed by prison inspectors. At Winchester: 'A fever has prevailed in the town since my last visit, but only one case of it occurred in the gaol or house of correction';[482] at Leicester county gaol: 'There is very little diarrhoea on the whole; it is less frequent in the prison than in the town';[483] at Lichfield city gaol: 'There was no influenza in the prison, but a good deal in the town. The cholera did not show itself here at the time of the epidemic visitation';[484] at Coventry city gaol: 'There was not one case of cholera in the prison, while there were 117 cases in the workhouse, of which more than 50 were fatal, if I am rightly informed';[485] at Derby county gaol: 'There has been considerable epidemic disease in the town. Diarrhoea has been very prevalent, as also low fevers, with typhus. The cases of diarrhoea within the gaol have proved of a light character, and yielded to ordinary treatment';[486] at Folkingham house of correction: '... in the last autumn, when the English cholera was extremely prevalent in the county, not a single case occurred in the house of correction. Influenza has also been prevalent in the vicinity but not in the prison',[487] and at Bedford house of correction: '... while scarlet fever and typhus have been prevalent in the neighbourhood they have not appeared in the gaol'.[488]

There were also comments on the generally better health of prisoners and on the gratitude they showed. At Bristol city gaol: 'The Governor believes

---

[480] *Report*, PP, 1843 (463), XLIII, 375, pp. 29-30.

[481] LCRO, QGR/4/11.

[482] *Sixth Report of Inspector, Southern and Western District*, PP, 1841 Sess. 2, V, 177, p. 99.

[483] Ibid., p. 196.

[484] *Fourth Report of Inspector, Southern and Western District*, PP, 1839, XXII, 215, p. 142.

[485] Ibid., p. 145.

[486] *Eleventh Report of Inspector, Northern and Eastern District*, PP, 1846, XXI, 483, p. 37.

[487] Ibid., p. 62.

[488] *Thirteenth Report of Inspector, Midland and Eastern District*, PP, 1847-48, XXXVI, 1, p. 12.

that the prisoners usually leave the prison in a much better state of health than that which they enjoyed at their entrance';[489] at Lancaster the surgeon stated: 'The labour in the prison is less, and the prisoners enjoy a superior diet to those of their class beyond the walls: at the same time I think it is not a particle more than they ought to have, for the long time they are shut up, and the depressing nature of the confinement';[490] at Devizes house of correction it was stated that the prisoners 'look healthier on discharge than on admission and usually gain weight'[491] and at Derby county gaol, the surgeon (referring to A.B., alias A.C., who had spent a great deal of time in prison nearly all of it under medical care before she died):

> I stated before the coroner that she died from chronic inflammation of the lungs, and she had been a great invalid for many years, that she always wished to live in the prison, and that she always appeared comfortable, as far as circumstances would permit, and that she expressed herself most grateful for all she had had done for her in prison, and that she did so a few hours before she died, as well as at other times.[492]

In at least one instance prisoners actually wrote to express appreciation and the surgeon at Salford was not too modest to show the inspector their letters:

> Sir, I wish to return my thanks for the benefit I have received from your kind attention during my late illness. (M.B., February 22nd 1837). Sir, I cannot leave this place without expressing a deep sense of the obligation under which I am laid to you for the kind and prompt attention you have paid to me during one of the most painful afflictions I have ever felt or endured. If you will have the goodness to accept of my sincere thanks for the benefits I have received at your hands since I have become afflicted, it will much oblige. (J.G., May 3rd 1837). I desire to return my most sincere thanks for the cure you have made in me; and if it had not been for your kindly interference I should have been a dead man, and had I died in that state I should have lost both my soul and body. (J.W., September 28th 1837).[493]

Reports of individuals contriving committal in order to get treatment are fairly common. 'I have just been to see Michael Kirwin who has venereal disease very bad and he tells me he got committed on purpose to get it cured. I have given him the proper remedies' (13 May 1837, Northleach). At Portsmouth borough gaol the surgeon 'thinks he has met with several instances in which prisoners have come in for the purpose of being cured

---

[489] *First Report of Inspector, Southern and Western District*, PP, 1836, XXXV, 269, p. 62.

[490] *Second Report of Inspector, Northern and Eastern District*, PP, 1837, XXXII, 499, p. 42.

[491] *Second Report of Inspector, Southern and Western District*, PP, 1837, XXXII, 659, p. 11.

[492] *Eleventh Report of Inspector, Northern and Eastern District*, PP, 1846, XXI, 483, p. 37.

[493] *Third Report of Inspector, Northern and Eastern District*, PP, 1837-38, XXXI, 1, p. 117.

of some disease'.[494] The surgeon at York county gaol stated: 'The women who are committed as vagrants almost invariably come in with the venereal disease, and most probably for the purpose of being cured, as they are not admissible into the public infirmaries: they are sent in for one month, and in the state they are, generally remain in hospital until they are discharged'.[495] At Cambridge Spinning House: 'A very great proportion of the females received here are infected with venereal complaints, and when suffering in the extreme, proffer a request to the authorities to be taken in, which is granted, they are kept separate from those in health'.[496] At Stafford county gaol: 'These [venereal patients] said they procured their committal for the sake of the medical treatment. This is a common occurrence'.[497] At Wakefield the governor stated:

> I never knew so many persons committed looking haggard, thin, and in bad health, as at the present time; nor did I ever know so many persons committed to this prison who are strangers to this district. Many of these strangers have been committed for breaking windows, and it is my belief that these offences have been committed with a view to getting into prison.[498]

Of Leeds borough prison: 'The matron, indeed, expressed it as her opinion that some of the females were using the prison as an hospital, and came in with the express object of being cured of their disorders, a state of things not at all peculiar to the prison at Leeds'.[499] At Southwell house of correction: 'The itch patients are most numerous; the surgeon has ascertained that vagrants so afflicted occasionally commit minor offences in order that they may be sent to the prison to be cured of this complaint'.[500] At Salford, the chaplain stated: 'One female has been in here 200 times within the last six years; she comes here, generally, to recruit her health: another has been in fifty times, and cried when she was last discharged'.[501] At York county gaol the surgeon stated:

I am convinced that many persons, especially females, get committed to the prison

[494] *Fifth Report of Inspector, Southern and Western District*, PP, 1840, XXV, 721, p. 85.

[495] *Second Report of Inspector, Northern and Eastern District*, PP, 1837, XXXII, 499, p. 123. Most hospitals refused to treat venereal patients without payment. Williams, *The London*, p. 10. Later, "Lock" (a term descended from the old lazar houses) wards in naval towns were paid for by the Admiralty. Ibid., pp. 88 & 8.

[496] *Eleventh Report of Inspector, Northern and Eastern District*, PP, 1846, XXI, 483, p. 12. The Spinning House (a house of correction for prostitutes) was a constant thorn in the inspector's side. Run by the university authorities and open only in term time, discipline was virtually non-existent and little notice was taken of his recommendations for improvements.

[497] *Thirteenth Report of Inspector, Midland and Eastern District*, PP, 1847-48, XXXVI, 1, p. 109.

[498] Ibid., p. 38.

[499] Ibid., p. 44.

[500] *Fourteenth Report of Inspector, Midland and Eastern District*, PP, 1849, XXVI, 1, p. 50.

[501] *Second Report of Inspector, Northern and Eastern District*, PP, 1837, XXXII, 499, p. 72.

on purpose to be cured of attacks of syphilis. Many of them have admitted to me that it was so. A man from Bradford who went out last week told me he had been here before, and that he had got committed again in consequence of his having a return of his disease (syphilis) and that he came to be cured. The hospitals in the West Riding do not admit syphilitic patients, and hence I suppose it is that persons so attacked often look on the prison as an hospital for their disease, and by committing an offence force their way into it. Prisoners labouring under this disease often require a costly diet, as well as medical treatment, and they can do no work. They are therefore, among the most expensive prisoners that we have. One man who was here for a month last autumn, and who came in a very diseased state, but who left cured, required, during nearly the whole of his time, a pint of wine per day, beside malt liquor. It was a case of sloughing chancre,[502] in which a very liberal diet is necessary to preserve life; and it was requisite to have a prisoner, acting as nurse, to sit up with him through the night. The cost to the West Riding of this single case counting expenses of all kinds, could not have been less than 6*l*..[503]

At Reading Gaol 'Vagrants ... have subjected themselves to Imprisonment for the Cure of Disease, and have timed the Period so well, that during their Incarceration they are necessarily exonerated from Labour'.[504] And prison inspector, William J. Williams comments on:

> ... the common practice of tramps and prostitutes, when infected with foul diseases ... committing some slight offence for the purpose of obtaining medical treatment in prisons. Their committals are generally for one or two months to hard labour which they seldom or never undergo, often-times passing the entire of their term in hospital, and many of the females are scarcely discharged a month, ere they return again for surgical care. Such prisoners are more disorderly in behaviour, more pernicious in example, and more difficult to control, than any other class.[505]

The claim that medical care in prison was better than that in the workhouse may be regarded as a dubious recommendation, but is supported by a comment in the surgeon's journal at Horsley: 'Call'd upon to attend this prisoner [Mary Ann Mann, aged 27] in Labour who came in yesterday and became ill with labour pains, she was delivered safely in the night. This is her second illegitimate Child and she prefers the Prison accommodation to the Tetbury Poor House' (2 February 1843). Adverse comments were rare. The Board of Guardians of Warminster Union complained that six men 'have been committed to this House of Correction (Devizes) in good health, and to have returned very ill'. An investigation reached the conclusion that none

---

[502] Chancre: the primary lesion of syphilis, usually on the penis. A syphilitic chancre doesn't usually slough; this may have been chancroid, a self-limiting venereal disease.

[503] *Sixteenth Report of Inspector, Northern and Eastern District*, PP, 1851, XXVII, 461, p. xx.

[504] *Second Report*, PP, 1835, XI, 495, Appendix, p. 241.

[505] *Second Report of Inspector, Northern and Eastern District*, PP, 1837, XXXII, 499, p. 3.

had suffered anything worse than diarrhoea whilst in prison (for periods of one to two months) and although all had lost between 4 and 8 pounds in weight, there was no evidence of neglect.[506]

CONCLUSION

Several points emerge clearly from this material. The vast majority of complaints dealt with by the surgeons were minor and many were probably made with the hope of gaining some advantage in terms of a better diet, avoidance of work or admission to hospital. Nonetheless, surgeons took a generally tolerant approach, although as will be seen in the next chapter they were on the lookout for feigned or factitious illness. Despite this, prisoners were given the benefit of the doubt and were treated with the full range of remedies in general use at the time.

There is little evidence in this period of 'the dialectics of prisoner resistance', of '… deeply embedded and significant patterns of resistance developed by prisoners and prisoners' rights organisations and the strategies they have adopted to deny medicine a position of hegemonic domination within penal establishments'.[507] It could be argued that by making frequent and trivial complaints, prisoners were resisting medical domination – but this is not a strong contention. Nor, in this account of the run-of-the-mill doctor/patient encounters is there any evidence of the use of cruelty or violence on the part of the medical attendants. Whether such a charge can be sustained with regard to the management of psychiatric patients or of those feigning illness will be the subject of the following chapter.

---

[506] *Fourth Report of Inspector, Southern and Western District*, PP, 1839, XXII, 215, pp. 104-109.
[507] Sim, *Medical*, p. x.

5

MALINGERING AND INSANITY IN PRISONS: SURGEONS' RESPONSE

The conflation of malingering and insanity may seem unfair – unfair that is to the genuinely insane who by definition lack total control over their actions. However, prison surgeons could find the distinction difficult to make – malingering prisoners often convincingly assumed insanity. Both groups provided a challenge to the authority of the medical officer: the malingerer attempting to deceive by pretending symptoms or fashioning factitious physical signs, the insane by failing to follow those rules of behaviour needed for the doctor/patient relationship to function properly.

MALINGERING: HOW SERIOUS A PROBLEM?

The frequency of malingering is difficult to assess but at one prison (Northleach, 1817-1840) an attempt has been made to quantify its extent. During this period, from a total of nearly 3,300 complaints to the surgeon, 83 (2.5%) were apparently made with the intention of avoiding work – initially on the handmill and latterly on the treadmill. Of these complaints, 32 were allowed and 51 disallowed.[508] These figures might be interpreted as indicating that the problem was of little significance but nonetheless it

---

[508] Higgins, 'Medical Care in Three Gloucestershire Prisons', p. 31 and pp. 52-56.

was a matter greatly exercising the minds of surgeons and inspectors.[509] The reason is stated succinctly in a comment made at Warwick county house of correction: 'There is no situation in life in which it becomes so strongly the interest of an individual to feign or to prolong sickness as here'.[510] At Salford, Henry Ollier speaks from the heart in his quarterly report: '... as usual much of the Surgeon's time has been occupied in judging between feigned and real sickness'.[511] Later, his successor echoed these sentiments:

> As usual, the most laborious part of the surgeon's duties consists in the application of malingerers and others slightly indisposed as out-patients. Many thousands yearly of such cases are met with and they not only consume much time and attention, but consume in the aggregate a large quantity of medicine.[512]

A note of despair rings down the years from Carlisle county gaol and house of correction showing that, sadly, the better the care the greater the problem: 'In consequence of visiting daily, as he [the surgeon] supposes, the cases of simulated disease has greatly increased, for whenever the prisoners see him, they appear to be possessed with the desire of complaining'.[513]

THE WHY AND HOW OF FEIGNED ILLNESS

A perception existed among prisoners that at trial it was to their advantage to be seen as insane: 'John Mayo ... had heard a conversation between Williams and another prisoner in which he [Williams] was advised to affect insanity under the idea that it would be advantageous to him at his trial'.[514] Thomas Roberts (of whom more later), having been detected in his imposture:

> he fell upon his knees, with hands uplifted, and, in an audible voice, acknowledged that, all the various degrees of Insanity, Dumbness, want of feeling etc. were merely assumed, and with a view of being discharged without Trial; and that he was encouraged in this villainous pursuit, by one ward who has been appointed to look after him (who was, some time back dischargd, on condition of enlisting in the army, who also it is said immediately deserted).

At Liverpool borough gaol several feigned suicide attempts were made with a view to avoiding transportation.[515]

The prison infirmary offered a lure. At Northleach a prisoner enlisted the

---

[509] The Northleach figures may underestimate the extent of malingering. This was a small prison in a predominantly rural area – its occupants were probably less 'street-wise' than say the cockney inmates of Coldbath-fields (q.v.).

[510] *First Report of Inspector, Southern and Western District*, PP, 1836, XXXV, 269, p. 74.

[511] LCRO, QGR/4/31.

[512] *Fifteenth Report of Inspector, Northern and Eastern District*, PP, 1850, XXVIII, 291, p. 232.

[513] *Seventh Report of Inspector, Northern and Eastern District*, PP, 1842, XXI, 1, p. 6.

[514] *Justices' journal*, GRO, Q/Gc, 1/2, 1 February 1817.

[515] *Tenth Report of Inspector, Northern and Eastern District*, PP, 1845, XXIV, 1, p. 91.

aid of a physician in an attempt to produce a diagnosis of insanity:

> On visiting the prison today I found Dr Coley of Cheltenham conversing with
> the Revd Thos Hanbury now in confinement here and the Doctor requested
> he might be placed in the Hospital under the plea of insanity but as I could
> not satisfy myself that such was the case I declined so doing, until I saw the
> necessity of it (26 January 1835). Revd Thomas Hanbury – does not have the
> slightest symptom of insanity today (27 January 1835).

Others feigned sickness to avoid punishment. At Lancaster the governor discovered a prisoner (Hurst) in solitary confinement lying in a pool of blood. It seemed that he had cut his throat but further examination showed that he was bleeding from the nose. He was stripped, searched and a loom knife was found, leading to the governor's comment: 'If he has burst his nose on purpose to intimidate me, he will find himself mistaken' (15 August 1816). On the following day there was more bleeding and the nose was packed with lint dipped in turpentine. By the next day Hurst 'asked forgiveness for his misconduct and promised to behave well during his stay in prison'.[516] Another attempt to escape solitary confinement was reported at Boston house of correction where the keeper's journal reads: 'April 22, 1840. T.T. found at 8 a.m. laid on the floor of his cell, with part of his neckcloth tied tight around his neck, but, in my opinion, it was a scheme to get over the punishment of solitary confinement which was ordered him'. The surgeon found no bruises and so T.T. was ordered back to the solitary cell – the turnkey having been ordered to visit him every ten minutes.[517] The point was made strongly by the surgeon of Coldbath-fields:

> Q. Do you think they sham sick in any Instances?
> A. Repeatedly; I have sometimes thirty or forty come up in a Morning
> during the hot Weather; they do not care for the Punishment of being
> locked up on Bread and Water for Three Days at this Time of Year.
> Q. They wish to go to the Infirmary, where they live better?
> A. Yes; it requires a great deal of watching and a great deal of Experience to
> be alive to the Pretences they practise; Men will wound themselves so as to
> incapacitate themselves for the Wheel; but there is such a system of Vigilance
> there it is almost impossible for them to escape Detection.[518]

His opinion that the 'system of Vigilance' had deterred those wishing to escape the treadmill (the introduction of which produced what was almost

---

[516] *Governor's Journal*, LCRO, MF/1/37
[517] *Seventh Report of Inspector, Northern and Eastern District*, PP, 1842, XXI, 1, p. 122.
[518] *Second Report*, PP, 1835 (438), XI, 495, pp. 385-386.

certainly the major cause of the problem)[519] had changed a year or two later:

> I do not think the state of mind produced by tread-wheel labour is favourable to moral reformation. It is more severely felt by some prisoners than others. It decidedly gives rise to every deception and falsehood. The prisoners occasionally attempt to avoid taking their turn; they watch opportunities for this purpose; they deceive the doctor, they feign sickness of various kinds; seldom on meat days, however, unless after dinner. The following cases are instances: first, by raising "a fox" (their own term), that is rubbing and excoriating the skin of the leg or foot, and applying to the wound any irritating matter, principally lime scraped from the walls; and by other such means causing an inflamed sore. This has also sometimes been done to the hands, in order to avoid picking oakum. Secondly, by causing swellings of the feet, legs, and other parts of the body, by tying a string (if procurable), or a garter or brace, tightly round the part on going to bed at night. Thirdly, by derangement of the bowels by drinking large quantities of water (formerly by mixing and drinking salt and water), and by swallowing pills composed of soap and lime, and also soap-suds. Fourthly, by imitating itch by pricking their fingers with a sharp instrument, and by friction with string between the fingers, applying salt or lime. Fifthly, by rubbing chalk or lime upon the tongue, so as to make it furred. Sixthly, by putting their fingers into their throats and causing forced vomiting. Seventhly, by pricking or cutting their fingers, and sucking and spitting the blood into their pots; and also sucking their gums till they bleed, and spitting out the blood; expedients to feign spitting of blood from the lungs. Eighthly, by coming into the prison with trusses on, that they may appear to have ruptures; also wearing their arms in slings, and pretending that they are dislocated. Ninthly, by feigning madness. Tenthly, by throwing themselves off the tread-wheels in pretended fits; which is a very common trick. Such are the principal frauds resorted to. There is scarcely a man who comes here sentenced to hard labour, who, by his own account, has not had some most afflicting illness, or met with some serious accident, disabling him from hard work.[520]

Tricks were passed from prisoner to prisoner but it was probably false optimism on the part of the surgeon at Chester county gaol: 'Since the prisoners have occupied separate cells there have been few cases of simulated disease'.[521]

At Kirkdale a technique emerged which had not been thought of at Coldbath-fields:

> Simulated disease is very frequent. They feign rheumatic fever by tying tight the hands, or leaning the arm over the edge of a bed-stead until it swells. Eight prisoners were brought into the infirmary with violent purgings, vomitings, and the appearance of cholera. One man was so ill as to oblige me to tell him that

---

[519] Occasionally a prisoner preferred work to idleness: 'Visited the Prison. Samuel Toone complains of a pain in his side but he had rather work at the Mill with it – sent him a Sudorific Draught' (23 January 1824, Northleach).

[520] *Second Report of Inspector, Home District*, PP, 1837, XXXII, 1, pp. 94-95.

[521] *Eleventh Report of Inspector, Northern and Eastern District*, PP, 1846, XXI, 483, p. 72.

unless he told me how the illness was brought in, I could not save him; he confessed it was done by placing tobacco chews in the fundament.[522]

At Salford county house of correction:

> cases of simulated disease are frequent: he [the surgeon] has noticed that injuries inflicted by prisoners upon their legs and eyes, are generally from the greater facility of doing so, produced on the right side of the body. Soldiers furnish the most frequent cases; one of the 17th Lancers taught the manner of ulcerating legs to two or three younger prisoners, epilepsy, spitting blood from pressure upon the gums, itch from pricking the fingers with pins, dysentery from mingling the evacuation with blood, and various other artifices have been detected.[523]

Individual instances were regularly reported in the surgeons' journals. At Gloucester county gaol: 'On advice from the Govr late this night I visited Partloe [a debtor] in the Sheriff's ward who I found to all appearances speechless. After some little time I discovered the deception and forced down a stimulating medicine which soon brought him to his speech, he is now very abusive' (7 March 1793); 'Richard Griffiths complains of violent pain in his Head, but being such a scoundrel I cannot give full credit to anything he says. I have however ordered my Pupil to bleed him' (30 June 1817); and: 'Sent for to Wm Crosby Transport, who states he had suddenly lost his sight and totally unable to open his Eyelids. He is a direct Imposture proposing his Sight and power of the lids' (22 July 1819), then: 'is recovered his sight and acknowledges he is very well' (24 July 1819).

Surgeons were not heartless – suspected malingerers were usually shown compassion and given treatment. At Gloucester city gaol:

> Strain (who fainted yesterday) is better today and from his observations to me I have not doubt he was yesterday affecting to be much worse that he really was. He said he expected to have more justice done him at the Assizes than at the Sessions. I consider he has a disease in his chest requiring attention – which I shall of course give him (12 July 1825).

The surgeon at Lancaster, investigating an instance of fits which the prisoner claimed had occurred at another prison, writes: 'Mr Stott says in answer to my letter as to Gregory "She had no fits till she fully expected to be transported, and she had served six months previously". She is however a poor delicate woman and will probably require attention and to be taken in hospital' (29 October 1849); and on another occasion: 'Campbell has a sore

---

[522] *Second Report of Inspector, Northern and Eastern District*, PP, 1837, XXXII, 499, p. 123.

[523] Ibid., p. 71. For even more imaginative techniques of military malingering see Martin Howard, *Wellington's Doctors: The British Army Medical Services in the Napoleonic Wars* (Staplehurst: Spellmount, 2002), pp. 180-181.

on the top of his foot, this has obliged me to send him to bed which I regret for he is evidently throughout an imposter' (23 January 1845).

At Horsley, writing of John Holtham aged 60 who had been complaining of pain in the limbs:

> My opinion of this man is that he has a strong aversion to breaking stones or being on the wheel as he says he took cold on coming in from breaking stones in one of the cells and that he should not mind working in the Garden. I cannot undertake to say it is a case of sham at present but suspect some of it is. There must be many such cases in prisons but this being an elderly man and subject to Rheumatism cannot be put to the test of a younger man. (3 February 1843)

Oddly enough at Lancaster, one inmate seems to have malingered in order to stay in prison:

> Humphreys, in the Penitentiary, who is to be discharged this morning, talks in difficulty, and she will scarcely attempt to walk, she has also declined to eat her breakfast. I have told her she must take some food, and show herself in a fit condition for the journey or I shall send her to the hospital. I believe a great deal of her infirmity is put on, tho' it is hard to say how much (22 April 1844).

That is not to say that the authorities did not do their best to detect malingerers. State of the art technology was brought into play to expose an imposter at Spalding house of correction: 'I tried him in the first instance with the stethoscope, but could discover no symptom, and he has gone on working'.[524] A classical education could be useful in the detection of feigned disease. At Millbank in 1824 the chaplain was suspicious of a prisoner who had been taken to the infirmary with a bowel complaint:

> I looked into his cell, and saw in one part of it a quantity of flax. It led me in the evening to look into Pliny's natural history to see what the medical properties of flax were, and I found it would have the effect of producing sickness ... he acknowledged afterwards to me that he had sucked the flax on purpose.[525]

After a visit to Westminster house of correction, the inspector reports a downside to a surgeon's expertise in detecting malingering:

> The patient attention, kindness, and judicious management of both Mr Lavies and his son are highly and justly commended, although the latter from his skill in detecting feigned disease, has rendered himself obnoxious to the ill-conducted prisoners and to those injudicious officers who side with them.[526]

---

[524] *Ninth Report of Inspector, Northern and Eastern District*, PP, 1844 , XXIX, p. 67. The stethoscope had been invented by Laennec in 1819 but does not seem to have come into general use until mid-century. Roy Porter, *The Greatest*, pp. 309 & 676.

[525] *Report from the Select Committee on the Prison at Millbank*, PP, 1824, IV, 407, pp. 22-23.

[526] *Twenty-third Report of Inspector, Southern District*, PP, 1857-1858, XXIX, 69, p. 70.

As already noted, prisoners went to considerable lengths to deceive, often involving the production of factitious lesions. An incident of self-mutilation was recorded in the governor's journal at Horsley:

> December 13th 1804. George Smith, who on cutting Fustic has cut off the Ends of three Fingers, although particularly cautioned by the Keeper to be careful in using the Knife. The Surgeon proposes to attend on Saturday next but has now left Instruction with the Keeper for dressing the Wound if necessary. January 24th 1805. There is every reason to suppose that George Smith intentionally cut off the Ends of his Fingers. [527]

At Lancaster the surgeon had his own way of dealing with factitious leg ulcers: 'The practice with such malingerers is to send them to the hospital, put them upon a reduced diet, and confine them strictly to their beds, and if there be reason to suppose they continue their tricks, to lock up their legs in a tin boot'.[528] Prisoners at Lancaster were nothing if not determined: '[name not given] was brought out to me pulseless this morning, but suspecting the cause, I have his coat taken off, and found both his arms tied up – this is a trick requiring notice; he had half time at the mill and must now do full'.[529]

At Norwich factitious illness was less common but there was one interesting case. Thomas Sizer had been under Scott's care in prison on 8 April 1826 and was then transferred to the Norfolk and Norwich Hospital. Seventeen years later, on 30 April 1843 Scott saw the newly imprisoned Sizer again: '… in a very precarious state and he passes a large quantity of blood in his urine.' A week later he was still in a precarious state and consultations were held both with Alfred Master and Mr J.G. Crosse.[530] The latter wrote:

> Having learnt of the deception practiced by this Man when he was confined in the Jail eighteen years ago, and having examined fully into the history and present symptoms of the Bleeding from the Urethra, under which he now suffers, I entertain a strong suspicion that the passage has been intentionally lacerated and the blood has been produced therebye – were urine to get into the wounded part and become diffused, his case might quickly become dangerous, but such an evil being avoided and further injury by the patient's hands being prevented, healing might take place.

The evil was avoided and although Sizer had a single further episode of haematuria he was able to leave the infirmary on 19 May. On 30 March 1844 a feigned fit was recorded, but a much odder incident is recorded on

---

[527] GRO, Q/Gh 1/1.

[528] *Second Report of Inspector, Northern and Eastern District*, PP, 1837, XXXII, 499, p. 42.

[529] *Fourth Report of Inspector, Northern and Eastern District*, PP, 1839, XXII,1, p. 33.

[530] Having made the transition from general practitioner/surgeon to consultant surgeon at the Norfolk and Norwich Hospital, Crosse went on to win the Jacksonian prize of the Royal College of Surgeons for his treatise on bladder stone – a condition particularly common in the Norwich area. See Crosse, passim.

30 November 1844:

> The Governor having called my attention to the fact that William Jenkins of the 8th Class had made a sore on his arm, attempting to mark himself. I examined the arms of all the Prisoners in the Gaol and found that the evil had extended beyond the Ward in which Jenkins is kept. I would suggest that the Visiting Magistrates should take some notice of this and by ordering some shaming punishment prevent the recurrence of this practice.

Inevitably there were errors of judgement. At Northleach:

> Richard Brown ... complains he is unable to work ... he is perfectly capable (27 October 1837);
> Richard Brown ... refused to work and otherwise misconducted himself [I] ordered him to work tomorrow (4 February 1838);
> Richard Brown ... has not been fit to work. Ordered gruel, mutton broth and admission to hospital (6 February 1838);
> Richard Brown ... in a very critical state (8 February 1838);
> Richard Brown ... weaker, ordered Brandy and water; [later] worse rapidly – refuses food; [later the same day] in a Dying state (9 February 1838);
> Richard Brown ... Died (10 February 1838).

Brown's cause of death seems to have been intractable diarrhoea, presumably some sort of intestinal infection. It is unlikely that the surgeon's error, which resulted in Brown working on for a day or two when he would have been better resting, had much impact on the outcome, and it is clear that he was well cared for once the seriousness of his condition was realised. And at Lancaster there was a misjudgement:

> Guity is trying to impose upon me, I suspect, at any rate he does not speak the truth as to his ailments, this morning he sent early and said he had spit half a bucket of blood, fortunately it was not put away, the amount was trifling and produced, I suspect, by unlawful means (12 December 1843).
> Guity looks rather brighter but we suspect mischief in his chest and I look to applying for his pardon on the grounds of declining health (13 April 1844).

And on 29 April Guity was discharged by order of the Home Office.

Other inmates were prepared to report deception – as shown in evidence given by a prisoner to a committee of the House of Commons on Secondary Punishments in 1831.

> Two very bad fellows indeed were sent up from Staffordshire in order to be confined in the Penitentiary [Millbank]: they were in a diseased state when brought to London, and they were placed in the infirmary at Newgate to be cured; they were covered with itch. In a very short time they were all but cured by the surgeon of Newgate. I saw them every day and I know positively that they

gave themselves the itch in other parts of their body, in order that they might remain in Newgate a longer time.[531]

The object of this self-infection was to defer transfer to Millbank – an aim in which they succeeded, remaining at Newgate for two months.

Inevitably, one attempt to deceive went too far. At Chester county gaol a prisoner was so determined to avoid transportation that, having tried pepper in his eyes and soaking his blanket in water to catch cold, he burnt his legs with a red-hot poker but developed tetanus and died.[532]

MALINGERING AND THE TREADMILL

The initial impact of the introduction of the apparent cause of so much trouble – the treadmill – was examined in reports made in 1823, 1824 and 1825.[533] By 1824 fifty-four machines had been constructed in thirty-seven prisons, in all capable of employing 1,162 prisoners.[534] In general the prisoners were subjected to spells of work on the wheel alternating with spells of rest, the latter usually spent walking round the yard in order to avoid sudden cooling. Thus at Devon county bridewell: 'The male prisoners, when at work, are three-fourths on the Wheels, and one fourth at rest; the females, one half on the Wheel, and the other half at rest'.[535] Work continued for between eight and ten hours in summer and five to eight hours in winter.

Initially the wheel was greeted with enthusiasm. It did away with 'epidemical disease'[536]; prisoners didn't like the work but they gained weight;[537] one woman carried on knitting at the wheel,[538] whilst another breast-fed her baby in the rest intervals.[539] It cured amenorrhoea[540] although at another prison some women had to be taken off treadmill work until 'certain complaints' had subsided.[541]

Despite the apparently phenomenal workload (the height climbed every two or three days equalling that of Mount Everest), healthy prisoners who were adequately fed did not have too much difficulty. At Oakham county gaol and house of correction: 'The health of the prisoners has manifestly

---

[531] *Third Report of the Inspectors. Home District and Supplement to Part 1*, PP, 1837-38, XXX, 1, p. 38.
[532] *Sixth Report of Inspector, Northern and Eastern District*, PP, 1841 Sess. 2, V, 1, p. 27.
[533] *Copies of all Communications made to, or received by the Secretary of State for the Home Department, respecting the use of TREAD WHEELS, in Gaols or Houses of Correction*, PP, 1823, XV, 307; 1824 (247), XIX, 165; and 1825, XXIII, 567.
[534] *Copies*, PP, 1824, XIX, 165, pp. 45-46.
[535] *Copies*, PP, 1823, XV, 307, p. 8.
[536] Ibid., p. 6.
[537] Ibid., p. 11.
[538] Ibid., pp. 7-8.
[539] Putting women to work on the wheel at this period was not unusual but by no means universal.
[540] LCRO, QGR/3/15.
[541] Ibid., p. 8.

improved since the introduction of the treadwheel'.[542] One of the turnkeys at Cambridge county gaol and house of correction stated: 'The labour is nothing to the prisoners; talking cannot be prevented: the untried have frequently asked to placed on the mill [normally the untried were not subject to hard labour], or to be allowed to do something'.[543] And at Norwich castle gaol: 'The prisoners prefer labour to being locked up in their cells in the winter. The tread-wheel is hard work in the summer; it is an alleviation of their confinement in the winter. Men in solitary confinement frequently applied to be placed on the wheel'.[544]

Such unqualified approval was unusual; comments about its adverse effects on prison discipline and the frequency with which it inspired malingering are common. From Maidstone county prison:

> The surgeon, in his report to me on the cases of illness which have occurred in persons working on the Wheel, has premised many observations on the frauds and evasions practised by the prisoners; the purport of which is, that whereas he was at first continually called to prescribe for feigned disorders; these have been so generally detected, that the prisoners have now ceased to endeavour to impose on him; and [his] observations have led [him] to say, with some degree of confidence, that the Tread Mill has been beneficial to those employed on it.[545]

Prison inspector Frederic Hill had no doubt of the link between the mill and malingering:

> One great objection to such kinds of work as treadwheel labour is the practice of deception to which it gives rise. In my former district, Scotland, where there was not a single treadwheel, and where all the work was in some degree at least useful, I very seldom heard of any "malingering" among prisoners; but in the English prisons I find this practice common; and it appears that, to escape the treadwheel, not only is sickness often feigned, but it is sometimes wilfully produced. The following evidence on this subject will be found in the present Report:– The surgeon of Norwich Castle:– "There are always more cases of malingering in the prison than of real illness. The malingering is chiefly caused by a desire to avoid the treadwheel."[546]

Similar reservations were expressed by the surgeon at Bedford county gaol:

> I think that treadwheel labour is injurious to health; it distresses the men in very hot weather, and in winter it exposes them to great changes of temperature, draughts, etc. ... they become dissatisfied, sullen and morose, and they practice

---

[542] *Eleventh Report of Inspector, Northern and Eastern District*, PP, 1846, XXI, 483, p. 59.

[543] *First Report of Inspector, Northern and Eastern District*, PP, 1836, XXXV, 161, p. 7.

[544] Ibid., p. 42.

[545] *Copies*, PP, 1825, XXIII, 567, p. 10.

[546] *Fifteenth Report of Inspector, Northern and Eastern District*, PP, 1850, XXVIII, 291, pp. xiii-xiv.

every kind of deception to avoid the wheel: they feign sickness, they pretend to have looseness of the bowels, and severe pain in the loins, and to suffer from old hurts.[547]

There can be little doubt that many cases of malingering were a response to treadwheel labour.

INSANITY IN PRISONS: THE BACKGROUND

Prisons have long been used in the management of those deemed to be insane. In 1482 it had been established that a "dangerous lunatic" could be held in his own home or in the local prison.[548] In the early-nineteenth century it became accepted that a diagnosis of insanity could be accepted as a mitigating factor when sentencing a criminal and in 1816, a section for "criminal lunatics" (45 male and 15 female beds) was opened at the Bethlem hospital. The number held there had increased to 112 by the time Broadmoor opened in 1863.[549] Earlier, there was little provision for the insane – criminal or otherwise. Bethlem (or Bedlam), founded in 1246 as a religious institution, was given to the City of London by Henry VIII 'for the Cure of Lunaticks'. Rebuilt in 1676 for 150 patients it was described in some detail by Strype in 1720 who paints a much rosier picture of the institution than that bequeathed to us by Hogarth and his contemporaries.[550] Few provincial centres showed any enthusiasm for making similar provision. A charity was set up to build a bethel at Norwich in 1713,[551] followed by others at Newcastle-on-Tyne (1765), Manchester (1766), York (1777) and Exeter (1801); but it was not until the 1808 Act made provision for asylums for all levels of society that facilities became widely available.[552] Although Paul proposed a scheme (modelled on the asylum at York) in 1793 for an asylum in Gloucester and buildings were purchased, it was not brought to fruition for thirty years.[553] Not until

---

[547] *Second Report of Inspector, Home District*, PP, 1837, XXV, 1, p. 220.

[548] Sir Louis Blom-Cooper, 'The Criminal Lunatic Asylum System Before and After Broadmoor', in *The Health of Prisoners*, p. 152.

[549] Ibid., pp. 153-154. By 1903, despite Broadmoor's capacity of 566 males and 192 females, there were a further 109 criminal lunatics in county asylums and 40 at Parkhurst awaiting transfer. Ibid., p. 158.

[550] John Strype, *A Survey of the Cities of London and Westminster, Vol. 1* (Churchill: London, 1720), pp. 192-196.

[551] A full account of this remarkable institution is given by Mark Winston, 'The Bethel at Norwich: An Eighteenth-Century Hospital for Lunatics', *Medical History* 38 (1994), 27-51 (pp. 27-51).

[552] Leonard D. Smith, *Cure, Comfort and Safe Custody: Public Lunatic Asylums in Early Nineteenth Century England* (London: Leicester University Press, 1999), pp. 14-24.

[553] The delay was due to Paul's caution at proceeding without substantial funds, G.O. Paul, *Doubts Concerning the Expediency and Propriety of Immediately Proceeding to Provide a Lunatic Asylum in Gloucester*, (Gloucester, Walker, 1813), passim. However, it was Paul 'who provided much of the impetus toward the expansion of the public asylum system', Smith, *Cure*, p. 20.

1823, when a new asylum opened at Wotton just outside the city,[554] was there formal provision for lunatics; until then prison surgeons had no alternative than to manage mentally disturbed patients as best they could. A bill of 1814 authorised removal of insane prisoners to an asylum but 'this measure was by no means universally enforced'.[555]

Earlier, Paul argued: 'If Lunatics are to be so confined … places suitable for their case must be constructed'.[556] His concerns were financial as well as medical: some of these unfortunates were inappropriately confined in prison at unnecessary expense to the county and to the detriment of other members of both prison community and the general population. He cites the instance of a debtor confined for five years at Gloucester gaol, making the point that it was simply not practicable to ignore the problems posed by a seriously unruly prisoner:

> in his paroxysms is frequently heard in the streets at Gloucester, and disturbs, not only the persons within the prison, but also the inhabitants of the neighbourhood to a considerable distance, and has frequently excited, in the minds of the populace, an idea that some cruelty was exercising within the walls of the prison.[557]

Neild also felt strongly about the inappropriate confinement of the insane in prisons. At Horsham county gaol:

> At my several visits here, I recollect to have seen one *Simon Southward*, a Debtor, who is said to have been committed to Horsham Gaol so Long ago as the 22nd of February, *one thousand seven hundred and sixty-seven*. He styled himself "*Simon, Earl of Derby, King in Man*"; and was very orderly and inoffensive, though evidently deranged.[558]

At the town gaol, Kingston-upon-Thames: 'I have not met with one Criminal here at any of several visits' (five in all), the only inmate was 'a raving lunatick'; at Northallerton bridewell, 'one poor *Lunatick*, who has been here ever since the year 1782'; and at Spalding (Lincolshire) bridewell he found (as one of only three or four prisoners): 'Mary Allan, a Lunatick, who has been confined there *four and twenty years*'.[559] His views can be summarised in this comment on Lancaster:

---

[554] *Victoria History of the County of Gloucester, Vol. IV: The City of Gloucester* (Oxford: Oxford University Press, 1988), pp 273-274.

[555] Webb and Webb, p. 70.

[556] Sir G.O. Paul, *Suggestions on the Subject of Criminal and Pauper Lunatics*, letter dated 11 October 1806 to the Home Secretary. *Report from the Select Committee appointed to enquire into the state of Lunatics*, PP, 1807, II, 69, p. 17.

[557] Ibid., p. 20.

[558] Neild, p. 279.

[559] Ibid., pp. 314, 432 and 539

At my visit October 1805, there were no less than *five Maniacs*, two of whom were furiously Frantick. From the want of proper places to keep them retired, I could conceive that the personal safety of the Keeper and his Turnkeys may, at sometime or other, be greatly endangered. I am anxious to leave it on record, That to my mind it is very desirable that Beings of this most pitiable description should be kept either in *an Hospital*, or as similar to it as possible.[560]

An 1814 report noted: 'Four lunatics are now confined at Newgate; two of them separately, but two with other Prisoners, one of whom would, but for his insanity, have been executed for murder … it is hoped that when the new Bedlam is finished, they will be removed'.[561]

INSANITY: MANAGEMENT AFTER 1820

The availability of lunatic asylums from the 1820s onwards did not entirely relieve surgeons of problem prisoners; magistrates were often reluctant to accept insanity as a mitigating factor in sentencing and those known to be insane still found their way into prisons. Clearly this was still happening at Newgate in 1835 when the surgeon gave his opinion that those who had been acquitted as insane should not be confined in gaol: 'I have occasionally … had handcuffs put on them, and had them put into bed, and had their feet chained occasionally'.[562] An apparent plea for discharge on psychiatric grounds was made at Horsley in respect of George Loneysome aged 30:

This man has been repeatedly seen by me, Mr Stokes has also visited him. He is undoubtedly a man of weak intellect and of eccentric habits, but I do not now consider him to be of unsound mind, but I think it highly probable if he continues long under confinement, that he will become a decided lunatic. This opinion is founded, first upon the circumstances under which he was committed and secondly upon the peculiar and eccentric state of his mind (31 May 1843).

When circumstances seemed clear, action was taken promptly as at Gloucester city gaol when on 3 June 1830 the surgeon saw Nathaniel Payne in the lock-up house – he was diagnosed as insane and sent to the lunatic asylum. An equally peremptory approach was usually taken at Norwich. 'Removed Kenney to Bethlehem Hospital pursuant to the warrant for that purpose' (21 February 1829); and: 'warrant to convey Richard Scott to the Lunatic Asylum at Thorpe' (11 November 1829).[563] Later at Norwich: 'Sunday night 9 o'clock June 30ᵗʰ [1844]. Visited William Frost and found him in a such an excited state, that I considered it to be my duty to confine

[560] Ibid., p. 329.
[561] *Report*, PP, 1813-14, IV, 249, p. 7.
[562] *Report*, PP, 1836, XLII, 231, p. 36.
[563] NCRO,MF/RO 576/1.

his arms to prevent him doing an act of violence to himself or the four men who remain with him night and day'. On 1 July Frost was seen in consultation with Mr Cooper, senior surgeon at the Norfolk and Norwich hospital; he was still 'in a violent state of excitement' and on the following day: '[has] torn his clothes and destroyed everything when his arms were released. They must again be confined'. Daily visits with Mr Cooper were made and there was gradual improvement, allowing his arms to be released on July 4, but evidently all was not well: 'William Frost was removed from the Castle on the 9th to the Criminal Lunatic Asylum Saint George's in the County of Surrey' (14 October 1844).

By the 1840s at Lancaster, as at other goals, the days of 'five maniacs, two of whom furiously frantick' in the prison were, in theory at least, long gone but occasional problems occurred. 'I have sent John Hawkins an insane prisoner just arrived from Preston where he has been tried, into hospital. I shall write to Mr Dixon the surgeon about his case' (2 March 1846). This is probably the same individual to whom Captain Hansbrow was referring when he wrote: 'I have received a perfectly insane convict from Preston'.[564] Hawkins was transferred to the lunatic asylum 'by order of the Home Secretary' on 18 March 1846.[565] Others were dealt with similarly:

> I did not think Ashbourne a fit subject for a gaol when she was here before and
> now it is evident she will be worse to control (24 May 1844);
> Ashbourne has been noisy all night (27 May 1844);
> Ashbourne is so disturbed she must have the muff[566] (28 May 1844);
> Ashbourne has been very quiet all night but she does not sleep. The nurse will
> be allowed a little coffee, sugar and milk (30 May 1844);
> [and finally] Ashbourne is gone to the asylum (5 June 1844).

Berry also posed problems: '… out of order, pulse quickened, he appears to be a man of weak mind' (13 April 1849). Medicines were prescribed, his hair was cut short and although he was able to leave hospital on 30 April, he was described as an 'untamed brute'. By 24 June 1849 he was in solitary confinement and after consultation with two local surgeons, Berry went to the asylum on 29 June. On another occasion an improvement in the patient's condition seems to have obviated the need for the asylum: 'Nelson is very noisy' (15 June 1847); 'Nelson is quiet but stupid' (16 June 1847); and: 'Nelson is become so violent I have been obliged to certify his insanity' (18 June 1847). Over the next few days Nelson improved and there is no mention of his being transferred.

---

[564] DeLacy, p. 198.
[565] *Governor's Journal*, LCRO, MF 1/37.
[566] Muff: A means of restraint, leather or iron handcuffs.

The Lancaster record provides another example of the difficulty experienced in making the fine distinction between insanity and bad behaviour:

> Rebecca Boyd has been put into one of the punishment cells for three days, she has been kept in hospital but not as a patient, and she evidently dislikes the restraint[567] and wants to be amongst the other women. Now from what I saw of her when she was last here I thought we could best manage her in the hospital and I therefore placed her there. She is reported to be liable to fits. She may become insane (20 March 1846).

She was quiet on the following day but on 25 March was noted to have tape-worms and returned to the hospital 'where I hope she will behave better'. On 22 May she was noted as 'being a little more disturbed this morning, expecting to see her husband' and although on 26 May her 'mind [was] more disturbed' she was 'improving' four days later. Things got worse – on 4 July: 'Boyd was violent yesterday, she has been removed to a punishment cell. I shall take away the milk from her and Ellison' and the following day: 'Ellison may keep Boyd company'. Two days later: 'Boyd has bled herself in both arms with the intention (she says) of destroying herself. She must wear a strait waistcoat and have someone in the cell with her', but such is human ingenuity that on 9 July: 'Boyd gets the jacket off, or rather some of the prisoners interfere with it. Perhaps the muffs will answer better'. She only rates one further mention: 'Boyd is feverish and out of sorts, I believe first from misconduct' (4 September 1846). A female prisoner even more determined to resist prison discipline was Julia St. Clair Newman, committed to Millbank on 11 March 1837 for theft. She threw a can of gruel over the governor, blackened her eyes when in the dark cell, made several half-hearted attempts at suicide and generally made life difficult for the authorities. By secreting a pair of scissors she was able to escape from a special strait-waistcoat, resisted restraining collars, strapping and a spell in Bethel hospital before being transported to Tasmania over a year later. Griffiths' account shows that the surgeon did what he could to mitigate her punishment.[568]

INSANITY IN GLOUCESTERSHIRE PRISONS

As already explained, prior to the availability of asylums for the mentally disturbed (and even to some extent afterwards), prison surgeons had little alternative than to do the best they could for these individuals in the prison

---

[567] I think this means the restraint of being in hospital. The relaxed discipline at Lancaster led patients to prefer the greater degree of "freedom" and, perhaps more importantly, the company of friends in the prison itself.

[568] Griffiths, pp. 269-288.

environment. Examples occur in all the Gloucestershire surgeons' journals of the difficulties faced in navigating that fine line which sometimes lies between distinguishing feigned illness or simple bad behaviour on the one hand, and real insanity on the other. Equally, their comments illustrate compassion and consideration for the patients.

Surgeons were involved in the management of bad behaviour at all levels. At Gloucester county gaol: 'Two Debtors ... singing loudly and extremely abusive' (21 August 1813); and: 'Stephen Harwood has placed his bed against the door which prevents its being opened. He is very impertinent' (28 July 1817). At Northleach:

> Visited Jane Smith ... She proposed herself much worse this morning and refused to attend in the Chapple and has also been guilty of very abusive language and refractory conduct ... But I know the woman to be of so violent a disposition that she will set all order at defiance if she possibly can (15 January 1834);

'Charles Gerrard ... labouring under great mental excitement apparently proceeding from too much drink' (28 April 1834); and:

> Edwin South ... the middle of the night ... became exceedingly refractory calling Murder and disturbing the Gaol in consequence of which the Governor very properly removed him into a more private part of the prison where his noise would not be so much heard ... on visiting him I found him labouring under a considerable degree of excitement and evidently requiring restraint, therefore ordered his head to be shaved and such other medical treatment as I conceived his case to require (15 June 1835).

These measures did the trick. Clearly this was not a punitive shaving – it was doubtless done to reduce "cranial overheating".

The surgeon at Littledean made the distinction between punishment and treatment: 'I beg to observe that in separating [Thomas Morgan] from the other prisoners and placing him in the hospital during a paroxysm of insanity I did so not for the purpose of punishment but merely until his attack was over and it was safe and justifiable to place him again with the other prisoners' (4 August 1846). However, Morgan continued to be a problem and by February 1847 had been transferred to Gloucester asylum.

More bizarre was the method of managing William Clutterbuck. A seventy-one- year old illiterate pin-maker, committed to Littledean in 1827 for two years after the attempted rape of a little girl, he refused food and smeared himself with his own excrement. As a last resort he was dressed in petticoats in an attempt to shame him into better behaviour.[569] This was not entirely successful but two years later: 'William Clutterbuck ... leaving

[569] *Justices' journal*, GRO, Q/Gli, 1/1, 28 November 1827.

the Bridewell in perfect state of good health and for which I consider he is much indebted to the humane and kind attention he has experienced from the Rector and Turnkey' (30 August 1829).

The earliest detailed accounts of managing prisoners apparently bordering on the insane are found in the surgeons' journals at Gloucester county gaol. Although the control measures used may seem foreign – barbaric even – to the modern reader it should be remembered that such techniques were standard practice at the time. Indeed the monarch of the day was subjected to the strait waistcoat, handbolts, blisters, and cooling.[570] The last technique was widely used in various forms for treatment of the insane until the 1830s, the principle being that a reduction in temperature would diminish excessive humours.[571] At the Quaker-run (and highly regarded) York Retreat the cold bath was used frequently on a 'maniacal' patient in 1808 and again in 1809[572] – the same method was used at Gloucester county gaol and has attracted criticism from Joe Sim (see chapter one). I will now examine the cases in which the cold bath was used in order to demonstrate that surgeons, in managing these patients were motivated not by cruelty, but by a genuine desire to ameliorate their condition.

The first to experience it was Thomas Roberts, committed on 30 June 1796[573] and found to have a 'very foul ulcerated state of the Itch'. Admitted to the foul ward he attempted escape by 'letting himself down from the Parrapet [sic] wall by the help of the sheets etc.' but was caught and on his return to the foul ward from a spell in dark solitude was 'sullen and inattentive to what I said respecting the use of the medicines'. Although his physical health improved, he remained uncommunicative: 'sullen and seems to put on a kind of childishness that savours mental derangement' (17 August 1796). He became 'more deranged' but significantly: 'he refuses nothing that is offered to him, either food or Physic'. On 20 October he seemed to have had a fit and was bleeding from the nose but his pulse was normal. On the following day: 'found Roberts in the same insensible state … I am at aloss how to account, and doubt the reality of disease'. The affair came to a climax on 27 October:

> Visited the Prison in company with Dr Cheston[574] found Thos Roberts, apparently as insensible as human nature could appear, this has been coming on ever since

---

[570] Christopher Hibbert, *George III: A Personal History* (Viking: London, 1998), pp. 264, 278.

[571] Smith, *Cure*, pp. 202-204; and Andrew Scull, *Social Order/Mental Disorder: Anglo-American Psychiatry in Historical Perspective*, (London: Routledge, 1989), pp. 68-69. Immersion in cold water was also used in the Army for treatment of fevers, Howard, *Wellington's Doctors*, pp. 164-165.

[572] Anne Digby, *Madness, Morality and Medicine: A Study of the York Retreat, 1796-1914*, (Cambridge: Cambridge University Press, 1985), pp. 269 and 271.

[573] Sentenced to death for theft he was reprieved, and pardoned on 11 April 1799.

[574] Dr Cheston, a physician, provided his services *gratis*.

Hydropathy. Lithograph, Charles-Émile Jacque, 1843.

he attempted his escape, and from that period he has appeared in all the various states, and degrees of Insanity; and who for some time past has appeared a perfect Mope,[575] totally insensible of every Person or thing. He has even been fed for some time. Various methods were tried to procure some idea of sensation but in vain, at length determined to try every effort to bring him (if possible) to some degree of sensation; he was led into the yard and placed upon one of the large stones, from which he fell, and lay upon the ground, quite motionless. Application was then made to the cat o' nine tails, he had two or three lashes given him; but of which he seemd to be quite senseless; these trials proving ineffectual, and Dr Cheston witnessing, the cold bath, had been tried with success. The apparent Mope, was orderd to be led to the Bath and to be plunged in; during all this, he had never utterd a syllable, when he was first immersed in the water, I immediately perceived, that he seemd to recover strength, this occasioned some suspicion in my mind which the event fully justified. After some 10 or 20 minutes immersion he appeared to increase very sensibly in strength, and made several indirect attempts to relieve himself by creeping to, and leaning against the sides, but was pushed off, and told he shd be kept there, till he walked from the further end of the Bath, directly to, and up the steps, this at length he condescended to do, but still was silent, it however confirmed my suspicions that he could both feel and hear, when rubbed down and clothd, he was told that his imposture had been discovered and, that it would be in vain to carry on the artifice any longer; that if he would directly own the truth, we would forgive him the trouble he had given us, as well as the trick he had for upwards of two months been playing us, but if he still continued obstinate, he should be conveyed to a dark solitary cell, kept without food, and be treated with the utmost rigour, upon which he fell upon his knees, with hands uplifted, and, in an audible voice, acknowledged that, all the various degrees of Insanity, Dumbness, want of feeling etc. were merely assumed ... .

On the following day Roberts was perfectly normal: 'and I think it will be long, 'ere he again attempts to pass for a Maniac'. This success with Roberts prompted Parker to try the cold bath treatment on Honora Oliver[576]: 'the Gypsy woman ... troubled by violent Fits of the Hysterical kind [which] were often assumed, or arose from irritability of Temper' (28 October 1796):

when I directed her to be taken to the cold Bath – after three several dippings, she received great benifit [sic] from the Operation, as she walked back perfectly well. I then directed her to be put in bed and strapped down (as is done with maniacs) with every necessary care, and have great reason to believe, that the cold Bath, will prove in the end, as efficacious to her as it has done to Roberts.

Two days later Roberts' improvement was maintained but Oliver was still needing straps at night – after that neither caused trouble. Another woman prisoner, Sarah Pullen[577] 'who for several nights past has had fits, ... supposed

---

[575] Mope: a state of unconsciousness, to move and act without the impulse and guidance of thought.

[576] Aged 18, she was sentenced to seven years' transportation for grand larceny on 22 July 1795 but was reprieved and left prison on 7 July 1798 having been given a pair of stays, a pair of stockings, a pair of shoes, a petticoat, a handkerchief and five shillings.

[577] Aged 16, sentenced to twelve months' hard labour for felony.

in great measure to arise from irritability of temper, I directed her to be taken to the Cold Bath, the good effects of this immersion was [sic] instantaneous and effectual for a time, she immediately went to bed, and had a very good night, and is now well' (7 January 1797). John Roberts (no apparent relation to Thomas), a recently committed felon[578], appeared deranged and refused to answer questions: 'Roberts has been more noisy last night and today than usual, he also weted [sic] his bed tho' for the first time' (5 July 1798). He was seen both by Dr Cheston and Dr Fox of Bristol (who happened to be in town) but the latter, even 'with his extensive practical knowledge of the various appearances of Insanity' (10 July 1798), was still unsure of the diagnosis. On 16 July Roberts was immersed in the cold bath and after 'considerable delay' walked out and 'acknowledged that the whole appearance of Derangement was merely assumed to avoid being brought to Trial, weakened as he was, I ordered him to be taken to a warm bed and every proper attention was paid to him' (17 July 1798). An identical result was achieved in the case of John Ireland.[579] Twenty minutes in the cold bath 'obliged him to drop the mask of Idiotism ... and brought him to his natural senses. He confessed that he assumed the Idiot to prevent being brought to Trial. Every necessary care was ordered for him after Immersion' (9 October 1798).

Sometimes the threat alone of the cold bath effected a remedy: 'I was required very early this morning to visit John Williams whom I was informed was speechless and insensible but both of which he was in full possession of, when the cold bath was named to him, he is now getting up and is perfectly well (4 August 1812). On another occasion, when used, it was instantly successful. Daniel Bishop, aged twenty-two, who was charged with stealing a mare and who, on receiving the death penalty: 'assailed the judge in horrid language and threw his hat at a witness',[580] attempted escape and then: 'affected to be insane ... the advice I could give produced no good effect ... the Cold Bath ... a very few minutes operation of this kind induced him to acknowledge his Roguery' (10 September 1811). Compassion was shown by modifying its use if the patient was not fully fit. Hester Harding had been behaving improperly and showing signs of insanity (apparently feigned) for some weeks (as well as having treatment for venereal disease) when the surgeon decided that a cold bath was the only option. Because she was still not fully recovered from mercury treatment, hot water was added

---

[578] Aged 31, he was charged (with four others) of the theft of 80 guineas, three £10 notes, a £25 note, two five guinea bills, 23 one guinea bills and several £1 bills. When the journal ends in April 1799 he was described as 'declining'.

[579] Aged 19, he was later sentenced to two years for stealing heifers. On discharge (11 March 1801) he was given a shirt, a jacket, a pair of shoes, a pair of stockings and three shillings.

[580] Whiting, *Prison*, p. 44. He was hanged on 11 April 1812.

and unsurprisingly: 'it has not as yet had the <u>full</u> effect' (20 December 1811). A promise of good behaviour was not kept and by 13 January 1812: 'her conduct resembling somewhat that of Insanity … however the use of the <u>Cold Bath</u> produced a good effect tho not a cure'. By 10 March 1812: 'Hester Harding (Fine) has conducted herself properly for some time past and prays for forgiveness'.

A technique used only once at Gloucester county gaol was the electric shock. Martha Jeynes[581] 'appears Melancholy and for the two days past has refused her food. In her bodily health she seems quite well' (5 November 1813). She was given medicine and seemed to improve but continued to refuse food and on 10 November: '[her] apparent indisposition arises in great measure from obstinacy of Temper'. On the following day: 'taking all circumstances into consideration I was induced to believe it was hypocrisy and resolved to try the Effect of an Electric Shock, which I am pleased to say produced the desired effect, she fell on her knees, confessed and promised to conduct herself properly in future'. Sadly this promise was not kept and a few days later she was 'again as obstinate as before and has not taken any nourishment since yesterday morning' (24 November 1813). On 25 November: 'I had again recourse to the Electric Machine which had not such an immediate good effect as before. I directed to the Turnkey to drench her with a Beer Caudle … this operation being performed, producing an amendment in this Woman, and she took this Evening her Tea as usual'.[582] Two days later she had 'taken her Food regularly'.

The use of electricity as a treatment for refusal of food may seem rather drastic but two matters should be taken into consideration. First, the surgeon was seriously worried about her health and secondly, at this time electricity was in the nature of a party entertainment rather than a punishment although its use had been tried for the treatment of various complaints.[583] This was not in any sense 'a form of electro-convulsive therapy' as suggested by Sim.[584] That the Gloucester surgeon was far from heartless when managing disturbed patients is shown by an entry regarding John Williams who had been troublesome[585] for some time, 'affecting Insanity' and refusing food, and at various times had experienced both the cold bath and the dark cell:

---

[581] Serving two months for stealing butter.

[582] Caudle: a sweetened hot drink. The word drench is here used in a sense now familiar only in veterinary parlance: to pour down the throat; c.f. Mrs Murrow who had been refusing food: 'if she does not [eat] I must be under the unpleasant necessity of Drenching her' (28 June 1810).

[583] Uglow, pp. 10-14. For its use in medicine generally see Roy Porter, *Bodies Politic: Disease, Death and Doctors in Britain, 1650-1900*, (London: Reaktion, 2001), pp. 217-219. For its use in lunatic asylums see: Smith, *Cure*, p. 205.

[584] Sim, 'The Health', p. 117.

[585] 'The <u>inconceivable</u> trouble which Mr Wilton as well as the officers of the Prison have had with John Williams who has for nearly two months feigned insanity, is beyond calculation' (14 January 1817).

Dispensing medical electricity. Oil painting, Edward Bristow, 1824.

I have this day again examined John Williams. I am fully satisfied that his insanity is not real. But from the obstinacy which he has shewn, the impaired state of his health and the very little benefit which repeated punishments have hitherto produced, I am decidedly of the opinion that that system cannot be carried further without great risk ... For this reason I recommend that every care be bestowed to bring him into good health by giving him a more generous diet and preserving him from the effects of cold. Every attempt also ought to be made to gain his confidence by mild and kind treatment, and no further restraint should be imposed upon him than is required to prevent him from injuring himself and others (1 January 1817).

To no avail. Williams became progressively more emaciated and died on 15 February. There was an even more poignant example:

Ann Tye under Sentence of Death has refused to take any nourishment since Thursday last and still refuses to do so ... ordered Tea, toast, a warm cell, gruel ... I have also informed her that unless she takes it, that tho' so very unpleasant to my feelings I must compel her to do so (12 April 1818).

Two days later: 'Ann Tye now takes her food'. Ann, a widow aged thirty-eight, had been employed by the parish to care for an old woman at Dowdeswell. Noticed by others to be pregnant, she was seen crouching in a field where shortly afterwards a new-born baby was found with its mouth full of moss. Attempts at resuscitation failed and two autopsy examinations suggested that the child had died either from strangulation or from injuries to the inside of the mouth and throat. Sentenced to death, at her execution 'she was so weak as to require the support of one or two persons till the last minute of her existence, and she was then launched into eternity in view of an immense crowd of spectators'.[586]

The cold shower was used in 1847 as a method of control in Dickinson's case at Lancaster. 'Dickinson, a lad for trial has twice tumbled himself over the landing rails. I have doubled him with the cleaners for the night. On second thoughts I think it would be best to take him into the hospital' (13 June). Six days later: 'Dickinson is crying violently, he wants to go home he says' and on 22 June: 'Dickinson is constantly crying and asking to go home'. Two days later: 'I have been obliged to give Dickinson a shower bath' and on 28 June: 'Dickinson is uneasy, I have given him another bath'. On 1 July: 'Dickinson attempted to strangle himself yesterday, he must have the muffs', but thereafter he seems to have settled.[587]

Clearly these were difficult patients and it was impossible to avoid taking some sort of action. However, I hope I have made it clear that in doing so,

[586] *Gloucester Journal*, 13 April 1818 and 11 May 1818
[587] The cold shower was still in use at the York Retreat in 1874; of one of the patients: 'Has continued very much the same, the dread of shower baths has kept him in better order'. Digby, *Madness*, p. 76.

prison surgeons were using techniques which were standard at the time and were thought to be therapeutic. Indeed it is probable that they showed more compassion than was general in private madhouses of the time.[588] Madness was a 'bad' disease[589] and if some of the treatments used seem cruel (and to some extent were intentionally cruel[590]), that was hardly the fault of prison medical officers practising conventional medicine.[591] Happily there is no record of any prisoner being subjected to the truly unpleasant swinging chair.[592]

SUICIDE IN PRISONS

At Lancaster, apart from Dickinson, there were no serious suicide attempts but there were a few threats: 'Murphy was sent to the hospital for a time, he had threatened to commit suicide' (27 March 1845); 'Brideoak [in solitary confinement] asked for his gruel yesterday, today he says "by his maker" if he is not more food allowed he will put himself away' (20 November 1848); and 'Isabella Monkhouse aged 20 is admitted into hospital. She will be well watched as she has threatened to destroy herself' (11 December 1848).

Gloucestershire prisons saw more convincing suicide attempts. Of a death on 13 July 1791 (only two weeks after the opening of Gloucester county gaol) we learn only: 'William Birt, found hanging in his cell, stiff and cold' – he was due to be executed two days later. Parker was more forthcoming on another occasion:

> Immediately on notice from the Govr attended, find Priscilla Fudge has Hangd herself to the Barr [sic] of the window in her Cell, was cut down as soon as possible after being discoverd but quite motionless. However by the immediate and well applied assistance of the Govr and Medical aid, was soon recoverd – Her appearance was frightfull [sic], – nor could she give any satisfactory reason for committing so rash an action. This afternoon she appears more composed and much better (4 March 1792).

Priscilla Fudge, aged 21, was sentenced to seven years transportation for theft from a house. Departing on 30 May 1792 she was fortunate to sail on the *Royal Admiral*, the first transport to have a naval surgeon on board – previous vessels carried a surgeon paid by contractors whose only interest was maximising their profits. And, although 'no mere medical officer could

---

[588] Jonathan Andrews and Andrew Scull, *Undertaker of the Mind: John Monro and Mad-Doctoring Eighteenth-Century England*, (London: University of California Press, 2001), pp. 153-160.

[589] Porter, *Bodies*, p. 95.

[590] 'Cold or tepid shower-baths or cold spongings were used ... the tonic effect may have involved an element of discipline as well'. Digby, *Madness*, p. 134.

[591] For a discussion of the rationale of "cruel" treatments of insanity see ibid., pp. 119-122.

[592] Scull, pp. 69-73.

tell a master what to do on his own ship', the naval surgeon's presence was felt and the death rate was markedly lower than on earlier transports.[593] Elizabeth Bliss, in the dark cell as a consequence of some unspecified act of misbehaviour, attempted to hang herself: 'She now declares she will destroy herself one way or the other. Great attention shd [sic] be paid to this vile woman to prevent her horrid design' (8 February 1810). She rates no further mention. There were no instances of suicide at Northleach, whereas Littledean had one successful episode and one fairly serious attempt. The successful suicide was Richard Goulding, committed to prison on 2 April 1821 for three months on a charge of destroying game, who hanged himself on 29 April. The attempted suicide took place before the surgeon's journal starts, indeed this event brought to the visiting magistrates' attention the fact that no such record was being kept. Describing the episode their journal (1 September 1806) reads:

> On visiting the prison this day I am sorry to find that George Gwilliam attempted to destroy himself during the last night. It appears that his Wife who had visited him yesterday brought him a Razor with which he cut three gashes below his elbow, and the loss of blood was so great that he appeared perfectly dead when the keeper opened his cell between six and seven o'clock this morning. The Surgeon reports to me that he is in a very fair way of doing well, but, as he attempted to pull off the bandage as soon as it was tied on the arm, he thinks it necessary that some person should sit with him.[594]

Happily, Gwilliam, a thirty-year old nailer sentenced on 24 July 1806 for taking bark from a forest oak tree, seemed to settle and on 8 September was reported as being 'sensible of the impropriety of his conduct' and of expressing 'a strong wish to enter into His Majesty's Service either by Sea or Land'. This sensibility as to the impropriety of his conduct did not last and on 20 September 'he made a second attempt to destroy himself by running with his head against a wall'. This apparently improbable method of attempting suicide was not unique. Of a prisoner at Millbank who tried the same technique: 'a special head dress was provided, a sort of Turkish cap padded at the top, merely to save her skull'.[595] Gwilliam survived to be discharged on 11 November 1806, his fine having been paid.

During these six years for which the surgeons' journals are available at Norwich there was only one successful suicide:

> I was suddenly called in to see William Arthur a prisoner for examination for forgery who was found by Robert Tidman a warder hanging from the iron

---

[593] Hughes, *The Fatal Shore*, p. 148.
[594] GRO, Q/Gli 1/1.
[595] Griffiths, p. 268.

grating over the cell door. He was quite dead on my arrival and I feel no doubt
that he was dead when he was cut down – I was in attendance within a quarter
of an hour of his discovery (20 February 1849).

There was also an apparent attempted suicide: 'Skipper has feigned twice to
destroy himself, but I am convinced it was only done with a view to excite
alarm, and his hands have been confined for 2 days, and now that he is
released, he is gone to work' (15 June 1844). Skipper is not mentioned again.
The keeper's daily journal (covering 1822 to 1835) records two successful
and three unsuccessful attempts. In the first category, each hanged himself
from the cell door: 'William Howchen tried and convicted of Sheep stealing
but not sentenced strangled himself with his Neckhandkerchief fastened to
the bar of the Pothole of the cell door' (31 March 1832) and the other similar
event took place on 16 May 1834. Of the unsuccessful attempts, two were
hangings (24 June 1828 and 16 November 1828, the latter a twenty-one year
old received into custody the previous night) and the third 'tried to bleed
himself to death with a nail' (31 March 1832).

The prison inspectors also report suicides – some successful, some not. One
of these was in relation to the rarely-commented-on problem of homosexual
activity within a gaol – at Giltspur Street compter. The prisoner, who had
been 'convicted of an assault of an abominable nature' was confined with
twelve others, one a fourteen year old boy, with whom he was found to
have 'perpetrated an unnatural offence ... in the privy of the ward'. He was
to have been transferred to Newgate for trail but was found hanged in his
cell.[596] At Bristol city gaol, an old woman who had already spent three years
in prison having been sentenced to transportation for coining 'succeeded in
hanging herself' with a handkerchief.[597] At Bodmin county gaol: 'in 1839 a
man cut his throat outside the walls on his way to the prison, with a knife
which had been taken from him at first, but given up to him again within
four miles of the gaol. He died three or four days afterwards'.[598] A woman
brought into Lancaster castle: 'on a Saturday night on a charge of felony.
She was in liquor and extremely violent. She was found the next morning,
suspended to the bars of the window, and had apparently been dead for some
time'. According to her mother, she was the seventh member of her family
to commit suicide.[599] Remarkably, at Derby county gaol, in the space of just
over a year there was one successful suicide, three fairly serious attempts and
two others who seemed about to try. All were male: the man who succeeded

[596] *Second Report of Inspector, Home District*, PP, 1837, XXXII, 1, p. 192.
[597] *Sixth Report of Inspector, Southern and Western District*, PP, 1841Sess. 2, V, 177, p. 131.
[598] Ibid., p. 178.
[599] *Fourth Report of Inspector, Northern and Eastern District*, PP, 1839, XXII, 1, p. 27.

had apparently just had a visit from the young woman whom he was engaged to marry and had been given a lock of hair from her head 'after which he appeared much depressed'; of the others, one feared that if he became sick during his transportation voyage he would be thrown overboard, one had seen the devil three nights in his sleep and another was a fifteen year old boy who wanted to see his mother. Conditions at this gaol do not appear to have been particularly harsh – certainly not bad enough to account for this rash of suicide attempts.[600] Unsuccessful attempts were recorded at Leicester county gaol, at Stafford county gaol and house of correction, and at Walsall borough gaol, where: 'Since my last visit a woman of the town tried to strangle herself with her garters, but ineffectually'.[601] One attempt was both bizarre and determined. The unnamed male prisoner was transferred from York to Wakefield house of correction where he was to remain for one year prior to transportation for life. At York he had attempted to divide 'the veins at the bend of the elbow' and at Wakefield he broke the glass of his cell window and swallowed the pieces (one of the recovered fragments is illustrated and is 3 cm. x 2 cm.). This was discovered and after 'Copious draughts of thick gruel, followed by an active emetic, ejected nothing particular' he was given 'large doses of castor oil, and repeated glysters'[602] resulting in the passage of 'several angular fragments of glass and pieces of broken pot, quite unaltered'. The surgeon extracted other pieces from the rectum where they had become 'entangled' and 'altogether, the fragments of glass passed, when united together, formed a pane nearly the size of the broken glass in his cell. Upon enquiry, he stated that he had enveloped the glass in bread, and in that manner prevented it irritating in the act of swallowing'. After two weeks he returned to his work as a comber but made further attempts, first by cutting his throat 'with a piece of old iron that he had sharpened and secreted', then, having destroyed with his teeth the straps that confined him, cut the veins in his elbow again. To prevent further episodes he was constantly attended by two wardsmen but he managed to tear open his wounds, and finding a large needle in the coat of one of the wardsmen who had fallen asleep, plunged this several times into the pit of his stomach. 'From these various attempts he lost a large quantity of blood, and consequently became much reduced: by nutritious diet and attention he soon was restored, and enabled to return to his work; and as a preventative of the future, he is constantly attended by a wardsman during the day, and placed in a cell without a window in the night, being carefully searched by a turnkey previous to locking-up'.[603] This

---

[600] Ibid., pp. 147-148

[601] *Sixth Report of Inspector, Southern and Western District*, PP, 1841 Sess. 2, V, 177 pp. 195, 213 and 219.

[602] Glysters: doubtless clysters (enemas).

[603] *Second Report of Inspector, Northern and Eastern District*, PP, 1837, XXXII, 499, p. 124.

last is an extreme example but (along with the heroic attempts to save life detailed in chapter four) illustrates the lengths to which prison staff were prepared to go in caring for these unfortunate and unhappy individuals.

CONCLUSION

So far as feigned or factitious illness was concerned, it is clear that the methods some prisoners displayed in their attempts to deceive medical officers showed a remarkable degree of ingenuity and determination. The response of medical officers – in detecting attempts at deception and at times conniving in its punishment – could be construed as participation in the process of controlling and dehumanising those in their charge. This I am sure would be a facile reaction to a complicated question. With or without the constraints of prison discipline, the practice of medicine necessitates that the patient should be truthful. If not, medical authority is challenged, making it impossible to establish a satisfactory patient/doctor relationship. This challenge – not to the authority of the prison but to the authority of the doctor *qua* doctor – has to be met.

Before making a judgement on the management of those thought to be insane, it is important to realise that prison surgeons had to take some sort of action – doing nothing was not an option. An individual refusing to eat might starve to death or become more prone to illness than otherwise would be the case, and a prisoner causing a disturbance would affect other inmates adversely. In dealing with these men and women, prison surgeons were of course undoubtedly part of the control process – it could not have been otherwise. Nonetheless, I would again assert that this exercise of control was largely an exercise of the power which is implicit in the practice of medicine, and that this power was exercised in as humane a manner as possible, using techniques that were normal for the time and that, on the whole, seem to have been remarkably effective.

6

DEATHS IN PRISON

The risk of death in prison – to staff and inmates alike – has long had a high profile; for example: 'in the year 1414, the gaolers of Newgate and Ludgate died, and the prisoners in Newgate to the number of sixty-four'.[604] Death is the medical outcome attracting most attention, and since as it happens is also the outcome most easily and accurately measured, death rates might be expected to provide a yardstick of prison care standards. In reality meaningful comparisons are hard to achieve. This is particularly true of the early part of the period where statistical information is scarce.

At Newgate (where most prisoners lacked the benefit of separation being confined in "wards") in the twelve months from 28 September 1785, 1,325 prisoners passed through the gaol; of these 294 were transported,[605] 176 whipped, 61 hanged, 1 burned,[606] 613 acquitted and 16 died. In the following twelve months the figures were 1,454, 364, 63, 87, (none burned), 615, but with 56 deaths.[607] The increase from 16 deaths to 56 strongly

---

[604] John Stow, *The Survey of London* (London: 1603; facsimile edition, London: Dent, 1977), p. 35.

[605] In this post-American independence but pre-Botany Bay era, a sentence of transportation meant confinement in a hulk.

[606] Until 1790, women found guilty of high or petty treason (which included coining) could be burned at the stake. They were usually strangled first. Clive Emsley, *Crime and Society in England 1750-1900*, (London: Longman, 1996), p. 249.

[607] Babington, p. 137.

suggests an epidemic (probably of typhus) in 1786-1787. The situation had apparently improved by 1814 when the average annual number of deaths in the prison between 1802 and 1814 had been nine.[608] It is also stated that 'in 1801, forty-five died. It was a mixed case of typhus fever with influenza'.[609] Clearly, the absence of separation resulted in high deaths rates during epidemics.

In his 1812 reports, James Neild gives some mortality figures. In 27 years at Bodmin county gaol there had been 15 deaths among 3,877 prisoners committed: 2 in 1,258 gaol prisoners (0.16%), 5 in 1,846 bridewell prisoners (0.27%) and 8 in 773 debtors (1.03%).[610] Mortality rates in relation to committal number are of limited value, an error made by Edwin Chadwick when he came to the ridiculous conclusion that prisons with the poorest dietary had the lowest mortality. He failed to allow for the fact that in such prisons the average stay was only 34 days whereas in prisons with a better diet the average stay was 82 days.[611] A leading article in *The Lancet* noted that the death rate in the houses of correction was low relative to that in the gaols and drew the (probably correct) conclusion that this was the result of shorter sentences in the former.[612] Exceptionally for Ilchester county gaol, Neild gives average prisoner numbers allowing the calculation of an annual mortality rate: 'Six only have died during the last seven years, out of seventy-eight, the average number of Prisoners here confined'.[613] This equates to a mortality of 1.1% per annum but many of those imprisoned were short stay.

In 1814, the surgeon at Newgate was Mr William Hutcheson Box, who had been in post since 1802. He claimed that since his appointment – no doubt we may infer, on a *post hoc ergo propter hoc* basis – the mortality rate from typhus had fallen dramatically.[614] Box was asked:

Q. What is the general nature of the illnesses, of which the nine upon the average have died?
A. Mostly, last year, pulmonary complaints; but there were two cases of mortification, and the rest old pulmonary cases; several Lascars were brought in there in a wretched state of health, and from change of climate became worse,

[608] *Report*, PP, 1813-14, IV, 249, p. 8.
[609] Ibid., p. 55.
[610] Neild, p. 56. Bodmin employed a surgeon, Mr Hamley, at £30 per annum. The prison held between 40 and 70 inmates.
[611] Wiener, 'The Health', pp. 44-58.
[612] *The Lancet*, 2, 1839-1840, p. 428.
[613] Neild, p. 289.
[614] This despite Neild's comment: 'I have so often witnessed the very distressful state of apparel, and filthy appearance of the poorer Females, particularly Convicts, crowded together in few rooms, like sheep in a pen, that it was a matter of surprize [sic] there should be, comparatively, so small a number on the sick list, or that the Gaol-Fever did not prevail'. Neild, p. 423.

and died of pulmonary consumption.[615]

The committee of inquiry concluded:

> Your Committee find that the Gaol of *Newgate*, as at present regulated, is able
> conveniently to hold 110 Debtors and 317 Criminal Prisoners; and it is of the
> opinion of the Surgeon, that when the whole number exceeds 500, great danger
> of infectious disorder is to be apprehended. On April the 5th, it contained 160
> Debtors and 326 Criminals, and in January last the whole number amounted
> to 822.[616]
>
> Mr Box states, that since his appointment in 1802, no fatal cases of infectious
> disorder has occurred. Pulmonary cases are the most difficult of cure in this
> and every other gaol; but Mr Box has not observed any disorder to be unusually
> prevalent. The average yearly number of deaths since 1802 has been only nine;
> and Your Committee have every reason to be satisfied with the liberality of the
> City, and the attention of Mr Box to this department.[617]

Assuming an average occupation of 500 (probably an under-estimate), the
mortality rate between 1802 and 1813 was about 1.8% per annum. Another
enquiry into conditions at Newgate in 1818 reported:

> It is most gratifying to Your Committee to state, that although numbers are
> committed to this prison in a state of disease, yet on referring to the lists in the
> Surgeon's book, and comparing the numbers with those in confinement, though
> the numbers of sick in the last year has been great, the proportion of deaths is
> much less than Your Committee was prepared to expect. Great praise remains
> due to Mr Box for his attention and medical skill.[618]

When Dr Babington (who had inspected the prison) was questioned, the
exemplary Mr Box again received praise:

> I learned that there had been, in the course of this last year, an unusual number
> of sick, and was surprised at the proportion of deaths stated by that gentleman
> [Mr Box]; that is to say, the number of deaths compared to those that were ill.
> Q. The number of deaths being many or few?
> A. Few.[619]

In 1835, the surgeon, Mr Macmurdo, provided some impressive statistics
(table 6:1):

---

[615] *Report*, PP, 1813-14, IV, 249, p. 55. Lascars (seamen) were a problem, if only because of the language barrier. 'I have visited a Lascar of the 4th Class who appears very ill, but I am unable to converse with him' (4 April 1845, Norwich).

[616] Ibid., p. 3.

[617] Ibid., p. 8. As noted earlier, Mr Box's memory seems to have been at fault as regards infectious disorders, at least in the early part of his tenure.

[618] *Report*, PP, 1818, VIII, 297, p. 8.

[619] Ibid., p. 205.

Table 6:1 Committals, sickness and deaths at Newgate prison 1826-1835[620]

Year	Commitments	Cases of sickness	Deaths
1826	2,702	174	4
1827	3,045	221	2
1828	3,085	175	4
1829	2,974	196	4
1830	2,762	185	4
1831	2,971	188	3
1832	3,277	231	4
1833	2,414	227	2
1834	1,821	140	6
1835	2,877	140	3

These figures may not be totally reliable – the 1836 inspector's report lists four deaths in 1835, but are still quite remarkable indicating a relative freedom from epidemic disease and perhaps surprisingly the 1832 cholera epidemic (in which London suffered 7,000 deaths [621]) evidently had little impact. Two of the deaths in 1834 were said to be due to 'spasmodic cholera' but this is almost certainly not Asiatic cholera. One of the 1835 deaths was caused by smallpox; evidently the disease did not spread within the prison. It is hardly likely that there were fewer inmates than in the first two decades of the century so, although accurate calculation is not possible, it seems likely that in the 1826-1835 period the mortality rate fell.

With the advent of the prison inspectorate in 1835, accurate statistical information was collected and it became possible to relate deaths to the average number of prisoners throughout England and Wales (table 6:2), providing a standard for comparison, and also showing that the death rates at Ilchester and Newgate earlier in the century were about what would be expected.

The cause of death was also more accurately recorded. For the year 1847 by far the commonest were 'Fever' (60 cases, 24.9%) and 'Consumption and Diseased Lungs' (65 cases, 27%). 'Dysentery, Diarrhoea, and other Bowel

---

[620] *Copy of a Report etc.*, PP, 1836, XLII, 231, p. 46.

[621] Porter, *The Greatest*, p. 403.

**Table 6:2 Deaths in the prisons of England and Wales
in the years 1839-1847[622]**

Year	Number of deaths	Daily average number of prisoners	Proportion of deaths to daily average (%)
1839	225	14,453	1.56
1840	246	15,883	1.55
1841	246	16,557	1.48
1842	236	17,718	1.33
1843	243	18,538	1.31
1844	160	17,415	0.92
1845	166	14,716	1.13
1846	128	14,624	0.88
1847	241	16,167	1.49
Annual mean	210	16,230	1.29

Complaints' accounted for 16 deaths; 'Apoplexy', 'Bronchitis and Congestion of the Lungs', 'Diseases of the Heart' 10 each; 'Debility and Atrophy' 7; and 'Dropsy' and erysipelas 5 each.

The figures given in table 6:2 conceal variations from prison to prison – revealed in table 6:3, compiled by inspector Frederic Hill from the largest prisons in the north of England.

For the year 1850, a satisfied Hill noted: 'the prisoners in my [Northern and Eastern] district have been unusually healthy, the average amount of mortality (2 removals on health grounds = 1 death) having been less than 1.5% of the average number of prisoners'.[623] Similarly satisfactory figures were achieved at Pentonville where the actual mortality was 1.215%, or adding 60% of those pardoned on medical grounds, 1.95%. At Parkhurst the actual mortality was only 0.3%.[624]

There were bad years: in 1849 the national toll was 341 (from 267 in 1848), virtually the whole of the excess (99 deaths) resulting from cholera.[625]

---

[622] *Twelfth Report of Inspector, Home District*, PP, 1847-48, XXXIV, 373, p. x; and *Thirteenth Report of Inspector, Home District*, PP, 1847-48, XXXV, 461, p. xviii.

[623] *Sixteenth Report of Inspector, Northern and Eastern District*, PP, 1851, XXVII, 461, p. xiv.

[624] *Reports of the Directors of Convict Prisons etc.*, PP, 1851, XXVIII, 1, pp. 51 and 32.

[625] *Fifteenth Report of Inspector, Home District*, PP, 1850, XXVIII, 1, p. xi.

Table 6:3 Deaths in larger prisons in the Northern District, year ending 30 June 1848[626]

Prison	Average number of prisoners	Deaths	Liberations or removals on account of illness	Percentage of deaths to average number of prisoners*
Carlisle	82	1	0	1.2
Newcastle	102	0	0	0
Morpeth	54	1	0	1.9
Durham	213	3	0	1.4
Lancaster	298	2	2	0.7 (1.0)
Preston	256	1	2	0.4 (0.6)
Liverpool (county)	363	8	1	2.2 (2.3)
Liverpool (borough)	822	16	7	1.9 (2.4)
Manchester	641	8	0	1.2
York	166	3	14	1.8 (6.0)
Beverley	72	3	1	4.2 (4.9)
Wakefield	547	7	1	1.2 (1.4)
Hull	142	1	1	0.7(1.1)
Northallerton	122	7	1	5.7 (6.1)**
Chester	115	6	0	5.2
Knutsford	283	7	0	2.5
Total	4,272	74	30	1.7 (2.1)

*The figure in parenthesis is arrived at by counting two discharges on health grounds as one death – this or similar approximations were widely used (q.v.).
**The unhealthy nature of Northallerton gaol had already been noted.

[626] *Thirteenth Report of Inspector, Northern District*, PP, 1847-8, XXXVI, 361, p. vii.

COMPARATIVE MORTALITY RATES

The availability of detailed statistical information stimulated attempts to compare prison mortality rates with those in the community at large. Bizarrely, a comparison was made between mortality amongst prisoners with a similar sized group entering the Equitable Assurance Society in 1837 – a group with a totally different social composition. Unsurprisingly, the prisoners' mortality rate was almost five times higher.[627] In a leading article in *The Lancet*, mortality rates in 93 prisons between 1826 and 1831 and in a similar sized population group aged between 20 and 30 years are compared. The annual mortality rate amongst prisoners was 1.6% but only 1.0-1.1% in the chosen control group. On this basis, and also on the basis that in the cholera epidemic of 1832 the Middlesex house of correction suffered a death rate two or three times higher than the metropolis, the inference was drawn that a prisoner was more likely to die than a free man by a factor of at least one half.[628] This inference is dubious because it fails to allow for the fact that many deceased prisoners were elderly or already ill when committed. A mistake was also made in the analysis of deaths in serious outbreaks of cholera at Millbank between October 1848 and February 1849, and between June and September 1849 in which 98 males and 12 females were affected, of whom 39 males and 9 females died. There were simultaneous epidemics in London and in an analysis of mortality rates, William Baly found the metropolitan mortality rate to be 0.66% whereas among prisoners it was 4.33%.[629] However, his conclusion that this indicates a higher degree of risk in the prison is erroneous. Cholera did not affect the population of London uniformly – the disease occurred in clusters (had it not been so, John Snow would never have made his epic observation with regard to the Broad Street pump) and if Baly wished to make comparisons he should have taken his control group from one of these clusters.

Baly produced an exhaustive statistical survey of prison death rates in general.[630] He analysed figures culled over a period of years from such diverse sources as England, France, Switzerland, the United States and Norway. Taking the five years to 1841 he found that in 36 largest gaols and houses of correction in England there had been 823 deaths among the average prisoner total of 8,657 – an annual mortality rate of 1.90%. However, this figure pales into insignificance when compared with the 1,980 deaths (average 3,389 prisoners) in the English hulks in the fifteen years to 1841 (3.89%) and a massive 1,981 deaths from an average 1,423 prisoners at the Maison Centrale at Eysses (France) in the years 1822-1837 (8.70%).[631] The

[627] Wiener, 'The Health', p. 57 (fn. 22).
[628] *The Lancet*, 2, 1839-40, p. 530.
[629] *Report, Millbank, 1849*, PP, 1850, XXIX, 73, pp. 10-12.
[630] Baly, pp. 113-272.
[631] Ibid., p. 126.

Photographed by MAULL & POLYBLANK, 55, Gracechurch Street, and 187a, Piccadilly, London.

William Baly. Photograph, circa 1860. Baly, born in 1816, became physician and lecturer in forensic medicine at St Bartholomew's hospital and physician to the Millbank penitentiary. On 28 January 1861 he was called to a consultation at Guildford. The train in which he travelled was derailed at Epsom junction by faulty track and he, along with several others, was crushed to death. According to *The Illustrated London News* (9 February 1861): '... the medical profession lost one its brightest ornaments.' (see also: *The Times*, 31 January 1861)

FUN.—August 18, 1866.

DEATH'S DISPENSARY.

OPEN TO THE POOR, GRATIS, BY PERMISSION OF THE PARISH.

Death dispensing disease from a pump. Although Snow had the Broad Street pump closed in 1854, the date of this cartoon from "Fun" magazine (1866) indicates that his beliefs were not immediately accepted.

best result among those he examined was achieved by Devizes house of correction with a mortality rate of 1.5%. Baly attributed the high rates in the hulks and in the French prisons as being – to some extent – due to the lack of any mechanism for pardoning on health grounds. In France an effort had been made to relate death rates to class: it was found that in the years 1815-1818 there was one death per 40 prisoners drawn from good or tolerable circumstances compared with one in four amongst beggars and vagrants. It was felt this was in part the result of the latter group lacking the means to purchase extra items of diet and clothing but it must also have related to poorer health on committal.[632] Baly also noted that in the United States "coloured" prisoners suffered a higher mortality than whites.[633]

Using figures from Millbank, Baly showed duration of imprisonment to be a contributory factor (table 6:4).

Table 6:4 A comparison of mortality rates in the year 1841[634]

Population under study	Mortality rate (deaths per 100)
London aged 15-70	1.54
Liverpool aged 15-70**	1.82
County prisons of England*	2.28
Millbank penitentiary (overall)*	3.10
Millbank penitentiary (3rd year prisoners)*	5.23

*In compiling these figures, Baly has factored in an allowance for those prisoners prematurely discharged on medical grounds, arguing that about half of those would have died and should therefore be included as prison deaths. He arrived at this factor by going through the notes of all those so discharged from Millbank and assessing the likelihood of their early demise.
**Liverpool, he felt, was less healthy than London due to its population of Irish immigrants.

In English county gaols and houses of correction where the average stay was 1 month and 12 days, mortality ran at 2.28%, in the hulks with an average stay of 10 months and 12 days it was 3.90%, whereas at Millbank with an average stay of 2 years it was 3.10%.[635] This last figure concealed the fact that the rate (including the pardoning factor) rose from 1.31 in the first year to 3.56 in the second year, 5.23 in the third year, 5.71 in the fourth year, but fell slightly to 4.42 in the fifth year – presumably on a "survival of the fittest" basis. In the first three months (during which time there were no pardons) the mortality was only 0.11%.[636] The mortality at Millbank resulting from 'consumption, haemoptysis and other tubercular

---

[632] Ibid., p. 134.
[633] Ibid., pp. 138-139.
[634] Ibid., p. 189. Throughout, Baly calculates in deaths per thousand and with three places of decimals. For clarity, I have altered his figures to deaths per hundred with two places of decimals at most.
[635] Ibid., p. 142.
[636] Ibid., pp. 150-151.

diseases' was 0.29% as compared with 0.03% in London.[637] Although many prisoners arrived already showing the signs of tuberculosis (1.35% of those committed to Millbank had 'external scrofula'),[638] Baly's data suggest that many of those dying of tuberculosis developed the disease in gaol.[639] In English county prisons the excess mortality from tuberculosis was lower than at Millbank the result, Baly felt, of the shorter sentences served in the former.[640] He detected the same tendencies in gaols in the United States, particularly among black prisoners.[641] Other conditions causing more deaths among prisoners than among the population at large – making due allowance for age – were fevers (4-5 times more risk) and bowel complaints (4 times greater risk).[642] On the other hand, prisoners were less likely than the general population of London to die as a result of heart disease, diseases of the respiratory organs (excluding consumption and haemoptysis), and diseases of the urinary generative apparatus.[643] He affirmed, almost certainly erroneously, that the drinking water (even that taken from wells fed by the Thames, as at Millbank) was not a problem: 'that the bowel complaints so common in English prisons, workhouses and lunatic asylums do not depend on the quality of the water, I am perfectly satisfied'.[644] Nor did he feel the location of prisons to be a problem: serious disease came 'not from noxious influences peculiar to the locality but from causes which were likely to be common to most if not all prisons'.[645] On the other hand he was ready to blame damp since many of the diseases were the result of 'some form of malaria[646] floating in the atmosphere' and was unhappy with the often predominantly liquid diet which he felt gave rise to diarrhoea.[647] His belief in the miasmic theory was strong; faced with the cholera outbreak of 1853 (with eight deaths at Millbank), he noted that Queen's prison, Horsemonger-lane gaol and Bethlehem – all just as close to the river as Millbank and all in areas severely afflicted by the disease but with the significant difference that they drew their water from artesian wells – had escaped cholera, he still remarked: 'I doubt the inference which is drawn from these facts.'[648] Even when the following year's outbreak at Millbank (with 28 deaths) terminated

---

[637] Ibid., p. 198.
[638] Ibid., p. 230. It is clear that Baly recognised that consumption and scrofula were manifestations of the same pathological process.
[639] Ibid., pp. 202-203.
[640] Ibid., pp. 205-206.
[641] Ibid., pp. 219-220.
[642] Ibid., p. 172.
[643] Ibid., p. 198.
[644] Ibid., p. 181.
[645] Ibid., p. 116.
[646] He is of course using "malaria" in its literal sense (Italian = bad air) rather than its modern meaning.
[647] Ibid., p. 170.
[648] Reports of the Directors of Convict Prisons, PP, 1854, XXXIII, 501, p. 102.

within a day or two of changing from river water to that from an artesian well at Trafalgar Square, he was still unconvinced.[649] This reluctance to abandon the miasmic theory – even when faced with what seems incontrovertible evidence – now strikes us as extraordinary.

So far as the excess mortality from tuberculosis was concerned he was on firmer ground. The explanations he offered were: (1) deficient ventilation, (2) cold, (3) lack of exercise, (4) 'listless state of mind', and (5) poor diet: 'for the diet of prisoners, though often perhaps more abundant than the agricultural labourer usually enjoys, yet has generally been less stimulating, and also less nutritious, than seems requisite for the health, under conditions so unnatural and depressing as are those almost necessarily attended on the state of imprisonment'.[650]

Millbank remained an unhealthy prison. In the three years to 1850 the death rate among males was 2.2% and among females 2.6%. An additional 11 prisoners had been pardoned.[651] After studying the usual thorough analysis provided by Baly the inspectors arrived at what seem to be entirely reasonable conclusions – emphasising the importance of overcrowding, the poor state of health of arriving prisoners and lengthy detention:

> 1st. That the diseases which caused the most numerous deaths were chronic diseases, of which the chief is consumption and various epidemic diseases; namely small-pox and influenza, cholera, fever and erysipelas. 2nd. That the unusual mortality from these diseases was not caused by any change of discipline, or any alteration in the internal arrangements of the prison. 3rd. That the increased mortality from chronic disease arose from the removal to Millbank of convicts who had lost their health in other prisons, from the longer detention at Millbank of the prisoners, especially of those who were feeble and prone to disease; and lastly, from the discontinuance of the practice of transferring the feeble and diseased to an Invalid or hospital hulk. 4th That the mortality from epidemic disease in the prison was primarily due to the prevalence of these diseases throughout the Metropolis, but that the mortality from fever appeared to have been increased by the too great number of prisoners in the prison, and especially in those rooms in which many men were congregated together.[652]

Baly's interpretation of his data supported the contention that an individual unfortunate enough to be confined to gaol had a greater chance of dying from disease than had he or she not been imprisoned. On the other hand, Dr William Guy (who succeeded Baly at Millbank) in an analysis of figures

---

[649] *Reports of the Directors of Convict Prisons*, PP, 1854-5, XXV, 33, pp. 108-111.

[650] Ibid., pp. 234-235.

[651] *Reports of the Directors etc.*, PP, 1851, XXVIII, 1, p. 22.

[652] *Sixth Report, Millbank*, PP, 1850, XXIX, 55, p. 8. As a postscript the inspectors add: 'The necessity of almost daily attendance at the prison, ... has afforded us abundant opportunity of observing the zeal, attention, and ability manifested by the superior officers, and the general good conduct of those in subordinate situations .... Ibid., p. 9.

from a few years later reached a different and more convincing conclusion: that the convict death rate was no higher than amongst free men of the same social and residential status – those '[inhabiting] the worst districts of the metropolis'.[653] Table 6:5 shows Guy's comparison of the actual number of deaths in prisons with those occurring in cohorts of the same size and age distribution (figures provided for him by the Office of National Statistics).

Table 6:5 A comparison of mortality among different population cohorts 1857-1861[654]

Category	Male deaths	Female deaths
Prisoners	83 incl. 6 pardons (35*)	18 incl. 4 pardons (8)
Population of England	75 (24)	12 (6)
Population of London	88 (25)	11 (4)
Population of St George's & Southwark	89 (34)	14 (5)
Population of Westminster	110 (42)	14 (4)

*The figure in parenthesis is the number dying from consumption

Guy argued: 'It would be both reasonable and fair, therefore, to substitute for these mixed populations those of certain metropolitan districts in which the criminal classes are known to live mixed up with more respectable person of their own rank in society'.[655] If this perfectly reasonable argument is accepted, it is clear that for males the risk of death in prison is no greater (or even less) than had they been at liberty but for females the risk is slightly increased – particularly from consumption.

DeLacy, from the vantage point of the late-twentieth century, made an exhaustive analysis of statistics collected from the prisons of Lancashire (more comprehensive than is available for most counties) between 1825 and 1843. She reached a similar conclusion to Guy's: 'On the whole, the average person's chances of dying probably increased slightly upon commitment and rose with the length of imprisonment; although this was not true for certain groups of prisoners, particularly those in Preston and those already sick or starving'.[656] Significantly, like Guy, she too concluded that prison mortality rates were lower than those in the notoriously unhealthy Lancashire industrial areas (from where of course, most of the prison population was drawn).

---

[653] Guy, pp. 19-20.

[654] The number of prison deaths (106 when corrected for discharges on health grounds) is appreciably lower than some of those quoted earlier. This is partly because the count is of felons only, and partly because the prison population was already in decline. The prison mortality rate is the expected level: 1.47%.

[655] Ibid., p. 19.

[656] DeLacy, pp. 185-186. Preston was an exception by virtue of its consistently low mortality rate (see table 5:3).

It seems therefore that in most prisons the mortality rate was in the range of 1%-2%, the rate rising with duration of stay. It was higher than this if the site's water supply was contaminated, as at Northallerton and Millbank. It is impossible to state with certainty whether an individual's risk of death increased with imprisonment; if there was an increase it was small. Epidemics, particularly of Asiatic cholera, inevitably added to the mortality rate, but not necessarily to a greater extent than in the community. Ironically, in some epidemics a prison might offer safety.

INDIVIDUAL DEATHS: THOSE ILL ON COMMITTAL

In this section I will concentrate on individuals rather than statistics: examining the manner in which dying and seriously ill patients were managed. First, I will give examples of a factor already touched on: the influence on prison mortality figures of those already terminally ill when committed. The inspectors' reports provide many examples. The surgeon at Salford house of correction is reported as stating, rather sanctimoniously, but doubtless truthfully: 'It is a melancholy fact that habits of intemperance have been equally the cause of death and disease as of crime'.[657] A more specific example comes from Oxford city gaol where the only death in 1843 was a 34 year old male 'Mad Drunk' on admission who died six days later as a result of delirium tremens.[658] At Coldbath-fields, (where from a daily average of 1,062 prisoners there had been 17 deaths in 1840 (1.6%) and from 1,048 prisoners, 24 deaths in 1841 (2.3%)), it was stated: 'In by far the greater number of these cases, the individuals were admitted in a bad state of health, and were only in confinement for very short periods before their death'. Of the seventeen who died in 1840, nine had been imprisoned for less than one week. These were mostly in their twenties or thirties.[659] The surgeon at Salford describes a case in detail: 'a poor emaciated, almost bloodless, creature; long ill, and complaining of severe cold and cough' when she was admitted (for trial) on 5 March 1845. She was put to bed, given a variety of treatments, anything she chose to eat with wine and porter to drink, but died on 29 March. Autopsy showed extensive pulmonary and renal tuberculosis.[660] More details of the sad state of some prisoners on their arrival is given in the following extracts from the journal of the surgeon at Kirton house of correction:

[657] *Third Report of Inspector, Northern and Eastern District*, PP, 1837-38, XXXI, 1, p. 117.
[658] *Ninth Report of Inspector, Southern and Western District*, PP, 1844, XXIX, p. 344.
[659] *Sixth Report of Inspector, Home District*, PP, 1841 Sess. 2, IV, 1, p. 250.
[660] *Tenth Report of Inspector, Northern and Eastern District*, PP, 1845, XXIV, 1, p. 121.

On April 13, 1847, at half-past six o'clock in the evening, I was sent for to visit a prisoner who had been committed after my visit to the prison in the forenoon (eleven o'clock): ... I found him in an insensible state, speechless, having no pulse at the wrist, the pupils of his eyes dilated and not sensible to the light of a candle; administered to him an emetic, and again visited him at half-past ten o'clock. The action of the emetic had expelled some strong liquid from his stomach, which was strongly impregnated with a small of liquor; his pulse was then quick, and his breathing stertorous, and he appeared to be dying of apoplexy. A vein was opened, but with no relief: he died at five in the morning April 14, 1847. On July 19 1847, ----- was committed in a bad state of health. He had been lying in a lodging-house with six Irishmen, all ill of a bilious typhoid fever, and he died of that disease on July 25. On February 22, 1848, ------ was committed, labouring under bilious typhoid fever and purging; he was immediately sent into the prison infirmary. He died on March 12, 1848, of bilious typhoid fever.[661]

At Spilsby house of correction a man, aged about 30, whose name never became known, died 14 days after committal:

He was found in a ditch ... having eaten all the grass within his reach. When brought into the prison he was in the greatest state of exhaustion from the privations he had endured; all his excretions had passed involuntarily, which had excoriated the parts with which they had come in contact; he was in a most miserable situation. After getting him thoroughly cleaned, I endeavoured to obtain, by suitable diet and medicine, a reaction in the system, the establishment of which caused the disease to manifest itself in its true character, as one of tubercular consumption; he gradually sunk and died. He never spoke after his committal, therefore it was impossible to ascertain his history, although the governor was very assiduous to obtain it.[662]

Presumably this man had been committed as a vagrant – the magistrate concerned opting for prison rather than the workhouse – and it is clear that such a practice was widespread and undoubtedly made a contribution (largely beyond the influence of prison surgeons) to death rates.

Some prisoners arriving in very poor health survived. George Gabb (aged 26), committed to Horsley on 20 February 1843 was not a suitable subject for imprisonment by any standards. In the entry for that day he is described as: 'Blind in both Eyes, Disease of the Bladder, unable to hold his urine. Disease of hip joints, a seton[663] being over right hip joint on his coming into the Prison'. Later he was diagnosed as a 'bad scrophulous case' and then on 5 March: 'Keeps to his bed as he is unable to stand' but he improved and could hold his urine. Given broth twice weekly in place of potatoes, and tea and bread and butter in place of gruel, he was due for discharge on 28

---

[661] *Fourteenth Report of Inspector, Midland and Eastern District*, PP, 1849, XXVI, 1, p. 17.

[662] *Fifth Report of Inspector, Northern and Eastern District*, PP, 1840, XXV, 565, p. 35.

[663] Presumably the hip was infected – probably with tuberculosis.

March but was unfit due to 'disordered bowels', and on 4 April the surgeon commented that Gabb, although sent for six weeks hard labour had spent nearly all that time in bed and was still unfit to leave the prison. Another example is seen in the following extract from the journal of the surgeon at Dorchester county gaol and house of correction:

> June 29th [1840] – Thomas **** – This prisoner, committed on Saturday, appeared to me to be in a state of starvation when I saw him on Saturday, and totally unfit for any labour. He nearly approached the condition of a living skeleton. He was committed, as I was informed, for stealing a loaf of bread.[664]

INDIVIDUAL DEATHS: GLOUCESTERSHIRE, LANCASTER AND NORWICH

To detail the deaths in all prisons for which journals are available would be tedious; I have therefore listed only the thirty-eight in Gloucester county gaol (table 6:6).

Table 6:6 Deaths at Gloucester county gaol: 31 July 1791 to 11 March 1799 and 2 Jan 1809 to 20 February 1820

Date	Name	Cause of death
13 July 1791	Thomas Barr	Suicide, found hanging in cell
24 July 1791	Thomas Barnard	Fever and jaundice. Aged 84
18 Jan 1792	Edward Ifield	'Epilepsy' – possibly cerebro-vascular accident. Aged 74
22 July 1792	John Burrows	Unknown, a debtor, ill on admission who died after 6 days
30 Sept 1796	Thomas Cooke	(possibly) chronic heart failure. Aged 70
24 April 1794	Benjamin Heague	Drowned in River Severn attempting escape
31 Jan 1796	(male) Meek	Gastro-intestinal infection
6 Feb 1796	(male) Poulson	Gastro-intestinal infection
24 Dec 1796	Joseph Holford	Probably heart failure
8 Feb 1798	(male) Humphries	Gastro-intestinal infection
8 Feb 1798	(male) Still	Gastro-intestinal infection
11 Feb 1798	(male) Coates	Gastro-intestinal infection
31 Nov 1798	(male) Wakeland	Gastro-intestinal infection
4 Feb 1809	Jonathan Hall	'Affection of the Brain' (possibly meningitis)
17 Dec 1810	Joseph Brown	'Diseased Viscera' (possibly tuberculosis)
2 Jan 1811	Joseph Bryant	'Pulmonary Consumption' (tuberculosis)
11 Jan 1811	Joseph Tackle	'Asthmatic Affection' (probably chronic bronchitis)

[664] *Report of Inspector, Southern and Western District*, PP, 1841 Sess. 2, V, 177, p. 107.

Date	Name	Cause of death
6 July 1811	Mary Rodway	Puerperal fever (peritonitis, possibly criminal abortion)
31 July 1811	Septimus Ludlow	'Fit of Apoplexy' (probably cerebro-vascular accident)
7 Feb 1812	Edward Tanner	'Low Fever' (possibly typhoid)
9 April 1812	Richard Day	Gastro-intestinal bleeding (possibly typhoid)
1 Oct 1812	Enoch Pegler	'Diseased Lungs' (possibly tuberculosis)
16 Jan 1814	Thomas Pittman	'Dropsical Affection' (probably congestive heart failure)
20 Mar 1814	William Jenkins	'Low Fever' (probably typhus or typhoid)
7 April 1814	Thomas Gardner	'Effusion of the Brain' (possibly typhus)
30 April 1814	Elizabeth Brinkworth's child	'Its death Hastened by Mother's Negligence' (aged two weeks)
19 May 1814	Samuel Bryant	'Debility'
12 Aug 1814	Mary Evans's child	Two weeks old. No cause given – never thrived
11 Feb 1815	Joseph Harper	'Low Fever' (possibly typhoid)
26 April 1815	Thomas Herbert	Typhus
18 April 1816	Joseph Clark	'Affection of the Brain' (possibly neurosyphilis)
8 Oct 1816	Joseph Teackle	'Inflammation of the Bowels' (possibly dysentery)
15 Feb 1817	John Williams	'Determined and Obstinate Conduct' (possibly neurosyphilis)
19 June 1817	Peter Aldridge	'Disordered Liver'
26 June 1817	(male) Broad	Old age and 'Exhausted for Want of Support'.
11 Sept 1817	John Hancock	'Consumption' (tuberculosis)
8 Feb 1819	Edward Green	'Infirmity and Old Age' (probably congestive heart failure)
10 May 1819	(male) Comley	Typhus

In addition there was one stillbirth (born to Mary Hicks, 21 December 1792).

As regards the other county prisons in Gloucestershire, there were five deaths (excluding a stillbirth) at Littledean 1807-1850 (representing 0.37% of those reporting sick), and eighteen at Northleach 1801-1841 (0.52%), as compared to the thirty-eight at Gloucester (1.11%). The higher percentage at Gloucester may partly reflect longer sentences but is also almost certainly a consequence of the fact that more of the gaol's inmates, particularly debtors, were ill at the time of their committal. An example is debtor Thomas Pittman. Committed suffering from a 'Dropsical Affection' was admitted directly to the gaol's hospital, failed to improve on treatment and died a week or so later, on 16 January 1814. Mary Rodway's death in 1811 at Gloucester is suspicious. On 29 June 1811 she miscarried and was ordered to bed. On

30 June the entry reads: 'Mary Rodway miscarried last night, she seems today easy, she was yesterday desired to keep in Bed, but contrary to my request she has chosen to be below, subjecting herself to cold and other consequences that are likely to take place from such imprudence'. Whether because of, or coincidental with this perverse behaviour she was taken ill with a fever on 2 July, and, although treated in hospital died four days later. An autopsy showed 'Inflammation of Intestines', which must raise the possibility that she or another prisoner carried out an instrumental abortion resulting in perforation of the uterus, peritonitis and – inevitably – death. Of other deaths at Gloucester, there is no reason to doubt the surgeon's diagnosis of tuberculosis in Joseph Bryant, (2 January 1811), whilst Joseph Brown (17 December 1810) and Samuel Bryant (19 May 1814) may well have suffered the same disease. These three patients, as well as Joseph Teakle and Enoch Pegler, had been in the prison hospital for several months before they died. The illnesses of Joseph Clark (died 18 April 1816) and John Williams (died 15 February 1817) are interesting in that they followed something of the same pattern with spells of disturbed behaviour, refusal to eat, and unexplained pains, interspersed with spells of normality. It is possible that they were victims of neuro-syphilis – the existence of which in its various manifestations was not recognised at this time. In nearly every case at Gloucester county gaol seriously ill patients had the benefit of a physician's opinion.

It is difficult to ascribe a precise cause of death in many instances. Usually the age of the deceased is not given and even when autopsy examinations were performed the diagnosis is not always clear. Of John Jacques (ill with a gangrenous leg since his committal about a month earlier, died 17 December 1835, Northleach). Thomas Cheatle of Burford, the acting surgeon, wrote that he had examined the body and:

> found many marks of previous disease such as scrophulous scars ... From the appearance of the feet and the history of the case ... I have no hesitation in attributing his death to mortification of those parts which is a common occurrence in advanced life where the system has been exhausted either by previous disease or great privation. I am further of the opinion that every medical attention has been shown to him and every comfort administered that the nature of his case required.

At the inquest death was ascribed to 'natural debility'.

As regards the death of Jane Smith's child at Northleach house of correction on 24 February 1832, the surgeon's journal for 25 February records the inquest verdict of: 'Visitation of God, its death accelerated by its removal from Cheltenham on the 24th'. Jane Smith would have walked the fourteen miles from Cheltenham to Northleach carrying her child. An 1843 report[665] criticised this arrangement and by 1848 the journey had become easier: 'At the foot of Dowdeswell Hill I passed a coach full of convicts from Gloucester gaol going to the Northleach House of Correction, with four horses'.[666] In general however, prisoners were expected to be able to walk: 'In 1822 it was the practice in the West Riding "for the prisoners ... to be marched from Wakefield to the place where the court is to sit, chained two together by their necks, besides the usual handcuffs on their wrists; in this way they are marched sometimes to Skipton, nearly thirty-five miles; to Knaresborough twenty-five miles, and other places of shorter distance to take their trial"'. After 1827 a covered van was provided.[667] However, even in the late 1840s prisoners in Lancashire still had to walk from Manchester to Liverpool, or even further.[668] Later, the transport provided was not necessarily suitable: 'The prisoners are sent [from Petworth] to Lewes for trial in a caravan drawn by four horses, which I am informed, is generally 17 or 18 hours on the road!'[669] The inspector felt the journey would be more appropriately made by train.

To return to the subject of deaths in Gloucestershire prisons. At Horsley house of correction in the period 3 January 1843 to 27 April 1844 there were just two deaths. John Bown, aged 38, died on 19 January 1843. He had a fit three days earlier and never recovered. The surgeon wrote:

> The prisoner had been paralytic in the lower limbs for a considerable time and had been discharged incurable from the Bath and Gloucester Hospitals. He had recovered the use of his limbs sufficiently to totter and stagger about but it appears while he was in the prison he had not the usual command over his bowels and bladder so that he required a good deal of waiting on.

Hester Wakefield died on 10 June 1843 having been ill for over a month. The journal entry states: 'This poor woman had been in a bad state of health for a long time before she was admitted a prisoner. Her mental faculties were in my judgement so weak that she could hardly be considered a responsible agent'. Clearly, both were suffering from a chronic wasting disease, perhaps neuro-syphilis.

In these Gloucestershire prisons the range of causes of death is sufficiently varied to make it unlikely that conditions within the prison were responsible

---

[665] *Report, Northleach*, PP, 1843, XLII, 375, p. 10.
[666] Verey, p. 171.
[667] Webb and Webb, p. 79.
[668] Dixon, p. 320.
[669] *Twenty-third Report of Inspector, Southern Division*, PP, 1857-1858, XXIX, 69, p. 126.

– but with some exceptions. At Gloucester county gaol, the clusters of deaths from gastro-intestinal infections in the early months of 1796 and 1798, and that of William Jenkins in 1814 suggest that drinking infected water from the well was probably responsible.[670] The cause of the death of Sarah Bettridge's child (Northleach, 18 January 1818), is not stated but the surgeon had previously noted that 'The Children [are] suffering in their health from being confined with their Mothers' (1 January 1818). This prison was prone to damp in winter.

Of those who died at Lancaster, six are described as old (with various qualifications) and all but one of these were debtors; in total there were at least seven debtors among the sixteen dead. R. Scully was a touching case. The prison inspector quoting from the governor's journal describes the unusual circumstances: '22nd May 1844. Debtor R.S. departed this life at 7.30 p.m. The gentleman was visiting magistrate for two Irish counties. He got himself arrested and sent hither on friendly process, merely to be with his nephew, whom I hold for a large sum of money'.[671] Another, (Forbes) was described as 'patience itself' twelve days before he died. Catherine Hacking had already been in hospital with a prolapsed uterus but on 8 April 1846 she was noted to be 'ailing' and given tea and sugar. She had an ague and on 27 April: 'I begin to think Hacking's troubled mind will soon bring her down, she has a turbulent heart and cough with some expectoration'. Although 'A little better' on 28 April, she died two days later. Mr Peers (probably a debtor) was already ill on admission: 'he has a very threatening looking inflamed foot' (30 December 1848) and went directly to hospital where he died seventeen days later. There were two infant deaths. The mother of one of these, Caldwell, had been noted on 23 September 1845 as being: 'out of order this morning, her child is delicate and does not keep the breasts down'. When the child died two weeks later the surgeon wrote: 'Caldwell's remaining twin child has gradually declined and died' (7 October 1845). Whether the other twin had died before Caldwell was committed to prison or whether its death in prison had not been noted in the journal is unclear but I suspect the former. Hewitt's child was only a few hours old: 'Hewitt was confined last night about 8 o'clock, the child was never likely for life and has since expired' (6 March 1847). A sudden and unexpected death, perhaps the result of coronary artery thrombosis or a cerebro-vascular accident, was that of Sween:

> Mr Langshaw and I have just seen James Sween, he fell back suddenly and died after he had partially dressed himself. He was occupied in reading at the time or immediately before his death. This man has occasionally complained of cough

---

[670] For details of contamination of the gaol's well, see chapter three.

[671] *Tenth Report of Inspector, Northern and Eastern District*, PP, 1845, XXIV, 1, p. 46.

but I believe he was quite well yesterday and even this morning. It is now 6 of a.m. (15 May 1848).

The only patient whose clinical history is given in detail is Ecclestone, in a lengthy note dated 19 August 1848:

> 3.30 a.m. Soon after two this morning I was called to visit Ecclestone who is suffering from apparent mischief in the head. He has taken no notice, [i.e., he was not responding to stimuli] it looks like a fatal seizure [Ecclestone died soon after 4 a.m.]. This poor man came here 28th February last, he then gave his age as 16. He was admitted to the hospital on the 25th March for headache and discharged cured on the 29th. At the time I considered him delicate. On the 3rd April he was admitted to hospital along with two other prisoners with symptoms of fever and discharged again on the 12th, he was induced to take his meals in the Trafficers, being a man likely to be imposed upon. Ecclestone complained of cough on the 28th May, of pain in the side on 4th July, and of headache on the 6th from disordered stomach he was treated on this day and again on the 10th. July 29th he asked for medicine for some slight eruption of the skin, which was cured on the 31st. On August 13th he had medicine for the stomach on 15th liniment for pain in the thigh. I inspected yesterday and he made no complaint. His life was terminated by apoplexy.

Even this detailed case history is not enough to establish the cause of death: Ecclestone certainly seems to have been a sickly youth but without any particular reason for terminal apoplexy – perhaps he suffered a fatal sub-arachnoid haemorrhage. There is a clue in the governor's journal for 19-20 August 1848[672] as to why the unfortunate Ecclestone warrants such a detailed journal entry. He notes that the prisoners refused to work, complaining that one of their number had been taken ill during the night and that the turnkey had been slow to answer calls for help. Captain Hansbrow told them that there had been too many instances of 'crying wolf' and the complaint was dismissed, but it seems that the mere whiff of trouble was enough to prompt the surgeon to write a note of justification in case the complaint should be taken further. Prison surgeons did not carry out their duties under a cloak of secrecy – they were well aware that any hint of malpractice could arouse public scrutiny. The only case which may perhaps have been the result of a prison-acquired infection was that of Brown whose death was quite sudden. 'I have cleared the Debtors' Hospital to admit Brown, a feeble old man, prostrated and almost pulseless from vomiting and purging'. He also had cramps and even though the surgeon or his assistant attended him constantly, he was dead within twenty-four hours. 'We shall have the inquest and interment as soon as possible. All clothing will be burnt' (30 November 1849).

---

[672] Quoted in DeLacy, p. 201.

In the six years covered by the surgeons' journals at Norwich there were 14 deaths (an uncorrected annual mortality rate of about 2.3%). Four of these were attributed to "debility" and it is impossible even to guess at a precise diagnosis, although at least some were probably tuberculous. George Butler, was already in the hospital on 1 January 1843 when the journal commences and although given a meat diet and tonic medicines, deteriorated and died. Jonathan Cook, already imprisoned for six years, had been in hospital for several weeks before death, but apart from the fact that he was 'sinking rapidly' no clues are given as to his medical problem. He must have developed bedsores because after his death it is noted: '[he] must be buried as soon as possible to prevent infection in the Prison, as his back is in a state of Mortification'. The hospital was white-washed and fumigated. George Ellis (died 19 July 1849) whose age is not given, had been intermittently ill for several months with debility and diarrhoea but it seems unlikely that the latter problem was the primary cause of death. Similarly, with Newton Crossfield (died 17 December 1849) we are given no information beyond his debility of about five weeks' duration and that he was treated with cod liver oil. George Thurthill had been ill for months with 'kidney disease' and at one stage a mass in the loin was noted, suggesting the possibility of a peri-nephric abscess, perhaps the result of a renal calculus. Poor Thurthill was not always treated as sympathetically as might have been hoped. On 15 April 1848 he was brought before the magistrates: 'in consequence of the report of the Medical Officer that he had been endeavouring to impose upon him, and [he was] admonished as to his future conduct'. [673] He too had diarrhoea latterly but this was probably an incidental feature; he died on 26 July 1848.

Such lack of sympathy was unusual – most seriously ill patients were treated liberally. At Gloucester James Harper (died 11 February 1815) was prescribed gruel and tea when admitted to hospital on 1 February, port wine and a pint of wine of 9 February, and 'at least a bottle of wine during the night' was prescribed on 10 February. Poignantly, Joseph Bryant (died 2 January 1811) expressed a 'strong desire to a little Chitterlings' (7 December 1810) and for turnips (10 December 1810). Both requests were granted. At Lancaster fairly typical was the case of Porter who, on 16 January 1847 became 'confused and generally out of order'. On 17th January: 'Porter's case assumes the aspect of fever' and on the following day: 'Porter is not worse this morning but I see no chance of his being in a fit state to discharge on Wednesday when his time is out'. On 20th January: 'Porter has passed a disturbed and rambling night but he is partly sensible this morning. Porter's

---

[673] *Visiting Justices Book*, NCRO, MF 880.

term of imprisonment expires today but as he is labouring under acute and dangerous distemper it would be unsafe to discharge him and of himself he is no state of mind to require it'. Later that day Porter was ordered mustard poultices for his legs, and 'the attendant and the two patients may have a bottle of porter'. By 22nd Porter was receiving port wine and a couple of eggs but he gradually weakened and died on 24th. At Norwich Mr Cole (debtor) had been confined for 15 years and at various times had been mentioned, once with 'purging' and once as being 'dropsical'. On 1 August 1846 he was seen with a severe nose-bleed and despite receiving a pint of porter daily he gradually deteriorated and died on 26 August. On 24 August: 'He expressed his grateful thanks for all the kind attention bestowed upon him during the many years he was confined in the Castle' and since he was 90 years old his death can hardly be put down as a failure of prison medical care. Also well advanced in age at 80 was William Cooper: 'This poor man was received into the Castle on 3rd of Fby 1845 in a most abject state of poverty as fully stated by myself and the Governor' (8 February 1845). Noted as being covered in sores and suffering from the Itch, on 11 February he was suddenly taken ill, put into the hospital: 'near a good fire, Brandy and Water was ordered for him, a Cordial Mixture' but he failed to rally and died. George Chamberlain was admitted to the hospital on 21 February 1846 and on 27 February is described as having 'diseased lungs' and being 'in great danger'. His condition fluctuated, he was seen regularly by Dr Tawke and, doubtless with the latter's approval, was given three glasses of port wine, four eggs and four oranges daily, together with mutton broth. Despite this lavish diet (or even because of it) Chamberlain developed abdominal pain and vomiting as a result of which Dr Tawke diagnosed peritonitis and stated 'he will not recover'. Nor did he, but on the day of death Dr Tawke wrote: 'during the whole period of his illness he has always expressed himself most grateful for the attention he has received and I can bear testimony to the humane treatment and anxious care with which he has been watched over by all the officers concerned with the Prison'.

Serious illness was not necessarily a prelude to death. At Norwich on 23 June 1843 Job Cattermaul became ill with a fever. Deteriorating ('[he is] very desponding') he was seen on 24 June by Dr Tawke who wrote:

> I this day visited Job Cattermaul in conjunction with Mr Scott and at his request. This young man is, without doubt, in considerable danger and requires much watching. I should say he could not receive more regular attendance in every way were he an inmate of a London Hospital. He has every attention paid to him.

On the following day Dr Tawke and Mr Scott gave their opinion that the fever was of the 'Typhoid form' but helped by regular doses of port wine Cattermaul recovered, as did William Barker who developed similar symptoms. By July 7 Scott reported that there had been no more cases but that every effort should be made to ventilate the prison. Both sufferers were discharged from the hospital on 28 July: '... they have been placed in a warm bath, and every possible care taken to prevent infection after such a severe fever'. At Lancaster, Perry was noted to be ill on 27 April 1848: 'his case assumes the aspect of a fever'. Daily entries record his alarming progress:

> a doubtful state, his head confused ... barely conscious at times but his pulse continues good (1 May);
> weaker but more like himself again, he will require a bottle of porter and the hospital mate may be allowed a little coffee and sugar in the night (2 May);
> Perry hardly so well as in the morning and I have ordered a little bread and cheese for the men who stay with him in the night' (7.30 p.m., 3 May);
> Perry has lost ground since yesterday, even since this morning. I have now much fear for him (5 May);
> I have inserted a catheter for Perry (9 p.m., 6 May);
> Perry is palsied in his speech but he appears to be recovering (15 May);
> Perry is going on well, he was put out of the way yesterday by some of the patients stealing his meat (23 May).

Surviving the attentions of both the surgeon and his fellow prisoners Perry left hospital, and although readmitted for a short spell on 31 August with 'distended bowels' he was discharged home on 7 September 1848. At Gloucester county gaol:

> James Dutton (debtor) has a very large unkind ulcer on the left side of his right foot – daily dressings (16 May 1797);
> [James Dutton] unwell and low...ulcer from the right side extended from the toes near halfway to the heel, in a state of inflammation tending to gangrene (17 June 1797);
> Notwithstanding the most powerful antiseptic medicines external and internal, mortification has taken place in a great degree. He has taken port wine (with and without bark) to the amount of a bottle daily, it being absolutely necessary (20 June 1797);
> [after consultation with another surgeon] it is my opinion that Dutton cannot survive this disease (25 June 1797);
> A line of Inflammation evidently appears between the diseased and sound parts, and he is better in himself (29 June 1797);
> Dutton mends very fast (23 July 1797); The Governor has just Informd me Sir G.O. Paul has granted Dutton leave to stay here till his foot is quite well, which is tending fast to that Period (23 August 1797);
> Yesterday James Dutton left the Prison in a much better state of health, than he had been for many months before, and gratefully thankful for all that had been done for him (1 September 1797).

COMPASSION RATHER THAN PUNISHMENT

Lancaster provides an unusual opportunity to study the practice of early discharge on medical grounds: during six years nineteen prisoners were recommended for reprieve on health grounds. There were sixteen deaths between 12 December 1843 and 30 November 1849, which in relation to an average occupancy of about 400 gives a highly creditable annual mortality rate of 0.66%, or making the usual adjustment, of 1.06%. A cynical view would be that reprieves were motivated by a desire to shed the work involved in caring for a difficult case and, on the assumption that the patient would die at home rather than in the prison, improving prison statistics. In fact, the journal entries demonstrate compassion – a desire to alleviate the sufferings of seriously ill patients and to provide for the comforting presence of family and friends in what might be the final part of life. Thus:

> Denby, a delicate lad spits some awkward stuff (12 December 1843);
> Henry Roberts is admitted to the hospital on the crown side. He spits blood and is otherwise threatened with disease of the lungs (28 December 1843);
> Denby and Roberts are failing, I shall recommend them to the Home Secty, as they cannot survive their terms of imprisonment (15 January 1844);
> Roberts is failing fast and Denby follows, I hope the order for discharge will soon arrive (20 January 1844);
> Roberts and Denby are gone home, the first cannot live long (27 January 1844).[674]

Sometimes it was a matter of fine judgement: 'I am rather doubting of Kay in the hospital should not be recommended for discharge on account of failing health, he has only to stay until July 5' (4 May 1847). And there were two apparently very close shaves: 'Williamson's pardon has arrived just in time, the old man is failing daily' (1 October 1847); and: 'Mr Coates is admitted into debtors' hospital. He has been seriously indisposed for some time before coming into prison' (18 October 1846) followed by 'I am glad to find Mr Coates is going home today, he cannot survive long' (28 November 1846). On another occasion an unexpected rally resulted in a change of mind: 'Myers ['a large collection of matter in the thigh'] fails, I shall have to take steps to get his time shortened' (7 October 1848), but two weeks later Myers had improved: 'I have not yet reported his case'. Most impressive was the speed with which the bureaucracy operated: the interval between the recommendation of discharge and the prisoner leaving goal was never more than two weeks – even less on one occasion: 'David Massey in hospital is failing, I believe I must intervene on his behalf soon' (28 May 1846) followed by: 'The Home Office considerately

---

[674] Both probably had pulmonary tuberculosis.

sent an immediate discharge for Massey' (6 June 1846).

Similar instances, eight in all, occurred at Norwich. A typical journal entry reads:

> William Tooley [of whom all we know is that on 29 June 1844 he was in 'a rapid decline' and that he had a large leg ulcer] under my care in the Hospital continues very ill, and the only chance of his ever being better will be in obtaining a free pardon and returning home for the benefit of country air as he has 8 months to remain in prison (20 July 1844).

The granting of a free pardon for Tooley is recorded on 3 August. On one occasion the gift horse of a free pardon was looked in the mouth:

> This day informed John Wright now under my Professional care in the Hospital that I was anxious to obtain a free pardon from the Secretary of State, as his general health is rapidly declining and he has 18 months to remain in Prison. This offer he refused to accept declaring that he was in every respect in a far better situation than he could be if discharged (27 October 1843).

Wright, half way through a three year sentence and suffering from 'great debility with a tendency to scurvy', was given meat broth, 2 pints of milk and a lemon daily. He improved steadily to the extent that on 1 December he decided he would like his free pardon after all. The recommendation was duly sent off to the secretary of state. A similar instance occurred at Springfield: 'A case of consumption died on the 21st instant, having been admitted on the 4th January last, then labouring under the disease, and although an offer of an appeal for the remission of his sentence was made to his parents, they declined any interference, being satisfied that he could not receive better treatment anywhere else'.[675] The practice of discharging prisoners whose illness appeared terminal was widespread: in 1850 the prison inspector noted that from all the county and borough prisons of England and Wales there had been 92 pardons on medical grounds, of which 49 had been granted on the basis of consumption or scrophulous diseases.[676] It is difficult to know when this practice was introduced – the earliest I could find was what appears to be a request for discharge at Gloucester county gaol on 5 February 1820: 'Henry Hastings who has been suffering severely with scrophulous affection, and which has increased ever since his confinement in the Penitentiary House is now become in so dangerous a state, that a continuance of confinement will deprive him of the most probable chance of restoration'. No further mention of Hastings is made so he may well have been discharged.

---

[675] *Seventh Report of Inspector, Home District*, PP, 1842, XX, 1, p. 72.
[676] *Fifteenth Report of Inspector, Home District*, PP, 1851, XXVII, 1, p. liii.

DEATHS IN THE HULKS

Whatever the death rate in prisons during this period, it is low compared to that in the prison hulks, which were unhealthy from their inception. This is hardly surprising since the men slept in holds battened down at night providing a perfect environment for spread of infectious disease. According to George Holford, after the hatches were closed:

> Neither the captain nor any other officer, ever visits the parts of the ship, in which the prisoners are confined after the hatches are locked down (in winter nearly sixteen of the twenty-four hours) except in some extraordinary emergency, or in cases of disturbance, which very rarely occur. And it seems doubtful whether, in some of the hulks at least, an officer could go down among the prisoners at night, without the risk of personal injury: the guards never go among them at night.

The prisoners occupied themselves in coining, drinking, trading stolen goods or in the manufacture of articles for sale, the least offensive of which activities seems to have been the making of peppermint drops. [677]

William Smith, as part of his survey of London prisons in 1776, visited the first prison hulk: the 300 ton *Justicia* which had recently been brought into use at Woolwich.[678] There was no medical help for the 89 prisoners of whom:

> Twelve are now sick, and unable to move their heads from the boards on which they lie. Most of them complain of diarrhoea, few are free from scorbutic blotches, some with bad sores and venereal complaints, and all look thin and pale. The dozen confined to the boards are ill of a low nervous fever, mostly accompanied with a purging.[679]

Howard reported soon afterwards and his early impression was non-committal:

> I went one Sunday in October 1st [1776] to see the Men-Convicts on board the *Justicia* near Woolwich. I wished to have found them more healthy; and their provision good of the sort; and to have joined with them in divine service. But as the scheme is new, and temporary, I am not willing to complain.[680]

By 10 October there were 84 on board: 'none sick', but 64 more prisoners came and: 'the Infection then came among the Prisoners, as they began to droop and sicken very fast'. By 28 November three had died – they had apparently seemed sick when they arrived – and this was just the start as is

---

[677] George Holford (*The Convict's Complaint in 1815 and the Thanks of the Convict in 1825* (London: Rivington, 1825), pp. vi-viii.

[678] A French prize from the Seven Years War, *Justicia* had been in service since 1765 transporting prisoners to America and became a prison hulk in 1776. Campbell, *The Intolerable*, pp. 13-14.

[679] Smith, *State*, pp. 83-85.

[680] Howard, *The State*, (1st edn.), p. 75.

shown in table 6:7.

**Table 6:7 Deaths on the convict ships *Justicia, Jamaica* and *Censor*,
August 1776-March 1778[681]**

Dates	Deaths
August 1776-21April 1777	34
21 April 1777-30 May 1777	13
30 May 1777-27 October 1777	79
27 October 1777-19 January 1778	35
19 January 1778-26 March 1778	15

These 176 deaths occurred among 632 prisoners committed to the hulks –
nearly one in three. By any standards this is mind-boggling: by comparison
on most convict ships to the Americas a loss of about 10% might have been
expected.[682] Howard paid further visits in 1787 and 1788 and although giving
no details, it seems that health conditions had improved – but he reports that
the gaoler at Reading had informed him that of eleven prisoners conveyed to
the hulks on 1 April 1787, eight were dead ten weeks later.[683]

Medical care was soon made available – provided by Dr James Irwin
and Mr Dodo Ecken from the Royal Artillery, who were inclined to
attribute the high death rate to the poor state of health of arriving prisoners:
'as they generally died between their coming and the 10th or 12th day'.
This impression was contradicted by James Chapple, keeper of the gaol at
Bodmin:

> Sir, Yesterday I brought from Bodmin and Launceston Gaol eleven Male
> Convicts, and put them on board La Fortunée Hulk, in Langston Harbour. I
> inquired after ten others, which I put there on the 14th September, 1800. Six of
> them are dead, and the other four look very poorly. Upwards of one hundred and
> twenty died in 1801, and forty since this year began (24 February 1802).[684]

Neild quotes this letter and goes on to state that the convicts had told him
that they are half starved and blamed this want of food for causing so many
deaths. He undertook a special enquiry and found that in 1797, from an
average of 600 convicts on *La Fortunée* there had been nine deaths, but
that in 1801, from an average of 500, there were 120 deaths, with a further

[681] *Parliamentary Journals*, XXXVI, (1778), p. 927.

[682] Although one voyage had resulted in 50 or 60 deaths from 150 – mostly from fever and small-pox. The
average loss – in captivity and on board ship – during a seven year sentence was reckoned to be about one
in seven.

[683] John Howard, *An Account of the Principal Lazarettos in Europe etc.* (London: Rivington, 1828), pp.
216-219.

[684] Neild, pp. 615-626.

34 in the first 75 days of 1802. He states that the most prevalent complaint had been one which 'begins with a low fever, and ends with a diarrhoea, or dysentery'. With regard to *La Fortunée*:

> it appears to us that great neglect is to be ascribed in the medical department; though it cannot be imputed to the late Surgeon, who was bound by *contract to attend* at the Hulks three times a week only, be the state of the Convicts what it might. The contract appears to have been 70*l*. per annum, for attendance at four miles distance, and medicine.

Overall the mortality in the early years of the century was particularly bad: 72 deaths in 1800, 228 in 1801, 143 in 1802, 79 in 1803, falling to 47 in 1804.[685] Better results were reported in an 1812 enquiry: for the years 1804-1811 of an average total of 1,804 prisoners an average 49 deaths per annum – an overall annual mortality of 2.7%. The *Retribution* was particularly unhealthy with a rate of 4.0%, peaking at 11.46% in what must have been the particularly bad year of 1807.[686] However, this is probably explained by the fact that *Retribution* was a receiving ship and as we know, prisoners were at their most vulnerable in their first few weeks. Neild noted: 'The Surgeon, Mr Bowles, appears by the books, to have been very attentive to his duty'. At Portsmouth, the hospital ship *Sageuse* was 'both clean and quiet' and 'The sick appear to be well attended in every respect. They sleep single, on crib bedsteads, with hair and flock beds; two sheets to each, a blanket, and a rug: and wine, porter, and extra diet are allowed to them at the Surgeon's discretion'.[687]

In 1818 John Henry Capper, superintendent of the hulks, reported:

> The health of the prisoners has been very good, and when it is considered in what a state of disease and wretchedness many of them are brought to the hulks, the number of deaths within the last six months being Twenty-three (out of an average of Two thousand Four hundred and Eighteen prisoners daily on board the respective hulks) is much less than might have been expected.[688]

This is an annualised mortality rate of only 1.9% – a very good figure for the hulks but still no better than that calculated by Baly (who, it should be remembered, factored in an allowance for discharges on medical grounds, which Capper did not) for the larger gaols and houses of correction (q.v.). This level of mortality was maintained in the early 1820s (table 6:8)

---

[685] *A Return of the Number of Prisoners who have died in the Hulks*, PP. 1810, XIV, p. 547.
[686] *Select Committee on the Expediency of erecting Penitentiary Houses, and the State of Punishment in Hulks*, PP, 1812, II, 363, p. 165.
[687] Neild, pp. 627-633.
[688] *Reports of John Henry Capper*, PP. 1819, XVII, 319, p. 1.

Table 6:8 Deaths on prison hulks[689]

Year	Average daily number of prisoners	Deaths	Annual mortality rate
1820	2,800	65	2.3
1821	2,800	64	2.3
1822 (Woolwich)	650	18	2.7
1822 (Sheerness)	900	13	1.4

By 1839 there had been a deterioration: 111 deaths from about 2,500 prisoners (2,047 in custody at the start of the year, 2,859 at the year's end) – a mortality rate of 4.44%.[690] It was even worse in 1840-1841 when Capper reported: 'the deaths during the last eight months have been more than usual'. In the first six months of 1841, of a daily average of 628 prisoners, there had been 305 hospitalisations and 28 deaths (an annualised average of 8.9%). In the second six months, with an average 638 prisoners, health improved: 145 admissions to hospital and 10 deaths (3.13%). Capper called in 'The Senior Medical Officer belonging to the Establishment attached to another Station ... to make a full and searching inquiry'. Inspecting surgeon, Archibald Robertson, was not disposed to find fault. He was entirely happy with conditions on *Warrior* and *Justicia*, with the clothing and diet of the prisoners, and with their medical attendants. He attributed many of the deaths to influenza, complicated by bronchitis, pneumonia and typhus and he too blamed low resistance to disease among new arrivals.[691] In the autumn of 1848 there was an outbreak of cholera on *Justicia* and *Unité* (there were no cases on *Warrior*, moored nearby) throughout which the surgeon slept on board *Unité* (the hospital ship). The first case occurred on 2 October, the last on 11 November and of 54 cases, 20 died. According to Herbert P. Vowles, new manager of the hulks, the deaths were 'confined to the aged, worn-out, and diseased patients, one young and healthy man alone having died of the disease. I feel we are, under Providence, much indebted to the unremitting attention of the surgeon for the comparatively few fatal cases recorded'.[692] This was not the last cholera outbreak: in 1849 there were 47 cases with 30 deaths (out of the annual total of 53 deaths) at Woolwich, and 31 cases with 17 deaths (total 31) at Portsmouth. There, the surgeon notes that the overall mortality had increased to over 4%, but says that this is accounted for by the cases of cholera.

---

[689] *Report*, 1823, V, 403, p. 362.

[690] *Papers Relating to the Convict Establishments. Report of John Henry Capper*, PP, 1840, XXXVIII, 543, p. 6.

[691] *Two Reports of John Henry Capper*, PP, 1842, XXXII, 523, pp. 1-8.

[692] *Report of the Manager of the Convict Hulk Establishment for the year 1848*, PP, 1850, XXIX, 1, pp. 2-3 and 9-11.

Even in non-epidemic years many died in the hulks. At Portsmouth and Gosport there were 17 deaths in 1844, 25 in 1845 and 22 in 1846. At Woolwich, 25 in 1844, 42 in 1845 and 50 in 1846. Capper excused the high mortality:

> The only Convicts received on board the Hulks at home during the past year have been Prisoners received from the Pentonville and Millbank prisons, who were at the time, either from disease, old age or infirmity, wholly unfit for Transportation, Confinement in a Gaol, or for Hard Labour.[693]

The average number of prisoners is not given but it is likely that there were about 600 at Woolwich, suggesting that the mortality rate ran at around 4-8%. An interesting fact emerging is that about one third of those dying at Portsmouth and Gosport were "anatomised", as were about half of those from Woolwich. Their bodies were usually sent to one of the London teaching hospitals or (from Woolwich) to Cambridge.[694]

The commonest causes of death were those likely to spread in crowded confinement – tuberculosis and other chest diseases. These were also common in an analysis of inquests carried out on deaths on hulks at Portsmouth, 1817-1827. Interestingly, of the 222 deaths reported, 32 were accidental, 14 of these from drowning – reflecting the dangers of both environment and work.[695]

In conclusion it is clear that after a disastrous start, when no medical care was provided, fresh arrivals on the hulks continued to be susceptible to the new diseases and conditions to which they were exposed. Even at the best of times, the hulks were the sites of epidemics, particularly typhus, diarrhoea, cholera and influenza, and to tuberculosis, all diseases which the conditions of confinement favoured. There is more evidence of medical competence than of negligence.

INQUESTS ON PRISON DEATHS

For prison deaths a coroner's inquest (with a jury) was always held and the verdict was nearly always 'Visitation of God' (the equivalent of death by natural causes). At this point it might be appropriate to point out that a

---

[693] *Report of J.H. Capper*, PP. 1845, XXXVII, 315, p. 1.

[694] *Returns Relative to the Deaths etc. of Prisoners on Board the Hulks at Woolwich*, PP, 1847, XLVIII, 465, pp. 1-5.

[695] Thomas R. Forbes, 'Coroners' Inquisitions on the Deaths of Prisoners in the Hulks at Portsmouth, England in 1817-27, *Journal of the History of Medicine*, XXXIII, 1978, 356-366 (pp. 361-366).

TOP DECK OF THE "UNITÉ" HOSPITAL SHIP,
ATTACHED TO THE HULKS AT WOOLWICH.

**A ward on the top deck of the hospital ship *Unité* at Woolwich.
Engraving**

inquest at this period was not necessarily the thorough enquiry expected of the modern procedure. In a highly emotive letter to *The Lancet* a Colonel Blennerhasset Fairman[696] states:

> 'Died by the visitation of God' is the return nine out of ten times when the verdict ought to be 'a broken heart, through persecution the most relentless or unjust' – 'of disease brought in by a removal from a bed of sickness to a place of incarceration', – 'of abstinence and starvation through the absolute want of the comforts and necessaries of life' – or, perhaps, 'from excess of drinking brought on by anxiety and dejection of mind, through a long confinement'.[697]

Sim and Ward quote this letter and give other instances which they feel demonstrate an apparently casual approach to inquests on prisoners' deaths.[698] Further criticism is levelled by T.R. Forbes in an analysis of inquests on 291 men and 85 women dying at Coldbath-fields between 1795 and 1829:

> An apparent lack of official interest in determining why prisoners died. Indeed

---

[696] Surely a *nom-de-plume*? This letter was part of a lengthy correspondence on the subject of whether the coroner should be a lawyer or a medical man. Most contributors to *The Lancet* favoured the latter.

[697] *The Lancet*, 1, (1830-1831), p. 143-144.

[698] Joe Sim & Tony Ward, 'The magistrates of the poor? Coroners and deaths in custody in nineteenth-century England', *Legal Medicine in History*, eds. Michael Clark & Catherine Crawford, (Cambridge University Press, 1994), pp. 245-249.

one wonders whether the vagueness of the record represents an effort to conceal the actual cause of death – a state of affairs which would not be surprising in a prison of utter disrepute. No cause was recorded for almost one third of the deaths. Almost one-fifth were piously ascribed to a 'visitation of God', a whitewashing phrase also frequently used by coroners' juries of the time for deaths in prison; it was as nonspecific as it was unassailable. 'Decay of nature' referred to a decline in physical vigour and must have been nearly synchronous with 'debility'. 'Dropsy' of course we would regard as a symptom rather than a disease. These six [sic] listed causes account for 85% of the deaths; what actual diseases were responsible we can only guess.[699]

Forbes is unfair: he is evidently unaware of the prevailing standards of diagnostic precision, and although the verdict of the jury was indeed usually 'visitation of God', transcripts of inquests into the deaths of James Bryant and Joseph Honniball held at Ilchester gaol on 19 January and 20 January 1822 show these procedures were not the hasty formalities that might be inferred from arguments put forward by Sim and Ward and by Forbes. At each of these inquests (held before identical juries – but since they were on successive days this is understandable) evidence was taken from a relative, from the person providing nursing care during the final instance (in Honniball's case the deceased's son, also a prisoner in the gaol, acted as nurse), from prison staff and from the attending surgeon.[700] No punches were pulled, particularly in the case of Honniball where two local surgeons were very critical of the care provided by the prison surgeon, and although in each case the verdict was 'visitation of God', in the case of Bryant this was followed by: 'from debility and exhaustion, occasioned by an inflammation of the liver, and accelerated by the cold, inconvenience, and damp, proceeding from frequent inundations of the gaol'; and in the case of Honniball by: 'from dropsy, accelerated by the inhumanity of James Austin, the Sheriff's Officer, in bringing him from his home in such a state of health'.

Another instance of an assiduous approach by a coroner was shown at the inquest on Thomas Hopkins at Northleach house of correction, to whose death as a result of a pre-committal beating reference has already been made. The hearing was opened on 15 February 1841 but was twice adjourned because the coroner was not satisfied that all the evidence was available. On the 18th the coroner and jury assembled at 11 a.m., and proceeded with the inquest. At 3 p.m. the jury brought in their verdict: 'That the deceased died from a serous effusion on the brain, accelerated by blows received from T.B.

---

[699] T.R. Forbes, 'A mortality record for Cold Bath Fields', *Bulletin of the New York Academy of Medicine*, 53 (1977), 668-9. Forbes provides the ages of some of those who died – intriguingly, one of whom was in the 100 plus age group. To reach one's "ton" at that period was quite a feat, to achieve it whilst in prison was remarkable.

[700] *Copies of Coroner's Inquests on two Prisoners at Ilchester Gaol*, PP, 1822, XI, 757, pp. 1-3.

and J.J. of Cheltenham. The body of T.H. was buried this day in Northleach churchyard'.[701]

The minutes of the select committee enquiring into the 1823 outbreak of infection at Millbank includes accounts of thirty inquests held between January and early June. In all of these the governor and the prison surgeon gave evidence, in later instances Drs. Latham and Roget testified, and in several cases evidence was also provided by the chaplain, a fellow-prisoner or by a relative.[702] *The Times* of 19 July 1823 reports the inquest on Benjamin Johnson who had died at Millbank and it is clear that the jurors gave Mr Pratt (the surgeon) a rough ride. He endured hostile questioning and then the jury insisted on interviewing three prisoners. The eventual verdict was 'natural death occasioned by diarrhoea' but this only after the coroner had dissuaded them from 'natural death occasioned by the former bad dietary'.[703] In this they were of course mistaken; during the period of Johnson's illness prisoners at Millbank had enjoyed an unusually good diet (see chapter seven). Although these inquests were perhaps not as exhaustive as modern standards would demand, at least information on the clinical progress of the deceased, and of the management of the terminal illness, was placed in the public domain; and criticism was freely made.

Clearly it would be wrong to make too many inferences from these few examples of inquests out of the several thousands held during the period, but they are enough to show the inadvisability of drawing the conclusions put forward by Sim and Ward and by Forbes, at a time when there was so much variation in procedure. Those I have quoted were conducted according to the standards of the day and were not used to whitewash prison authorities. Juries were prepared to criticise when they thought necessary.

CONCLUSION

The figures I have given in this chapter show that the average prison, with an annual mortality rate of about 1-2%, was not a gateway to death. In many instances, this mortality rate would have been much lower but for the committal of those already mortally ill. It is interesting to note that in 1877 the rate was still running at about this level (1.08%) but that by 1898 it had fallen to 0.56%.[704] During the second half of the nineteenth century there had been many improvements in medical treatment – and more importantly in public health – so a reduction in the prison death rate is to be expected.

---

[701] *Seventh Report of Inspector, Southern and Western District*, PP, 1842, XXI, 193. p. 130.

[702] *Report*, PP, 1823, V, 403, pp. 150-165.

[703] *The Times*, 19 July 1823.

[704] Webb and Webb, p. 209.

In the earlier part of the period 1770-1850 it is highly probable, and in the latter part almost certainly true, that a prisoner's chance of dying in confinement was little different than had he or she been at liberty. This was not true of prisons in which the water supply was suspect nor of those where confinement involved close proximity to their fellows, such as in the hulks. Prolonged imprisonment increased the risk of dying, particularly from tuberculosis.

What is abundantly clear is that dying prisoners were cared for as well as was possible in the circumstances. They were visited regularly – at least daily – by the surgeon. That these visits (or indeed much of the treatment provided) made little or no difference to the clinical outcome is of no consequence – surgeons were doing what was expected of them in the management of any patient, and providing a service appreciated by that patient. Those near to death were allowed extra diet including items of their own choice. Wine or porter was prescribed liberally to the seriously ill, which may seem rather odd, but was standard practice. We can take as an example Princess Charlotte (second in line to the throne) who, in 1817, was delivered of a stillborn son (who would have been third in line) after fifty hours of labour. A few hours later she became unwell and her distinguished medical attendants 'poured brandy, hot water and wine down her throat ... "they have made me tipsy" she complained pathetically [and shortly afterwards], with a gentle sigh she expired'.[705]

The causes of death in prisons were sufficiently varied (except during occasional epidemics) to suggest that conditions – in the maintenance of which surgeons were closely involved – were not at fault. This cannot be said of the hulks, but even there little suggests that failure of medical care was responsible for the high mortality.

A prison surgeon was always subject to public scrutiny and knew full well that hostile criticism would adversely affect his private practice. Professionalism (which included a measure of self-interest) motivated these men to care for the seriously ill to the best of their ability. On the whole it is unreasonable to impute any serious criticism to prison medical staff in this aspect of their work.

[705] Christopher Hibbert, *George IV* (Harmondsworth: Penguin, 1976), pp. 486-487.

7

PRISON SURGEONS AND AUTHORITY

In the three previous chapters I have examined the manner in which prison surgeons cared for their sick and dying patients. In this chapter their contacts with prison management will be explored; in particular those areas of potential conflict such as the running of the prison, the quality and quantity of diet, and punishment. So far as diet is concerned, although Sim gives some prison surgeons credit for voicing concern at inadequate dietaries, his general theme is that they did not do enough.[706] I will counter this argument with examples from Lancaster and other prisons where surgeons went to considerable lengths to ensure that prisoners received sufficient food to maintain health. The most widely quoted example of dietary inadequacy leading to prisoner suffering – the outbreak of supposed scurvy at Millbank penitentiary – is examined in detail.

Surgeons' obedience to the rules in respect of attendance at the gaol and record keeping will be assessed. Examples gleaned from the inspectors' reports of less than perfect obedience to rules will be detailed and the impact these deficiencies might have had on patient care will be evaluated. Finally I will scrutinise some specific examples of alleged medical malpractice.

[706] Sim, *Medical*, pp. 25-26.

INTERACTION WITH AUTHORITY

Regular comments made by Gloucestershire magistrates in the surgeon's journal from 1791 show there was close supervision of the surgeon's activities at the county gaol. By contrast (particularly in the early years) at the Gloucestershire bridewells and at Gloucester city gaol (1825-1837) there was a relative sparsity of magisterial entries, indicative of a looser degree of control by county magistrates at smaller prisons and by city magistrates. Peel's Gaol Act of 1823 required magistrates to carry out inspections of the gaols under their jurisdiction three times each quarter but this requirement was often ignored, as were many other components of the bill.[707]

Surgeons' activities necessitated regular contacts with prison governors. The quality of these men varied greatly throughout the period of study and from prison to prison, although as time went by there was a general improvement in their educational and social status.[708] Many were former army officers; some were recruited from the lower ranks of prison staff (turnkeys or warders); in larger gaols they received a salary of £200-£500.[709] In general, the status of governor and surgeon was roughly equal, and usually they enjoyed a satisfactory working relationship. At Gloucester county gaol the governor was obliged to comply with the recommendations of the surgeon in matters where the health of prisoners was concerned, although any variations in regime had to be reported to the magistrates.[710] Both of course were much superior to the turnkeys, many of whom came from lower echelons of the social scale. On just one occasion it is noted that a surgeon – at Cambridge borough gaol and the Spinning House prison 'is likewise a Visiting Magistrate'.[711] Equally rarely the "surgeon" was a physician, as at Colchester house of correction where there was employed 'a physician at Colchester, who is assisted by his son, a surgeon, and another assistant'.[712]

Good relations between surgeon, governor and magistrates were not universal – as shown in a serious spat at Gloucester county gaol. Following the surgeon's complaints (already described) regarding nursing, Mr Parker carried the matter further, even enlisting support from prisoners:

> On my visit this morning, I was informed by Honor Oliver that King (the assistant turnkey) had behaved in a very disrespectful manner (at times) in

---

[707] Emsley, p. 270.

[708] McConville, pp. 300-307.

[709] Ibid., pp. 308-315 and 292-294.

[710] Ibid., p. 130.

[711] *Second Report of Inspector, Northern and Eastern District*, PP, 1837, XXXII, 499, p. 13.

[712] *Second Report of Inspector, Home District*, PP, 1837, XXXII, 1, p. 342. Physicians (cf. William Baly and William Guy) were employed to provide care at the larger national prisons later in the period under study.

my absence, on acct (I suppose) of my reproving his shameful neglect of duty, respecting the sick: they also said Sparrow had done the same. Olive Compton said the above acct was true, I reported this acct to the Govr who ordered King to be confronted by Honor Oliver, but he strongly denied the Charge, whilst the informants as strongly persisted in the accusation (13 March 1796).[713]

Inevitably word of this internecine strife came to the magistrates' attention – they were not impressed.[714] This despite Parker enlisting the support of Dr Roberts, whose evidence appears in the surgeon's journal on 5 April 1796: 'Having examined the Surgeon's Journal, I find it accurate in every Circumstance that I have had the opportunity of observing: and I take the liberty of remarking that his attention to the sick in respect of clean linens and diet, as well as in respect to medicines, merits every commendation. [signed] William Roberts'. The magistrates' examination of the prison revealed no problems with the bedding; nonetheless they accepted the charges 'with caution' feeling they should have been made 'in Time when Enquiry might not only have produced Proof as to Fact, but might have led to instant Remedy and Reproof'. And: 'On the whole, the Time and Manner of urging this complaint, appears to us rather to indicate a <u>Wish</u> to incriminate, when proof can<u>not</u> be had, either to convict or clearly acquit, than to cause a correction of the Evil'. Finally, and unkindest cut of all:

> We have only to add that we wish Mr Parker will confine his conversation with the Prisoners, his entries in his Journal, to the Medical Department, and by leaving his Book in the Office, let the Establishment have the full and intended Benefits of his Observation. [Signed] G.O. Paul, Thos. C. Bowey.[715]

The magistrates' comment about confining journal entries to medical matters relates to Parker's penchant for expressing interest in the general running of the prison. For example, although not required to attend executions, he did so and evidently felt it his duty to comment: 'The Prisoners (the Debtors excepted) were all Spectators at the execution of John Evans, a very old Offender.[716] The Behavr of the prisoners on this melancholy occasion was very decent and orderly' (12 April 1793). Much more poignant is his entry for 23 August 1794:

---

[713] Olive Compton was sentenced to two years hard labour for grand larceny (theft of various items) On her release she was given a pair of shoes, a gown, a petticoat, a handkerchief and five shillings to get her home to Purton (about 15 miles away). For Honor Oliver, see chapter five.

[714] *Justices' Journal*, GRO, Q Gc 1/1, 8 April 1796.

[715] According to Whiting (*Prison*, p. 41) Paul subsequently regretted the giving of this instruction.

[716] Aged 70 and from Newent, he was hanged for house-breaking.

This morning presented a more melancholy and affecting scene to a feeling mind than that of yesterday.[717] The unhappy sufferer, Hannah Wibley, attended divine service in the Chappel with a becoming conduct, and resignation. She afterwards receivd the sacrament consistent to her deplorable fate, steadfastly denying the fact to the last moment of utterance. The Prisoners who was [sic] at the front cells yesterday and today, to view the Melancholy sight, behaved with becoming decorum. Strong, very strong Circumstances has come to light in favour of this unhappy Victim's Innocence, since her condemnation, and from her own artless story (before and since her conviction). Of the manner and not infrequent way the child was born, I am inclined to think (notwithstanding the verdict of the jury) she was Innocent of the Charge (23 August 1794).

Before his reprimand, Parker frequently commented on prison discipline (5 March 1792, 3 April 1792 & 2 May 1792); on prisoners' demeanour (1 January 1795); and on the fact that they worked much better when consuming water rather than 'strong drink' (16 July 1793). He noted deficiencies in staff conduct impinging on health:

find Hester Sharpless very Ill, she appears to be much agitated and hysterical and I believe owing to improper words said by Edward Green [one of the turnkeys] who has been with her. He asked her if she intended to take her fine slippers to Botany Bay, or to mount the Square over the Lodge [the place of execution] (24 March 1793).

Poor Hester was so upset that she had to be kept in the hospital for a week. Happily, she appears neither on the lists of those executed nor of those transported.

Following his reprimand, Parker's comments became less discursive: 'This day the Execution of James Cornish and Thomas Smith took place' (30 July 1796)[718] – lacking his usual embellishments on the demeanour of other prisoners; although he could not resist: 'I went over the Prison with Dr Small and His Serene Highness the Prince of Orange, who expressed much pleasure and satisfaction at the order and neatness of the difft Parts thereof' (14 August 1796).

Parker's degree of involvement in prison matters was unusual, possibly he relished his historic role in providing care at a new prison. The Lancashire surgeons showed a more deferential attitude. Typical is a letter sent by Lancaster county gaol's surgeon asking magistrates to approve an increase in prison dietary: 'It is with utmost deference I do so, and trust I shall not be considered as exceeding the bounds of my Duty in the respectful expression

[717] The 'scene of yesterday' was the hanging of Hannah Limbrick, aged 26, of Westbury-on-Sea for murder. Hannah Wibley, aged 24, was hanged for the murder of her child – but – 'She denied the fact to the last moment and many circumstances afterwards came to light that left no doubt of her innocence'. *List of Criminals Hanged in Gloucester from the year 1786 to 1885*, GRO PS 17.

[718] Aged respectively 34 and 22, they were hanged for sheep stealing.

of my Opinion and apprehension ...'.[719] Sometimes comments verged on the sycophantic (as well as indicating an almost pathological state of prolixity), as shown by entries from the quarterly reports (addressed to 'the Worshipful the Chairman and the Magistrates') of Henry Ollier, surgeon at the Salford New Bailey prison:

> The prisoners confined in this House of Correction have been so healthy since the last Sessions as to render it perfectly unnecessary for him to occupy the valuable time of the Magistrates by any observation regarding the Medical department .... As however, it is much more agreeable to account for the existence of health than to give up reasons for the prevalence of disease, the Surgeon imagines that he would be not doing justice to the [reason] why this prison is comparatively more healthy than any in the Kingdom, viz: the excellence of the government. The Gaol is healthy not because it is unexposed to danger, for it is in the centre of a crowded and labouring population and the succession of its inmates undergoes a daily change. But it is healthy from internal causes, from that discipline which subjects the Prisoner – the moment he enters its walls to regulations which contribute to his health without affecting the Character of his punishment.[720]

And in the following year – thankfully at less length: 'The Surgeon has therefore merely to present his books for inspection, and (congratulating the Bench on the good order of the Gaol, with which the health of the Prisoners is so intimately connected) to cut short his Report for "lack of argument"'.[721] Similarly, Thomas Chalmers at Kirkdale waxed almost equally lyrical although with welcome brevity: 'The food is amply sufficient and the freedom from infectious disease, notwithstanding the quantity, introduced by the Vagrants and prisoners for short Periods, amply favours the judgement of the Gentlemen who consented to the Prison's erection in so healthy a Site'.[722] These examples indicate the obsequiousness towards their masters some surgeons felt necessary to show and illustrates the gap in social status between surgeons and county magistrates.

Surgeons and prison dietary: supplements and quality

Complaints drawing attention to the relationship between health and the quality of the food provided in confinement enjoy a distinguished pedigree. No less a personage than Sir Thomas More set a precedent; writing to secretary Cromwell from the Tower he pleads: 'My diet also – God knoweth how slender it is at many times. And now, in mine age, my stomach may

---

[719] LCRO, QGR/1/17.

[720] LCRO QGR/4/25. During the quarter there had been five births and two deaths: one of these an infant child the other a female with dropsy.

[721] LCRO, QGR/4/29. During the quarter there had been two births and no deaths among over 500 prisoners..

[722] LCRO, QGR/3/30. During the year there had been four deaths from an average of over 500 prisoners.

not away but with a few kind of meats; which, if I want, I decay forthwith, and fall into coughs and diseases of my body, and cannot keep myself in health'.[723]

More lacked the benefit of having a prison surgeon to supervise his imprisonment but from the late-eighteenth century onwards it is clear that surgeons recognised their responsibilities as regards diet, both in the form of supplements for the sick and as prophylaxis (examples of which were given in earlier chapters), and in ensuring an adequate intake of reasonable quality food for the prison population as a whole.

At Gloucester county gaol Parker regularly checked the quality of food eaten by the inmates, usually finding it wholesome but on 24 August 1794: 'Condemned the beef already being cooked and ordered fresh. It is to be remarked, this is the first instance of putrid meat'. Comments about food were general at other prisons – sometimes the surgeon agreed with prisoners' complaints, sometimes he did not. At Lancaster, on 5 July 1844 the prisoners complained about the sourness of the bread: 'I shall speak to the contractor about it'; on 28 September 1844: 'there is no reason why 7 and 8 class should reject the gruel this morning, I have tasted it'; on 17 June 1845 there was a complaint about potatoes but as the surgeon pointed out: 'it is difficult to find better at this time of the year'. Then: 'there is a complaint about the gruel being too thin, the men acknowledge it is good in taste. I think it is in every way good enough for them' (8 January 1846); 'the debtors' meat is very indifferent this morning, I have sent for the butcher' (4 December 1847); and: 'Some of the men decline their gruel because it is slightly bishoped' (8 February 1848). The verb "bishop" has an interesting pedigree: it means to let burn while cooking. It is northern dialect dating from the sixteenth century, when the populace had noticed the bishops' partiality for burning those citizens who disagreed with them, as in 'Bishops burn what displeases them'.[724]

At Newgate, the question was raised as to whether the bread (the daily allowance had recently been changed from 14 oz. of white bread to 16 oz. of brown) caused dysentery, and although the surgeon admitted: 'there was not a week that I went round the prison, that there was not some complaint about the bread', he dismissed this: 'I mean to give it as my medical opinion, that the brown bread we give them now is better than the white bread we got from the bakers'.[725] At Gloucester city gaol: 'Several of the convicted

---

[723] Dixon, pp. 39-40.

[724] OED.

[725] The daily allowance was 16 oz. brown bread, 1 pint good gruel for breakfast, and for dinner, on alternate nights: ½ pound beef (6 oz. when cooked) and, one quart of soup in which the meat was boiled the previous day with barley and a variety of vegetables. *Report*, PP, 1818 (275), VIII, 297, p. 66.

Prisoners complained this morning of their Bread being short weight. I found on enquiry this is quite true and that Mr Turner [the governor] has frequently returnd the loaves and got them changed' (22 March 1828); and: 'The Penitentiary Prisoners are complaining of their Bread being sour, whatever it might have been some days since I know not, but the present is very good' (13 August 1835).

SURGEONS AND PRISON DIETARY: QUANTITY

Prior to the 1820s, prison diet was a matter for the magistrates; subsequently guidance from central government was issued but this was only permissive instruction until the 1840s. Consequently, particularly in the later part of the period, the most intractable problem faced by prison surgeons was in relation to the on-going and inescapable dilemma of maintaining the "discipline of less eligibility"[726] – the differential between the conditions of the ordinary working man, the inmate of the workhouse, and the prisoner – with the prisoner at the bottom of the scale. In 1786 it is estimated that a labourer's family spent about 2s. per week per head on food at a time when the cost of the food for a prisoner in Lancaster gaol was 2s.7d.. A letter in the *Liverpool Courier* in 1837 pointed out that the weekly per capita expenditure on food at Kirkdale house of correction was 5s. and in the Liverpool workhouse 2s. ½d. DeLacy concludes that in general: 'Even by contemporary standards, therefore, prison diets were at a low level, although probably better than those of the worst-paid urban workers or country dwellers in years of dearth'.[727]

The surgeon at Knutsford intimated – an observation repeatedly made by prison medical officers – that diet was not the only problem:

> Ever since my appointment as surgeon to the goal, I have noticed with regret the gradual falling away of the men sentenced to long terms of imprisonment, and I have endeavoured by various means to obviate this. I have exempted them from ordinary gaol labour, employed them in irregular labour in the yards, increased and varied their food, but without any very satisfactory results. My conviction, after 15 years' experience, is that it is not possible to keep men under long sentences of imprisonment in robust health, it is not that they actually fall sick, but that they become pallid, care-worn and enfeebled, and lose all their energy and exertion. This is not the effect of the diet, or the labour, the locality or discipline of the gaol but arises I believe solely from their being in confinement and the depressing circumstances attending that confinement.[728]

---

[726] Wiener, 'The Health', pp. 47-48.
[727] DeLacy, pp. 167 and 109.
[728] *Further Papers*, 1843, XLIII, 355, p. 5.

He went on to say that he had recommended 'a general increase in food to the prisoners under long sentences' which had recently been agreed with, he thought, some benefit. Nevertheless, criticisms of what were regarded as unduly lavish prison diets continued. The Home Office ordered the introduction of an improved dietary in 1843, but this was not necessarily adopted and in any case could be attended with disadvantages: 'The gradual introduction of fixed dietaries lessened the prisoners' freedom of choice and, while saving a few from hunger or starvation, caused malnutrition in many'.[729] The magistrates at Reading refused even to 'adopt even the *minimum* of food proposed by [the Home Secretary]'.[730] As a result of this sort of attitude prison inspector William J. Williams felt he had to justify the apparent pampering of prisoners:

> Among other evils foretold as the certain result of this interference with the food for prisoners, there is one more warmly insisted upon than others, and which I advert to, rather from the strenuousness of its advocates, than its real importance. I allude to the anticipation that by the adoption of these dietaries, or their equivalents, the situation of the convict as to food, would be so superior to that of a considerable proportion of the humbler classes, that it would induce a preference for a prison, and therefore encourage crime. With every deference to those from whom the apprehension of such an evil proceeds, I do not hesitate to affirm that I have such a confidence in the moral feeling of the humbler classes, that even in the times of severe pressure and distress, I believe that few and but very few would break the law for the purpose of seeking an asylum in a prison.[731]

These views were repeated in 1849 by prison inspector D. O'Brien ,[732] but a leading article in the Lancet in 1858 shows the belief persisted that the principle of less eligibility was not being adequately addressed:

> A prison, it seems, may be coveted by the poor as a sort of temporary paradise and the union [workhouse] changed into an asylum which is viewed with ineffable disgust ... the prison is greatly preferred to the workhouse as a place of abode by the lower classes ... the prison offers a clean and comfortable lodging, food far superior to that of some of the workhouses, and comparatively kind and attentive officers of a higher grade than those provided for the simply unfortunate and starving.[733]

This was the climate of opinion within which prison surgeons had to work and I will now give examples of specific instances.

---

[729] DeLacy, p. 111.

[730] *The Lancet*, 1843, 2, p. 390.

[731] *Eighth Report of Inspector, Northern and Eastern District*, PP, 1843, XXV and XXVI, 249, p. 1.

[732] *Fourteenth Report of Inspector, Midland and Eastern District*, PP, 1849, XXVI, 167, p. viii.

[733] *The Lancet*, (leading article), 1858, 2, 284-285.

DIETARY AT LANCASTER CASTLE

Between 1826 and 1829 at Lancaster castle gaol, a running battle was fought between magistrates, concerned to keep down costs and not to allow prison to become a "soft option", and the surgeon John Smith, apprehensive that cuts would adversely affect the prisoners' health. In 1825 before the cuts were made, Smith had written: 'The improved Dietary [apparently ordered in July 1825] has had the most beneficial effects upon the general health of the Prisoners and has diffused the greatest satisfaction amongst them'.[734] The magistrates, having ordered this improved dietary, then apparently had second thoughts: evidently the diffusion of 'greatest satisfaction' amongst the prisoners was not one of their objectives. The diet was therefore reduced and problems caused by this reduction ('at the late adjourned annual session' – presumably in early 1826) prompted Smith a year later to address three pages of closely written A3 sheets to the magistrates.[735] He describes in considerable detail an outbreak of mostly dysenteric sickness sweeping the prison from mid-August, resulting in six deaths, four from gastro-intestinal infections.[736] His plea, despite its eloquence and submissive tone seems to have fallen on deaf ears for no change was made until June 1829. This was too late to prevent Smith himself from coming under fire, both for the increased number of deaths and for what his critics saw as excessive expenditure on medicines and medical "comforts" (see table 3:1). In his 1829 report he details the reductions in diet which had been made and to prove his case produced a table of statistics (reproduced as table 7:1) After making the obvious point that committal rates were fairly constant but the death rate rose sharply when the diet was reduced he concludes: 'It only remains to acquaint the Magistrates that the additional allowance of food granted on the 20th of June last, has already [been] productive of extremely beneficial effects, the prisoners in general are much improved in appearance and have expressed great gratitude for what has been done. [signed] John Smith, Surgeon'. He goes on to recommend an even better diet.[737].

Smith may not have been correct in his assertion that dietary reduction was the sole cause of the increased mortality but it was almost certainly a contributory factor – particularly as the table of 37 deaths to which he refers shows that 13 were caused by dysenteric diseases and 16 were probably cases

---

[734] LCRO, QGR/1/12.

[735] In addition to this reduction in diet, the prisoners' privileges of being able to spend a part of their earnings on food and of receiving food from their friends in the community had been withdrawn. LCRO, QGR/1/25.

[736] Although one of these was eighty-three years of age and another 'an infirm female [upwards of sixty] with broken constitution and who for the last two years had been constantly in the Hospital'.

[737] LCRO, QGR/1/25.

Table 7:1 Deaths in Lancaster castle 1822-1829

Year	Number of Prisoners committed	Number of Deaths	Ratio (omitting fractions)
1822	219	3	1/73
1823	218	0	
1824	261	1	1/261
1825	247	2	1/123
1826	377	10	1/37
1827	392	5	1/78
1828	277	12	1/23
1829 (to 20 June)	181	8	1/22
Total 1825-1829	1,474	37	1/39

of tuberculosis – both conditions in which death is likely to be accelerated by inadequate diet. Two facts are however clear: first he was deeply concerned to maintain both his professional integrity and the health of his patients, and second that Smith, literate and well educated as he was, felt he had to be exceedingly cautious and deferential in his dealings with the magistrates. His efforts continued to reap their reward. In 1831 he reported: 'Bilious disease and bowel complaints which have been exceedingly general thro' the County have been less frequent in the Gaol than usual at this season of the year'.[738]

Smith was not alone in exposing dietary problems. At Gloucester county gaol:

> Mr Wilton begs leave to state to the Magistrates of the Quarter Sessions, that ever since he has attended the Gaol as Surgeon he has observed in very many of the Penitentiary Prisoners a strong disposition to Scrophula and some have been afflicted severely. He attributes this Malady to arise from a want of more Animal Food and therefore submits to the Magistrates the propriety of allowing these Prisoners an additional dinner of Meat in each week (10 April 1815).

Reports of battles between magistrates and surgeons similar to that fought at Lancaster crop up regularly in the inspectors' reports. At Cambridge county gaol and house of correction the dietary for those working on the treadmill was reduced in March 1834. The prisoners had been getting two pounds of fine wheaten bread, one pound of inferior quality, and a pint of table beer daily. Evidently this was too lavish and according to the inspector:

> At the suggestion of the visiting magistrates the bread was reduced to two pounds of an inferior quality, and a quart of gruel was substituted for the beer.

---

[738] LCRO, QGR/1/34.

... The effect of this change was closely watched; as might be expected, the discontent among the prisoners soon became general; in a few days many struck work altogether, but finding it unavailing returned to it in a day or two, and others threw themselves on the sick list with a view to strengthen the general clamour.

The report goes on to describe the surgeon's efforts over the next few years – not altogether successful – to arrive at a diet acceptable to prisoners and magistrates alike.[739]

Surgeons' problems regarding diet were exacerbated with the introduction of hard labour. The following extract from the surgeon's journal at Northleach was written when prisoners were still employed on the hand-mill:

Those who are confined for some length of time and sentenced to hard labour, are extremely weak and languid, the diet in such cases does not appear sufficient; and I am of the opinion that after long confinement (aided by depression of spirits, hard labour and low diet) the constitution of many of them may suffer materially and it is not improbable that Chronic disease may eventually ensue, which may prevent them gaining their own livelyhood [sic] for some time after their periods of confinement expire (9 July 1826).

Prison inspector Frederic Hill, who was generally critical of the treadwheel, quotes surgeons at Spilsby, Hull, and Kirton-in Lindsay echoing these fears[740] and similar concerns were voiced by the governor of Coldbath-fields.[741]

The surgeon at Shepton Mallet noticed great loss of weight among the prisoners and recommended extra diet and a reduction in working hours from eight to six.[742] A similar problem was remedied by Kirkdale's surgeon: 'The period of working at the Wheel allotted to the female Vagrants and disorderly has been altered at my suggestion from six hours to four ... from the state of Exhaustion in which they come in [and] the absence of their usual stimulus (spirits) they are incapacitated from working the longer period'.[743]

Tables compiled by the surgeon at Guildford county gaol show that of 25 prisoners weighed over a period of four to five months, only seven gained weight – the others lost amounts varying from one to twenty pounds (the latter is exceptional, mostly the loss was of a few pounds only).[744] At Bodmin county gaol the recently introduced hand-mill 'produced much debility and consequent illness, but by timely application to the surgeon,

[739] *Third Report of Inspector, Northern and Eastern District*, PP, 1837-38, XXXI, 1, pp. 161-162.
[740] *Fifteenth Report of Inspector, Northern and Eastern District*, PP, 1850, XXVIII, 291, pp. xiii-xiv.
[741] *Second Report of Inspector, Home District*, PP, 1837, XXXII, 1, p. 94.
[742] *Copies*, PP, 1825, XXIII, 567, pp. 15-18.
[743] LCRO, QGR/3/22.
[744] *Second Report*, PP, 1835, XI, 495, XI, 495, p. 363.

who ordered such nourishing diet as he considered these cases required, the men are fast recovering'.[745] The surgeon at Stafford county gaol was particularly worried about prisoners on hard labour; the lengths he went to in detecting its worst effects and in circumventing these by giving extra diet are described by the inspector:

> The women and boys fatten on it [the diet]; but the men at the tread-wheel lose on an average 4 lbs. per month in weight, so long as they continue to work. The surgeon has a private weighing machine in his office. He frequently puts such prisoners on extra diet. He weighs them all, and keeps notes of their weight in his private journal. Those who have been in long give him much uneasiness: but at the end of six months they are usually put to head pins, break stones, pick oakum, or some other light labour.[746]

The inspectors provide numerous instances of similar concerns on the part of surgeons for the health of their charges undergoing hard labour. At Hereford county gaol and house of correction there had been a reduction of diet in the early part of 1847 and on 18 September 1847 the surgeon wrote to the magistrates:

> This reduction has been continued to the present time, and I now beg leave to report that I have watched its effects very closely, and have no hesitation in stating that [the dietary] is not sufficient to maintain the health of the prisoners under the present regulations for the hours of labour, and the present strict discipline of the prison.

He too had compiled tables demonstrating weight loss among those working on the wheel and recommended increases in allowances of bread, meat, and potatoes over and above the government scale. The inspector selected this (and other similarly themed documents) because 'They show much attention and acuteness to the observation of the condition of the prisoners' health, and are expressed in a tone of manly confidence, becoming a physician intrusted with a momentous responsibility with reference to a large number of his fellow-creatures'.[747]

To set against all these examples of surgeons' attempts at dietary amelioration I could find only a single record of a recommendation for reduction. The journal entry at Littledean (5 May 1849) reads:

---

[745] *Fourth Report of Inspector, Southern and Western District*, PP, 1839, XXII, 215, p. 133.

[746] *Sixth Report of Inspector, Southern and Western District*, PP, 1841 Sess. 2, V, 177, p. 214.

[747] *Fourteenth Report of Inspector, Southern and Western District*, PP, 1849, XXVI, 93, pp. 19 & 20. See also *Fourth Report of Inspector, Southern and Western District*, PP, 1839, XXII, 215, p. 103, *Fifth Report of Inspector, Home District*, PP, 1840, XXV, 1, p. 231, *Seventh Report of Inspector, Home District*, PP, 1842, XX, 1, pp. 72 & 185-186, & *Seventh Report of Inspector, Northern and Eastern District*, PP, 1842, XXI, 1, p. 137.

> I have to state that in the last quarter 55 prisoners have been admitted weighing
> 522 stone 3 pounds Upon being discharged they weighed 527 stone 11 pounds
> affording an average increase of one pound five ounces to each prisoner during
> his residence in the prison. Upon comparing the dietary for the Westbury-on-
> Severn Union with that of the prison dietary I find the prisoners from class No.
> 3 to be better fed than the paupers in the Workhouse. I recommend the quantity
> of meat in each class for males to be reduced to seven ounces instead of eight
> ounces.

In reality, this was still probably a reasonable allowance of meat at a prison
where there was no treadwheel in use, but it still seems rather a miserable
recommendation and could be seen as a solitary example of a surgeon
engaging in what a Marxist might interpret as subjection of the working
class. This must be set against the many instances of an opposite approach.

"SCURVY" AT MILLBANK PENITENTIARY[748]

Serious allegations have been made with regard to this episode, indeed
it has become something of a *cause célèbre* in the demonology of the
prison medical service. Sim claims: 'Millbank was at the centre of a major
controversy when an outbreak of scurvy occurred and 31 prisoners died.
The Prison Medical Service was deeply implicated. In particular the
physician and surgeon had cut the prisoners' already meagre diet ...'; and
he goes on to blame the physician in charge of engaging in experiments
with the bodies and minds of the confined.[749] Others, in less pejorative
tones, but still perpetuating the scurvy myth, write: 'In the winter of 1823,
the inmates began to succumb to typhus, dysentery, and scurvy. Thirty-
one died and four hundred others were incapacitated';[750] 'The decision [to
reduce the diet] was a major factor in the scurvy epidemic which followed
shortly afterwards, causing at least thirty deaths';[751] 'Fifteen months later,
after 30 had died, and the whole convict population had been evacuated
from the prison, Holford was convinced that the disease had been sea-
scurvy';[752] and: 'there was a serious outbreak of scurvy not long after the
new diet was adopted'.[753]

As a result of this apparent scandal a parliamentary select committee
enquired into the matter, and a cursory scan through the first six pages of
the resulting reports might seem to justify the claims listed above – of a

---

[748] For a fuller account see: Peter McRorie Higgins, 'The Scurvy Scandal at Millbank Penitentiary', *Medical History*, 50, (2006), pp. 513-534.
[749] Sim, p. 17.
[750] Ignatieff, p. 176.
[751] McConville, pp. 144-145.
[752] Evans, *The Fabrication*, p. 249
[753] Campbell, *The Intolerable*, p. 99.

serious outbreak of scurvy resulting from medically instigated tinkering

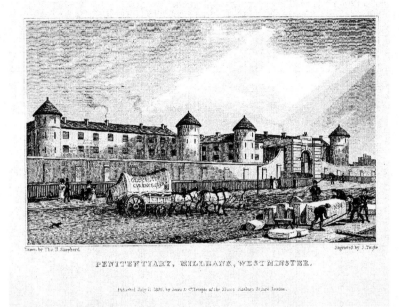

PENITENTIARY, MILLBANK, WESTMINSTER.

Millbank Penitentiary with a carrier's cart from Cirencester and Gloucester in the foreground. Engraving, Thomas Shepherd, 1829.

with the diet.[754] However, a close study of all 550 pages of the four reports comprising the document presents a completely different picture.[755] It is true that the management committee reduced the diet but the extent of reduction was mitigated – not enhanced – as a result of medical intervention. There were a few cases of mild scurvy – but most of the deaths were the direct result of unidentified gastro-intestinal infections or tuberculosis. None of the deaths can be attributed to scurvy.

As we now know, scurvy is the result of Vitamin C deficiency. Early signs are debility, with soreness of and bleeding from the gums; later spontaneous bleeding becomes more widespread, wounds fail to heal, old wounds re-open and death follows. It has to be said that diagnoses of scurvy made in the late-eighteenth and early-nineteenth centuries must be treated with caution. Howard was mistaken when he wrote of 'a contagious disease which in France they call *Le Scorbut*, the *Scurvy*' whose cause was 'generally

---

[754] Later in the report, the authors of this first part admit their mistake (*Report*, PP, 1823, V, 403, pp. 394-395).

[755] *First Report of the Physicians on the State of the General Penitentiary at Milbank* [sic], PP, 1823, V, 379 and *Further Papers (Correspondence)*, PP, 1823, V, 387. *Report from the Select Committee on the State of the Penitentiary at Milbank*, PP, 1823, V, 403. *Report from the Select Committee on the Penitentiary at Milbank*, PP, 1824, IV, 407.

thought to be *Want of Cleanliness in Prisons*', and which, he opined, could be cured by the provision of clean linen every week.[756] However, there were undoubted (if uncommon) instances of the condition in English prisons, notably from 1826 onwards at Springfield.[757] Other cases were recorded at Norwich county gaol,[758] Coldbath-fields,[759] Ilford,[760] and Swaffham.[761] A case was recorded at Portland, a man: 'who had imbibed the notion that potatoes and other vegetables were injurious to him…'. He was soon cured.[762] Factors involved in the appearance of scurvy were thought to be excessive treadwheel labour and, of course, dietary deficiencies.[763] Prison inspector John G. Perry made an intelligent observation:

> In connection with the subject of health, it is highly interesting to remark that the opinion which has lately so universally prevailed, of the value of potatoes as an article of Prison diet, in supplying the best preservative against scurvy, has met with strong confirmation from the effects which have attended the necessary discontinuance of that vegetable, during the late scarcity.[764] Scurvy, which since the universal adoption of potatoes, had become almost unknown in prisons, has reappeared during the last 18 months, although its ravages have been in all instances checked by the adoption of suitable measures.[765]

Despite its intermittent incidence, I was unable to find any instance of death in prison resulting from scurvy but there were deaths in the general population, many of whom did not have access to the alternative sources of Vitamin C provided for prisoners. Perry gives figures: 16 scurvy deaths in 1842, 13 in 1843, 21 in 1844, 25 in 1845, 28 in 1846, and 78 in 1847.

To return to Millbank. The penitentiary was run by a governor (salary £600) who, with the rest of his staff was responsible to a management committee of between ten and twenty members, appointed by the king in council, and required to make an annual report to parliament. They met

---

[756] Howard, *The State*, (1st edn.), pp. 83-84. He admits his mistake in a footnote on p. 101.

[757] *Second Report of Inspector, Home District*, PP, 1837, XXXII, 1, p. 304; and *Seventh Report of Inspector, Home District*, PP, 1842, XX, 1, pp. 71-72.

[758] *First Report of Inspector, Northern and Eastern District*, PP, 1836, XXXV, 161, p. 39.

[759] *Second Report of Inspector, Home District*, PP, 1837, XXXII, 1, p. 81.

[760] Ibid., p. 336.

[761] *First Report of Inspector, Northern and Eastern District*, PP, 1836, XXXV, 161, p. 49 and *Seventh Report of Inspector, Northern and Eastern District*, PP, 1842, XXI, 1, p. 141.

[762] *Reports, Convict Prisons*, PP, 1857-1858, XXIX, 483, p. 324.

[763] The means of prophylaxis was well known but nonetheless: 'scurvy remained common in convict ships until a late date'. Bateson, p. 57.

[764] 'The late scarcity' was of course the result of potato blight. The fungus appeared in Britain and Ireland in 1845; its worse effects were in 1846 and 1847 and it did not die down until 1850.

[765] *Twelfth Report of Inspector, Southern and Western Districts*, PP, 1847-48, XXXV, 1, pp. v-vi. A similar relationship between the appearance of scurvy and the absence of potatoes had been noted at Salford county gaol and at Kirkdale (where the condition was previously unknown) and in both cases relief was obtained by appropriate dietary adjustments. *Thirteenth Report of Inspector, Northern and Eastern Districts*, PP, 1847-48, XXXVI, 361, pp. 24 & 20.

once a month; much the most active member was George Holford. So far as medical care was concerned, it had been recognised from the outset that it was necessary to have '[a] resident medical gentleman' at the prison[766] and that he (and also the chaplain) should have a degree of independence from the Governor: 'they must neither be under strong obligations to the Governor nor subject to his power'.[767] The budget would not run to '[a] person of high standing in the medical line' so it was decided to employ 'such a medical resident as we could afford' together with an honorary consultant physician and an honorary consultant surgeon.[768] The last of these seems to have played little part in providing day-to-day care but the physician, Dr A. Copland Hutchison M.D., was involved to the extent that in May 1819 he was offered a salary of £300 (in the event he took £200).[769] The medical resident they could afford: 'competent to discharge the duties of Surgeon, Apothecary, and Man-Midwife ... a Member of the Royal College of Surgeons'[770] was Mr John Pratt who, in addition to his salary of £400 received free accommodation and heating. Situated on the upper floors of the central block were three infirmaries; for the care of the males there was a 'distinct warder' (later provided with an assistant);[771] and for the women, nurses were employed.[772]

Critics of the penitentiary thought medical provision on this scale lavish[773] but most of their scorn was targeted on the prison diet. Holford noted the heavy irony to which he had been subjected:

> The luxury of the Penitentiary was a standing joke. The prison was called "My fattening house". I was told that public economy might be safely [conserved] by parting with many of our officers, as it was unnecessary to keep up an establishment to prevent escape, though it might perhaps be proper to apply for a guard to prevent persons from rushing in.[774]

Accusations were made that food was wasted. Prisoners were overfed: 'symptoms of plethora were constantly showing themselves; and a general fullness of habit appeared to prevail among all the inmates of the Penitentiary'.[775] Furthermore: 'if we did not content ourselves with a less luxurious table of diet at Millbank, the annual vote for the expense of our

---

[766] *Report*, PP, (1823), V, 403, p.79.
[767] McConville, pp. 133-134.
[768] The latter was a hospital surgeon.
[769] *Report*, PP 1823, V, 403, p.79.
[770] McConville, p. 135.
[771] Holford, *An Account*, p. 94.
[772] Ibid., p. 56.
[773] McConville, fn. p. 149.
[774] *Report*, PP, 1823, V, 403, p. 114.
[775] Ibid., p. 29 and p. 5.

establishment would be opposed'.[776] Faced with such a threat, Holford and his committee gave way – it seemed reasonable to follow the example of other prisons, including Gloucester, and reduce the diet.[777] Dr Hutchison advised against too much reduction on the grounds that long term prisoners (they were all long term at Millbank) would suffer and he advised obtaining the opinion of other authorities.[778] Sir James McGrigor, Peninsular War veteran and director-general of the army medical department was consulted. He agreed that a reduction could safely be made[779] and this was done, but to a significantly lower level than Dr Hutchison had recommended.[780] The change was made in July 1822 and until January 1823 there were no adverse effects.[781] The first diagnoses of 'true scurvy' were made by Dr Hutchison, somewhere between 11 and 13 January. He said there were three female and two male cases by 8 February.[782] Mr Pratt first mentioned it on 4 February: 'We have five or six cases partaking of the nature of scurvy, which I fear can only be accounted for from the dietary'.[783] On 14 February the opinion of Sir James McGrigor was again sought. He took a sanguine view giving his opinion that all was well; indeed at that stage there had been no increase in the number of infirmary cases.[784] This was the lull before the storm – in late February infirmary numbers rose with, according to Dr Hutchison: 'One well marked case of scurvy, and two others of less distinct character' but, more seriously and as a harbinger of things to come, there had been cases of flux[785], one fatal. Hutchison made a diagnosis (probably incorrect) of scorbutic dysentery, but perfectly correctly recommended more vegetables in the soup, more meat and an ounce of lemon juice weekly for all prisoners.[786]

At this point the management committee became alarmed and on 28 February called in two physicians, Dr P.M. Latham M.D.[787] and Dr P.M. Roget M.D[788] to advise (Dr Roget was a substitute for the more eminent first choice, Dr Maton, who refused).[789] These appointments effectively

[776]   Holford, *An Account*, pp. xxxiv-xxxv.

[777]   George Holford, *An Account*, p. xxxvi. & *Report*, PP 1823 (533, V, 403, p. 109.

[778]   *Report*, PP, 1823, V, 387, p. 1-2.

[779]   *Report*, PP, 1823, V, 403, p. 333.

[780]   Ibid., pp. 73 & 333.

[781]   *Report*, PP, 1823, V, 387, p. 2.

[782]   *Report*, PP, 1823, V, 403, p. 36. One of these women died from long-standing consumption.

[783]   Ibid., p. 100.

[784]   Ibid., p.7.

[785]   Flux: a severe form of diarrhoea.

[786]   *Report*, PP, 1823, V,387, p. 6.

[787]   Later to become Physician Extraordinary to Queen Victoria.

[788]   Of Thesaurus fame. See D.L. Emblen, *Peter Mark Roget: The Word and the Man* (London: Longmans, 1970), pp. 255-285.

[789]   *Report*, PP, 1823, V, 403, pp. 335-336.

sidelined Dr Hutchison[790] who continued to attend the penitentiary, but his instructions were ignored and after a rather acrimonious exchange of letters with the management committee, he was dismissed on 19 April 1823.[791] This on the trumped-up charge that he had – inappropriately and whilst under the influence of alcohol – ordered a warm bath for a dying patient. These well-rehearsed accusations were made by Mr Pratt, the matron and the nurses[792] ('the old women' as Dr Hutchison refers to them), accusations strenuously denied by Dr Hutchison. A pantheon of distinguished medical men, including Sir Astley Cooper[793], attested to his habitual sobriety. Even Dr Bennett D.D., the chaplain (with whom Hutchison was not on speaking terms[794]), testified that Dr Hutchison had not been drunk at the relevant time.[795] All to no avail – a scapegoat was needed: news of sickness in the penitentiary was beginning to appear in the press and by sacking Dr Hutchison the committee sought to divert attention away from themselves – an aim in which they probably succeeded.

Meanwhile, Drs Latham and Roget approached their new task with enthusiasm and, although neither of them had any worthwhile experience of scurvy[796] they contrived to diagnose "scorbutic diarrhoea" in no fewer than 52% of the prisoners.[797] This, it seems, largely on the basis of small brown spots (possibly flea bites[798]) on the legs of affected prisoners, some of whom had, and some of whom had not, diarrhoea. Their diagnosis was given retrospective support by Sir Gilbert Blane M.D. who visited later and who, from second-hand descriptions, had no doubt that the prisoners were suffering from sea-scurvy.[799] A modern observer might feel that his position as an authority on scurvy (he had served four years in the navy, forty years earlier) is somewhat undermined by his assertion that 'oranges are perfectly inert in sea-scurvy'.[800] Drs Latham and Roget recommended still more meat in the diet, rice, white bread instead of brown, and three oranges each day

---

[790] Ibid., p.119.

[791] *Report*, PP, 1823, V, 387, p.14.

[792] Griffiths spoke of most of the officials resident at the penitentiary as being prone to 'Gossip of course – probably worse, constant observation of one-another, jealousies, quarrels ... subordinates ever on the look out to make capital of the differences of their betters, and alive to the fact that they were certain of a hearing when they chose to carry out any slanderous attack' Griffiths, p. 69-70.

[793] Sir Astley Cooper (1768-1841). One of the most eminent surgeons of the time and a great anatomist.

[794] *Report*, PP, 1823, V, 387, p. 11.

[795] Although he had been agitated because his sister, as a result of some unspecified misjudgement, had lost £400 of his money. Also, the fact that his front teeth were missing made his speech indistinct at times.

[796] *Report*, PP, 1823, V, 403, p.28.

[797] *Report*, PP, 1823, V, 379, p. 7.

[798] *Report*, PP, 1823, V, 403, p. 60.

[799] As distinct from "land-scurvy" which seems to have been a form of atopic dermatitis. Sir Gilbert Blane (1749-1834) had promoted the regular consumption of lemon juice in the Royal Navy. Porter, *The Greatest*, p. 196.

[800] *Report*, PP, 1823, V, 403, p. 33.

(subsequently reduced to one orange daily). A total of 86,009 oranges were bought, 'till we had spent £300 of the public money, and raised the price of the article in the market.'[801] Those with diarrhoea were given pills made up of chalk, opium, aromatic and mercury – this last component (given in direct defiance of the instructions of Dr Hutchison[802]) likely to produce the soreness of the gums previously lacking in the supposed cases of scurvy. It seems that many convalescent patients (sensibly we might think) threw their pills out of the window.[803] These therapeutic efforts were ineffective. The numbers of infirmary patients doubled in March and, more importantly, the number of deaths rose dramatically. In 1821 and 1822 respectively there had been 18 deaths (a mortality rate of 2.8%) and 22 (3.0%).[804] In the first six months of 1823, 33 prisoners died (25 of them after 1 March) – an annualised rate of 7.7%. Of the 33 deaths, 17 had gastro-intestinal symptoms, nearly all with severe diarrhoea; seven were probably the result of tuberculosis; and nine of other causes.[805] In none of the quite detailed descriptions of terminal illness given at inquests is there any indication of scurvy.

Before this episode, diarrhoea, genuine or contrived, had been quite common in the prison – up to 100 cases annually.[806] Most were mild: in the three years prior to January 1823 there were only seven fatal cases, the most recent of these on 2 July 1822.[807] In the first half of 1823 there was a huge increase in the incidence of diarrhoea and of resulting deaths – from seven in three years to seventeen in the space of a few months. Initially Drs. Latham and Roget clung to their diagnosis of scorbutic diarrhoea but, faced with evidence from senior naval surgeons with extensive experience of scurvy and from a committee appointed by the Royal College of Physicians,[808] admitted (on 4 July):

> Unquestionably, then, we do believe, that some injurious influence has been in operation over and above the causes to which the epidemic was originally imputed. This injurious influence may have been present from the first, or it

---

[801] Holford, *Third*, p. 70. His figures suggest that initially oranges cost a penny each.

[802] *Report*, PP, 1823, V, 403, pp. 135 & 137.

[803] Ibid., p. 237.

[804] Ibid., p. 362.

[805] Figures collated from inquest summaries in *Report*, PP, 1823, V, 379, pp. 150-165, pp. 311-313, and a note on p. 176 to the effect that there had been two further deaths from 'dysentery and flux' between 12 and 17 June.

[806] The diagnoses were based on the number of prescriptions given but it was alleged that the prisoners may have feigned diarrhoea in order to enjoy the opium in the medication (not containing mercury at that time) or in order to avoid work. (*Report*, PP, 1824, IV, 401, pp. 52 and 102). Also Dr Hutchison asserted that it was not uncommon for prisoners to feign diarrhoea. 'I have seen convicts ... break down with their fingers, in their urinary utensils, a good figured or formed motion, and intimately mix it with the urine, so as to induce the belief that it was in reality a diarrhoeal motion.' Ibid., p. 81

[807] *Report*, PP, 1824, V, 401, p. 24.

[808] *Report*, PP, 1823, V, 403, pp. 9, 175, 200 and 205

may have been subsequently super-added. Whatever it may be, it has hitherto eluded our detection; and, whether it is, or is not in operation at present, we cannot tell.[809]

In July, the decision was made to evacuate the penitentiary.[810] First the women moved to the ophthalmic hospital in Regent's Park, and a month or two later the men to hulks (where, significantly, they were free from diarrhoea). Diarrhoea continued among the women who were also moved to hulks and then, because of continuing illness, pardoned. This process was completed by 18 June 1824 after which most of the women recovered their normal health.[811]

It is abundantly clear that scurvy did not play even a minor part in the excess mortality at Millbank in 1823. Whether "scorbutic diarrhoea" even existed as a medical entity is dubious, if it did its incidence was grossly over-diagnosed by Drs. Latham and Roget. Rather, the principal cause of illness and death was some sort of gastro-intestinal infection possibly spread by a female carrier involved in food preparation.[812] The reduction in diet – opposed by medical staff – certainly did not help but probably did not contribute materially to the number of deaths, most of which took place after the diet – on medical recommendation – had been improved. Thus, accusations by modern commentators that this episode reflects badly on the prison medical service are totally without foundation.

PRISON SURGEONS' OBEDIENCE TO THE RULES

In the early years there were no national rules but in general the recommendations of a committee of aldermen seem to have been applied in larger prisons:

> That the Surgeon appointed should attend whenever required; and see every Prisoner *ill* or *well* at least once in the course of the week; that the Infirmaries should be entirely regulated by him, as to diet or otherwise; and he should keep a regular Journal for the inspection of the Visiting Magistrates and Quarter Sessions ...[813]

Later, more was expected, and Shrewsbury county gaol's surgeon was an exemplar:

---

[809] Ibid., p. 394.

[810] On the basis of the miasmic theory of contagion.

[811] Holford, *Third*, p. 151.

[812] The possibilities are amoebic or bacillary dysentery, campylobacter, or even cryptosporidiosis – it is impossible to be certain on the available evidence. For this information I am indebted to Dr. Stephen Morris-Jones, M.R.C.P., M.R.C. Path., D.T.M. & H., consultant in infectious diseases and microbiology, U.C.L. who has studied all the evidence and consulted with some of his colleagues.

[813] *Report from the Committee of Aldermen appointed to visit several Gaols in England*, (London: Nichols, Son and Bentley, 1816), p. 11.

> The medical officer visits the prison daily, and sees each prisoner on admission before he is transferred from the reception cell. He likewise sees the prisoners on discharge. He visits daily all sick prisoners and prisoners in solitary confinement. He makes a monthly inspection. He keeps a weight book, in which he records the weight of the prisoners both on admission and discharge. Each prisoner is bathed on his admission, and occasionally afterwards.[814]

As I will show, this standard of excellence was usually, but not always, emulated elsewhere.

So far as journal keeping and attendance were concerned, surgeons at the county gaols at Gloucester, Lancaster and Norwich could not be faulted on either count. All visited on almost a daily basis (including weekends and what would now be regarded as public holidays – Christmas day for instance), and often several times a day if a patient was seriously ill. Any exception deserved a comment: 'Having received a report that there were no sick and no fresh prisoners I did not attend yesterday' (24 July 1849, Norwich). On one occasion, after a particularly heavy spell of duty, it seems that the strain was telling: 'My duties at this time very heavy in the Prison, requiring many hours attendance' (15 March 1845, Norwich). Since there was no provision for holidays as such, absences were generally accounted for. At Lancaster Mr Langshaw always notes when he is to be away and writes that his work will be done by Mr Langshaw (presumably his brother or son). At Norwich Scott writes: 'Being obliged to go to the Ipswich Election, Mr Alfred Master, Surgeon, has been requested to attend to my duties daily at the Castle' (19 April 1843). Even at the less-well-supervised Gloucester city gaol where duties were frequently undertaken by pupils of the Wiltons (father and son, who were also contracted to attend the county gaol), it was always one of the latter making the journal entry. However entries were not necessarily made on a daily basis; on 29 October 1829: 'The Prison has been very healthy for some time, I have occasionally visited since the date of my last report [dated 11 September], but had no complaints'. As at the county prisons, whenever a patient was seriously ill visits were made daily or twice daily with a journal entry on each occasion.

At Northleach and Littledean houses of correction also, any really sick patient was visited frequently, but routine visits were on a less regular basis. Much of this apparent lack of enthusiasm can be attributed to the low level of occupancy – particularly at Littledean – during the early years. In the first seventeen years (1791-1807) there were 3,384 committals to Gloucester county gaol (an average of nearly 200 per annum). In the same period the bridewells were much less busy: 1,104 committals to Horsley (65 per annum), 702 to

---

[814] *Tenth Report of Inspector, Southern and Western District*, PP, 1845, XXIV, 207, p. 15.

Northleach (just over 41 per annum), and a paltry 195 (11.5 per annum) to Littledean.[815] After 1817 when prison occupancy rose (between 1823 and 1841, an average of 347 committals per year at Northleach) the surgeon's attendance improved to at least twice weekly. Not until 1834 was similar regularity of attendance achieved at Littledean where committals were slower to rise (an annual average of 122 between 1823 and 1834 and of 158 between 1836 and 1849), but eventually increasing numbers resulted in an improvement in the surgeon's attendance.[816] In later years at Northleach and Littledean the magistrates took their supervisory role more seriously: 'I wish to observe that the Act of Parliament requires the Surgeon to see every prisoner twice a week ... and I ask Mr Hadwen to record that he has done so in the Journal' (Northleach, 28 November 1833). Mr Hadwen's record keeping improved thereafter so as to conform to the Act of Parliament. Similar reminders were given at Littledean: 'The Act requires that the Surgeon should visit the prison twice every week, seeing every patient (28 December 1833), and: 'I beg to observe there appear to be not quite two visits a week as the Act requires' (4 April 1834). It is noticeable that the subsequent attendance record at Littledean showed a marked improvement with eventually (after two changes of surgeon) visits on almost a daily basis. Record keeping was still imperfect: the surgeon's journal contains a note that the 'County Chairman [of justices] declines to sign this journal – the Medical Officer not having made his Annual Report in accordance to the directions of the Act of Parliament' (Michaelmas 1847). This omission was promptly rectified.

Other small prisons with low occupancy had similar problems. At Lichfield borough gaol the inspector noted: 'The surgeon comes sometimes on passing by, to ask how the prisoners are, but only goes into the wards when sent for, or desired to do so, by the keeper. He sends in a bill, and has no salary'. Notwithstanding the surgeon's apparently casual approach, 'the health of this prison is good'.[817] The surgeon at King's Lynn borough gaol took a robust stance: 'I merely attend on the sick. I do not keep the books, or perform the duties laid down by the Gaol Acts; they were not stipulated to be performed by me when the agreement was made, which was to attend the sick at £10 a year'.[818]

Magistrates ran into difficulty on one occasion because of a too-literal interpretation of regulations. At Horsley house of correction on 28 July 1843 the surgeon, James Henry Wells, writes that he has received a letter from

---

[815] G.O. Paul, *Evidence to Quarter Sessions, 1809*, GRO, Q/Gh 1/1.

[816] Committal numbers taken from annual reports (1835 missing): GRO, Q Ag 19/1-19/26.

[817] *Sixth Report of Inspector, Southern and Western District*, PP, 1841 Sess. 2, V, 177, p. 211. At the time of the inspector's visit there were eight prisoners in this gaol.

[818] *Ninth Report of Inspector, Northern and Eastern District*, PP, 1844, XXIX, p. 43.

the magistrates dated 27 July 1843 pointing out that 'Sir James Graham's[819] last regulations for prisons' directed that the surgeon should visit 'daily or oftener such of the prisoners as are sick' and that such additional work would justify an application for an increase in salary. The surgeon agreed to visit daily, but on 1 September 1843 he notes that the magistrates were backtracking on this instruction (perhaps regretting their rash offer of more salary) and a niggling dispute regarding his attendance continued until April 1844 when the journal ends.

Earlier, Neild was critical of Stafford county gaol where no surgeon's journal was kept. 'I should be happy to see the same attention paid here to the Rules and Orders as I found to prevail at *Gloucester*; where these important regulations are punctually observed'.[820] Remarks on the subject appear frequently in the inspector's reports, some approbatory as at Southampton gaol: 'The surgeon's journal contains copious headings, including the date of his attendance, (which appears to be every day), the nature of the disease, the medicines daily administered, and the diet etc.'; and similarly at Dorchester county gaol and Stafford county gaol. However there was criticism of note-keeping at Penzance town gaol and at Exeter county goal.[821] At Ely goal there was a note in the surgeon's journal excusing himself from making entries because of the high number of prisoners. The inspector was not moved: 'The daily entries of the state of health of prisoners, by the surgeon, I conceive to be of such importance as not to be dispensed with under any circumstances'.[822] Equally strongly at Maidstone county gaol:

> The surgeon, who has a large private practice in the neighbourhood, has a salary of £200 for his services in the prison, including medicines. He does not appear to attend constantly himself, and has not signed the attendance book from 13th November to 11th January; but his assistant, who is also a regular surgeon attends daily. The circumstance of the surgeon not performing the whole of his duties is irregular and improper.[823]

Deputising arrangements at Knutsford also caused concern: the surgeon visited twice a week, also making a monthly inspection, but all the routine work was carried out by his assistant (a qualified surgeon) who kept the journal. W.L., the "hospital nurse" reported:

> The assistant doctor comes every day at 10, and on Tuesdays and Fridays at 1; on these days he goes through the day-wards when the prisoners are at dinner. Mr

---

[819] Sir James Graham: Home Secretary 1841-1846.

[820] Neild, p. 540.

[821] *Sixth Report of Inspector, Southern and Western District*, PP, 1841 Sess. 2, V, 177, pp. 92, 107, 213, and 193. *Tenth Report of Inspector, Southern and Western District*, PP, 1845, XXIV, 207, p. 108.

[822] *Ninth Report of Inspector, Northern and Eastern District*, PP, 1844, XXIX, 227, p. 30.

[823] *First Report of Inspector, Southern and Western District*, PP, 1836, XXXV, 269, pp. 361 and 379.

D. (the principal) comes regularly once a month, and at other times whenever prisoners request to see him. They do not all know his name, but ask for the head doctor. Mr D. was here twice last week

Although this sounds to have been quite an efficient system the inspector drew attention to Rule 156.[824] The rule stated: 'In case of sickness, necessary engagement, or leave of absence, he shall appoint a substitute, to be approved by one or more of the visiting justices; and the names and residence of such substitute shall be entered in his journal'. It is clear that strict adherence to this rule was not the norm and apprentices sometimes saw minor cases: 'The surgeon always attends three times weekly himself. He has four assistants, who enter their names and visits in the journal, but I believe they attend chiefly trifling cases, such as the itch, etc.' (Exeter County Gaol).[825] It is equally clear that in most instances, if a deputy was used, he was competent to perform the duties required of him.

SURGEONS AND DISCIPLINE

Surgeons were in a sense 'intimately involved in reinforcing the discipline of penality'[826] in that they were required to supervise floggings and solitary confinement. In either case, I will show that they were concerned with health, generally ensuring that the bounds were not exceeded.

Early in the period there is one record of involvement with fetters, Mr Parker at Gloucester county gaol having cause to ask for their removal:

Wm Sibley who had been afflicted for months with ulcers on his legs of the most inveterate kind, but was got nearly well, find that since the ring of iron has been round his leg, the completion of the cure is much retarded – therefore judge it necessary that the ring be removed, and that with care as the parts that had sufferd, are still very tender. N.B. The Collar he may wear round his Neck as mentioned in rule vii (19 April, 1792).

Floggings were used throughout the period under study: either as part of the punishment meted out on sentencing or ordered by justices for bad behaviour in prison; the surgeon was empowered to terminate proceedings. At most prisons this form of punishment was not common: the surgeon's journal at Northleach notes attendance at twenty-three floggings (usually two or three dozen lashes) between 1817 and 1841, whilst at the much larger Lancaster castle there were only four instances recorded in the six years of medical records available for study. There, the

---

[824] *Ninth Report of Inspector, Northern and Eastern District*, PP, 1844, XXIX, 227, pp. 133 and 134. In fact the rule to which he refers was number 137.

[825] *Sixth Report of Inspector Southern and Western District*, PP, 1841 Sess. 2, V, 177, p. 142.

[826] Sim, *Medical*, p. x.

surgeon's comments vary from: 'Bird was well whipped yesterday' (29 July 1844) to: 'Diamond is to be punished according to his sentence this morning but his health is so indifferent the punishment must be next to nominal' (25 May 1849). At Norwich, floggings were administered rather more frequently than at Lancaster and on several occasions the surgeon exercised his power to modify punishment: 'Attended the flogging of Robert Breeze. Only 10 lashes and very softly applied on account of his indifferent constitution' (6 December 1849); 'I certify that Michael Gathercole whose term of imprisonment expires today is unfit from his state of health to undergo the flogging sentenced by the Court' (13 June 1849); and: 'I was called to witness the flogging of William Gunn but on stripping him I found him too much emaciated to bear the punishment' (5 July 1849). Gunn was again spared on the surgeon's order on 1 August 1849. And: 'Attended the flogging of Neal Scott. I was obliged to stop the flogging after 17 lashes in consequence of the blood starting' (31 January 1850). At Littledean house of correction, the entry: 'Attended the punishment of John Bridgman and extended it as far as I considered it proper to proceed' (13 April 1819) suggests this was another occasion when mercy was exercised. The surgeon at Ipswich gaol stated: 'the ordinary amount of lashes inflicted to be from 12 to 20; that the skin is not abrased, and that he never had occasion to order a liniment'. He details one case: '[the prisoner] became ill, and I found him suffering under greatly increased action of the heart, the force and quickness of the pulsation being greatly increased ... but after all he was not a man who could prudently be subjected to such a punishment, or indeed any punishment'.[827] At Huntingdon county gaol: 'The surgeon is present at the infliction of corporal punishment. He describes it as being anything but severe, the skin not being abrased'.[828]

It has to be admitted that in some instances the surgeon appeared to feel that punishment was justified. At Norwich on 17 April 1849: 'Visited and attended the flogging of William Lambuck. 17 lashes were laid on. The punishment took place at the new post which ensures its performance thoroughly'. Similarly at Gloucester county gaol: 'Attended at the Punishment of Wm Boulton (guilty of stealing) by order of John Parker Esq. Visiting Justice. This was very prudent and necessary discipline. Penitentiaries present, this example promises good effect' (11 May 1793). The severity of these punishments seems quite light when compared with those described in the surgeon's journal at Spalding house of correction:

> This morning at 11 o'clock, I attended to witness the infliction of flogging upon the persons of Wm. B., John B., John P., and Charles F. for refractory conduct; 72 lashes were given to each, with the exception of Charles F. to whom were given 120 lashes, in consequence of his extreme gross language during the infliction of the punishment.

[827] *Eleventh Report of Inspector, Northern and Eastern District*, PP, 1846, XXI, 483, p. 22.
[828] *Seventh Report of Inspector, Northern and Eastern District*, PP, 1842, XXI, 1, p. 180.

The inspector was very critical of the arbitrary nature of this extra punishment but the surgeon noted: 'Each prisoner bore the punishment with much hardihood, and in no case was there much depression'.[829] The brutality of these punishments fades into insignificance contrasted with those administered in the Army: 300–1,200 lashes.[830]

The public whipping of women was not abolished until 1817[831] but there is only one mention of corporal punishment to a female: 'Mary Savage was afterwards Privately whipped according to her sentence, and then discharged' (22 August 1794, Gloucester county gaol).

The use of the treadmill at Northleach provides further examples of indirect medical involvement in the disciplinary regime. This came about because prisoners were occasionally prepared to go to considerable lengths in feigning illness to avoid work. Some responded to a reprimand from the magistrates but others were more determined. In the thirteen years of medical records when the mill was in use, four were flogged for refusing to work when certified medically fit. A similar instance is recorded at Norwich county gaol where, on 31 July 1845 George Windham was placed on the treadmill and after a few minutes 'declared he could not work. I am decidedly of the opinion that he <u>can</u> but will not work'. Windham was flogged as a result of this refusal. At Gloucester city gaol a prisoner named Price showed determination; he had already made a variety of complaints, had been treated with leeches, a blister, and gruel; and on 4 February 1830:

> On this night I was call'd in a hurry to Price who had been making a noise in his cell and declaring himself to be very ill. I found him perfectly well but in the describing his complaints I detected him in so many lies, that I believe he himself felt he was convicted and he finally declared he had nothing to complain of but weakness, his bodily power however appears good. I have expressed to him that if he persists in his present mode of conduct and refuses to go on the wheel I will assuredly request the attendance of the visiting Magistrates and obtain him the Punishment of the cat of nine tails.

On the following day: 'Price got up this morning and went to work without complaint' and on 22 February: 'Price who has given so much trouble did not complain and appears very well'. However, at the same prison a degree of adaptability was shown: 'Visited Frith, a boy who is subject to fits should not work on the Wheel at least not when he may be expected to have them; they are periodical being influenced by the particular state of the Moon, have given him Medicines' (3 February 1828).

I found just one similar example of a surgeon initiating punishment – albeit

[829] *Ninth Report of Inspector, Northern and Eastern District*, PP, 1844, XXIX, 227, p. 68.
[830] Howard, *Wellington's Doctors*, pp. 212-213.
[831] Emsley, p. 249.

indirectly: 'Jane Lyes[832] Incontinence of urine ... I have every reason to believe that this is the result of lazy and filthy habits and wish the Matron to punish her' (22 October and 1 November 1847, Littledean). The punishment book shows she was stopped extra food (that is given bread and water only) for three meals.[833] This seems harsh, but a punitive approach to what was perceived as wilful incontinence (which it may have been) was common in this period throughout society.

Surgeons were required to make daily visits to prisoners punished by solitary confinement or in the dark cell (usually accompanied by reduced diet). At Gloucester county gaol the inspector noted the surgeon's involvement in ameliorating hardship: 'Those who are in solitary confinement for a fortnight generally become very emaciated, and very frequently suffer diarrhoea; but then they have only a pound and a half of bread, and a pint and a half of mint-water during the day. The surgeon continually puts them on extra diet'.[834] Prisoners could be removed on medical grounds, as shown in these extracts from the surgeon's journal at Dorchester county gaol:

> March 18th 1840:– When we went into the solitary cell we found that Charles ***, a boy about 16 Years of age, had been very sick, and he complained of headach [sic], and of being generally unwell; the cell appeared to me to have a suffocating effect and I entered it, and I was not satisfied of its being sufficiently dry to confine a prisoner in it. I directed that this boy should be immediately sent into the infirmary; and it occurred to my mind that the most satisfactory method of ascertaining whether the cell was sufficiently dry would be to examine the state of the bed- clothes, and particularly the rugs. I therefore desired the matron to have the clothes carried into the laundry – and upon placing them separately upon a drying copper, she found the rug in a very damp state, and certainly unfit for use.
>
> June 29th 1840. – John ***, confined in one of the new seclusion cells, complained of headach, and his face appeared to be red and full, when the cell door was first opened. It appears to me that a sufficient quantity of air is not admitted into these cells; or there is something wrong. I observed the same effect produced upon the boy who was first confined in an adjoining cell ... I ordered him to be removed into one of the old seclusion cells.[835]

Similarly at Bodmin county gaol: 'the surgeon has observed incipient disease in several prisoners in solitary confinement, and has had such prisoners frequently removed during the last two years, in summer as well as in winter. The cells are not heated and in winter are necessarily very cold'.[836]

---

[832] She was imprisoned for two months for stealing 14s.4p. from a shopkeeper. Aged 13, her height was 4 *feet. 7 inches.*

[833] GRO, Q/Gli 12.

[834] *Fourth Report of Inspector, Southern and Western District*, PP, 1839, XXII, 215, p. 67.

[835] *Sixth Report of Inspector, Southern and Western District*, PP, 1841 Sess. 2, V, 177, p. 107.

[836] Ibid, 1841, p. 179

The surgeon at Lancaster also sympathised with the prisoners' problems and not infrequently recommended that the bread and water diet be enhanced: 'The boy put apart by sentence of the Court is very humbled, I must give him a little milk as he refuses other food' (2 January 1845); 'The two men on punishment diet in the back yard show signs of declining strength. They must have all our variety of food beginning with half the quantity' (17 April 1845); and: 'Instead of bread and water I have ordered all the men punished their gruel night and morning' (22 January 1849).

Strangely it would seem that the surgeon was not required to attend executions – but with one notable exception. This was at Norwich: 'Visited and attended the execution of James Blomfield [sic] Rush. Copy of certificate addressed to the Visiting Magistrates' (21 April 1849). Rush was a murderer whose trial attracted a great deal of newspaper attention and presumably it was felt necessary to have more than the word of the hangman that he was in fact dead. It is also noteworthy (although again the reason is not explained) that Mr. Master had to spend the days of 31 March and 1 April 'in attendance on Emily Sandford during her examination in Court'. She was housekeeper to Rush and chief prosecution witness.[837]

HEAD SHAVING

A problem for modern historians is that some medical treatments can seem like punishment. One such was blistering (of which more later); another was shaving of the head. It is true that Paul had ordered 'The heads of [male convicted felons] shall be shaved'[838] and Sim uses this shaving as evidence of medical involvement in salutary humiliation.[839] Not so according to the surgeons' journals, where the evidence is that it was only ordered for infestation or when a problem of "cranial overheating" or delirium was thought to exist. An example is seen at Gloucester city gaol where Henry Williams was delirious as a result of typhus. His hair was cut close and his head kept cool with vinegar and water (26 September 1836). He survived. Another indication for shaving was used at Gloucester county gaol: 'Jones [afflicted with Scrophula] has also a Disease on the head which requires its

---

[837] James Bloomfield Rush was the tenant of Potash Farm. Its owner, Isaac Jermy, lived at Stanfield Hall and was Recorder of Norwich. On the day before the mortgage on the property was due to expire Rush went to Stanfield Hall and shot Jermy and his son – as a result he became the last man to be hanged in public at Norwich Castle. Sandford, in addition to her housekeeping duties, is thought also to have filled the office of mistress to Rush. The event attracted such attention that pottery figures of Rush and Sandford, together with models of Stanfield Hall, were produced and are now of considerable value. Griselda Lewis, *A Collector's History of English Pottery*, Fifth Edition (Woodbridge: Studio Vista, 1999), pp. 222-223.

[838] G.O. Paul, *Rules, Orders, and Regulations for the Controul [sic] and Government of the Prisons of the County of Glocester* (undated, but appended to *Address (1809)*, p. 62.

[839] Sim, *Medical*, p. 14

being shaved twice a week. He should also have a bladder to wear over the application I have given him to use on it' (25 February 1819). At Salford house of correction the surgeon wrote: 'I gave instructions to the assistant governor and the matron that the hair of all prisoners on admission, and from time to time afterwards should be cut so short as to render disease or a filthy state of the head, easy of detection, due regard being paid to a decent appearance as to the breadth of the hair covering the forehead and temples'.[840] Perhaps at times there was some abuse but if so it was an abuse those in power were ready to curb. At Gloucester Epiphany Sessions in 1843, the Visiting Justices Report from Northleach stated: 'An order has been issued by the visiting justices that in future none but the turnkey should cut the prisoners' hair, that it should not be cut so close as to disfigure their persons, but merely sufficiently so for the purpose of cleanliness, and to serve as a mark in case of escape'.[841]

FAILURES TO ABIDE BY THE RULES

Inevitably, expected standards were not always achieved. A failure to carry out his duties "by the book" was provided by the surgeon at Kirkdale. In 1837 the inspector reported: 'I cannot but observe, that I think it absolutely necessary that the surgeon to an establishment of this magnitude should visit it daily, be present at corporal punishments[842] ... and examine the prisoners before they are classed'.[843] Evidence of the manner in which the inspector's remarks could be ignored is apparent six years later when the same surgeon evinced a remarkable degree of insouciance as regards his duties:

> *Evidence of Surgeon* – "I do not see the prisoners before they are classed; they come into the building and are sent directly to their class. They do not pass through the bath. There is no fumigating apparatus for their clothing. The itch breaks out among the prisoners frequently; I do not know who is to know whether they have it or not, I do not see them. I do not see the prisoners individually twice a-week.

However he had mitigated the severity of three cases of corporal punishment: 'The sentences were not inflicted with any degree of severity. I stopped after

---

[840] *Fourth Report of Inspector, Northern and Eastern District*, PP, 1839, XXII, 1, p. 67.

[841] *Wilts and Gloucestershire Standard*, 9 January 1843.

[842] There was another example – at Exeter borough gaol: 'The surgeon is sometimes present [at floggings] but not always' (*Sixth Report of Inspector, Southern and Western District*, PP, 1841 Sess. 2, V, 177, p. 158); and at the same prison: 'In cases of punishment by whipping, the governor is always present; but the surgeon only attends in cases of the of more than ordinary severity, as for instance when 40 or 50 lashes are ordered' (*Tenth Report of Inspector, Southern and Western District*, PP, 1845, XXIV, 207, p. 132). The inspector to some extent excuses this poor attendance by his remarks on the inadequacy of the surgeon's remuneration.

[843] *Second Report of Inspector, Northern and Eastern District*, PP, 1837, XXXII, 499, p. 62.

the infliction of three dozen lashes; no medical application was required'. He took a down-to-earth view of doling out medicines, responsibility for which, as already noted in chapter three, had been largely delegated to the "nurse":

> I never ordered the nurse to give medicines on his own responsibility. ... I won't say that there may be some opium pills under the care of the nurse. He has never given, to my knowledge, more than a dose of castor-oil to prisoners. I order the nurse a pint of beer daily. I keep him well, to prevent his robbing the patients. Another reason I have for giving the nurse extra food is, that being well fed, he is less likely to be infected.[844]

Despite these failures on the surgeon's part, this seems to have been a reasonably healthy prison. In 1836 its population averaged 449 with 5 deaths – a relatively low mortality rate of 1.1%.[845] There was a particular problem at this gaol in that magistrates were reluctant to replace the 'old and frail' governor and matron.[846] These officials were apparently too set in their ways to dance to the inspector's tune and not until 1845 was there any improvement. In that year: 'The medical officer visits the prison daily and complies most strictly with the Rules. His salary has been raised to £180. The medicines are furnished by a chemist in the neighbourhood'.[847]

Rules were also flouted at Liverpool borough gaol. The surgeon stated: 'I give the officers cough-pills, purging-pills, and cordial-pills, which they give to the prisoners, upon complaining, before I see them; likewise castor-oil and salts, to administer as wanted'.[848] Irregularities on this scale were unusual, but did occur elsewhere. The governor at Reading county gaol stated 'he had found it necessary to take upon himself to direct treatment for patients affected with the itch forty of fifty times in the course of the year'.[849] Medicines were also handed out by staff or the "nurse" at Woodbridge house of correction.[850]

On occasions the activities of surgeons were subjected to parliamentary enquiry. The subject of one of these was Charles Beale, who died on 10 October 1842 at nearly twenty-three years of age, some six weeks after his release from about six months of confinement at Northleach house of correction.[851]

---

[844] *Eighth Report of Inspector, Northern and Eastern District*, PP, 1843, XXV and XXVI, 249, p. 11.

[845] *Second Report of Inspector, Northern and Eastern District*, PP, 1837, XXXII, 499, p. 62.

[846] DeLacy, p. 196.

[847] *Tenth Report of Inspector, Northern and Eastern District*, PP, 1845, XXIV, 1, p. 62. Previously he had been paid £63 per annum plus whatever profit he could make from medicines – for which he had been charging between £124 12s.6d. and £144. 1s. per annum. The inspector thought this arrangement most unsatisfactory. *Sixth Report of Inspector, Northern and Eastern District*, PP, 1841 Sess. 2, V, 1, p. 98.

[848] *Third Report of Inspector, Northern and Eastern District*, PP, 1837-38, XXXI, 1, p. 126.

[849] *Fifth Report of Inspector, Home District*, PP, 1840, XXV, 1, p. 26.

[850] *Fifth Report of Inspector, Northern and Eastern District*, PP, 1840, XXV, 565, p. 140.

[851] *Report, Northleach*, PP, 1843, XLIII, 375.

He complained bitterly to his mother (at whose instigation the enquiry was set up) of poor diet, insufficient medicine and of being overworked. The autopsy showed death from extensive pulmonary tuberculosis and although the committee felt the outcome inevitable (as of course it was in the absence of antibiotics) they were critical of the surgeon (John Ralph Bedwell):

> We consider the surgeon to have been remiss in not having put Beale on an improved diet, in not having paid attention to his clothing and the temperature of his cell during the early stages of his disease or at least as soon as cough had so far exhibited itself as to demand medical treatment. [and] Owing to the loose and imperfect state of this document [the surgeon's journal] we were unable to trace the early progress of Beale's disease.

According to the report, the surgeon failed to examine Beale on his arrival at Northleach (from Gloucester gaol), nor did he examine him prior to his going on the treadwheel. He was taken off the wheel on 17 May (having arrived at Northleach on 8 March) and allowed extra diet and rest but was put onto other work (in the 'potatoe [sic] bury') until being admitted to hospital where he was: 'attended by the principal turnkey … and was not neglected while in the Infirmary'. Apparently for the last month before release (on 1 September) there were entries in the surgeon's journal on almost a daily basis regarding Beale's cough and chest pain. The general tenor of the report is that the surgeon was unsympathetic to Beale during the early stages of his disease. In view of these findings the motion was proposed at the following Quarter Sessions meeting of magistrates that Bedwell be dismissed. To this the Rev. Mr Price responded:

> … after referring to the high attainments of Mr Bedwell and to the extreme difficulty of the situation, [I] considered it extremely hard that that promising young man should be made the scape-goat of all the others involved. He (Mr Bedwell) had not been many years at Northleach, and he came recommended in the highest manner and his conduct had been such as to give the highest satisfaction to all who employed him. He trusted he would be retained ….[852]

And retained he was, the motion being defeated by a large majority: 'Mr Bedwell was therefore continued, but with an admonition to the future'.

Another enquiry touched on an apparently casual approach to the disposal of body parts from hulks: this was one of the accusations leading to a parliamentary enquiry instigated by Thomas Dunscombe M.P. and reported on in 1847.[853] It was said that 'Entrails are taken from the body [at autopsy], and thrown into the river, where dozens had gone before'.[854] Most of the

---

[852] *The Wilts and Gloucestershire Standard*, 22 April 1843.
[853] *Report and Minutes of Evidence taken upon an Inquiry into the General Treatment and Condition of the Convicts in the Hulks at Woolwich*, PP, 1847, XVIII, 1.
[854] Ibid., p. xi.

more serious accusations regarding medical care were not substantiated at the enquiry but it emerged that Mr Bossy, the surgeon, in addition to a salary of £250 for his part-time appointment 'enjoys a large private practice in Woolwich and its neighbourhood' and also was using his post as surgeon to the hulks in order to engage in what must have been a very lucrative sideline training apprentices. Large numbers of autopsies were performed – giving these young men ample opportunity to improve their anatomical knowledge – and additionally they had a (literally) captive population on which to practice their "skills". According to William J. Williams it was a great impropriety that they were:

> left in charge of the hospital in the absence of the Assistant-Surgeon, and ... prescribing medicines, and performing such operations as bleeding, and passing catheters, the latter requiring much experience with manual delicacy and dexterity. I must observe too, that the youthful appearance of these young gentlemen is very little impressive of confidence.[855]

The assistant surgeon (Mr Blyth) referred to was not qualified, and although he received a salary of £100 and slept on the hospital ship, he was allowed to attend lectures in London for four months of the year.[856] Although Williams was full of praise for Mr Blyth's skills and conduct he was highly critical of the system of medical care and as a result Bossy was replaced (receiving a pension) by a full time naval surgeon, Mr G.H. Dabbs, who seems to have shown more commitment to his work.

HENRY HUNT AND ILCHESTER GAOL

An event cited by Sim as evidence of medical involvement in the punitive regime related to a prisoner having a blister applied to his head – apparently as a punitive measure – with the surgeon's connivance.[857] This instance came to light as part of a parliamentary enquiry instigated by Henry Hunt following his imprisonment in Ilchester county gaol for involvement in the St Peter's Fields (Manchester) demonstration of 16 August 1819.[858]

The commissioners looked at thirteen complaints mostly directed at the governor, William Bridle. These ranged through gross neglect of duty, drunkenness, swearing, gambling, failing to attend divine service and impregnating two of the female prisoners; to cruelty to, and torture of, the prisoners.[859] Medical matters

---

[855] Ibid., p. xxx.

[856] Ibid., p. xxx.

[857] Sim, *Medical*, p. 22.

[858] *Reports from the Commissioners appointed to inquire into the state of Ilchester Gaol*, 1822, XI, 277 and appendix, 1822, XI, 313. *Reports relating to Charges made against the Keeper by one of the Prisoners*, 1822, XI, 733. *Copies of Coroner's Inquests on two Prisoners at Ilchester Gaol*, 1822, XI, 757.

[859] *Reports*, PP. 1822, XI, 277, p. 7.

The Peterloo massacre. Engraving, 1819. On 16 August 1819 a crowd of some 60,000 assembled in St Peter's Fields, Manchester to hear Henry Hunt speak on the subject of reform. Seeing the size of the crowd and fearing disorder, the magistrates ordered the local yeomanry to arrest Hunt. They got into difficulty, Hussars were ordered in and the resulting mayhem ended with eleven people killed and over 400 injured.

play a minor part, but are important in the context of this book; the charge of wrongly using a blister has to be taken seriously. The recipient was prisoner Gardner (or Gardiner or Gardener) and the governor stated:

> Goaded by Gardner's continued misconduct [which included conveying a note over the wall, kicking a prisoner in the leg, stabbing a man in the knee, assaulting another prisoner, picking a comrade's pocket and perhaps worst of all 'cursing and abusing the magistrates']. I applied to Mr Bryer for a blister, and desired it to be applied to his head. ... I sincerely and deeply lament the occurrence.[860]

It transpired that the blister had been ordered by the governor without the surgeon's knowledge; no journal entry was made at the time but this defect was remedied subsequently by the surgeon at the governor's request. Asked about this, Bridle said: 'One word as to the entry in the Surgeon's Journal. It was entered a considerable time after, perhaps a month; one of the turnkeys came up to me and said, the doctor had never entered Gardner's blister. I went immediately to Mr Bryer, and desired he would do it'.[861] Bryer had been told Gardner 'was very abusive, and behaved in an outrageous manner'. He agreed he had seen no medical symptoms: 'It was to relieve his head ... from phrenzy [sic], I should suppose', and in attempting to justify its use he said: 'Mr Bridle informed me, when I came the next time, that the man had become very civil, and had promised to behave better in future'.[862] He denied putting blisters on the heads of other prisoners solely because they had behaved in 'an outrageous manner'. The only excuse he could offer for the instance under investigation was that his partner, Mr Valentine, had thought Gardner was feigning illness when seen a few days previously.[863]

The conclusion was reached that the blister had been used primarily as punishment; other evidence given in the enquiry indicates a degree of laxity in the provision of medical care at this prison. In theory there was a female infirmary, but at the time of the enquiry this was occupied by Mr Hunt (who also had the use of the adjacent 'Refractory Yard') whilst the male infirmary was occupied by 'Misdemeanors'. If necessary the sick were sent to a spare ward (the boys ward) but this was not always available and Mr Robertson, a surgeon from Northover who frequently deputised for Bryer, gave evidence that this lack of adequate accommodation for the sick could be a considerable problem.[864] Bryer seemed reluctant to attend emergencies, such patients were usually seen by one of the other local surgeons. The regime at Ilchester had become lax, the commissioners thought, partly because:

---

[860] Ibid., p. 38.
[861] Ibid., p. 39.
[862] Ibid., p. 127.
[863] Ibid, p. 363.
[864] Ibid., pp. 127, 131 and 212.

the internal government of this Gaol appears to have been considerably deteriorated since the declining health of Sir Richard John Palmer Acland [chairman of the magistrates for many years] has deprived the county of Somerset of the advantage of his unwearied and vigilant superintendence.[865]

So far as Bryer is concerned, there is little reason to doubt that he was, to say the least, lacking in enthusiasm in the pursuit of his duties, and it seems that he was replaced shortly after the commission finished their enquiries. The reason for assuming this is that in inquest evidence all references to the medical attendant after 16 October 1821 are to 'Mr William Tomkins, surgeon to the gaol'.[866] If nothing else, the happenings at this gaol indicate the value of enthusiastic magisterial supervision.

A PEEP into ILCHESTER BASTILE

**'A Peep into Ilchester Bastille'. *Investigation at Ilchester Gaol,*
Henry Hunt (London: Dolby, 1821). A depiction of Ilchester gaol owing far
more to the imaginations of Hunt and the artist than to reality.**

Sim also makes much of another matter dealt with in the enquiry: the death of James Bryant (a debtor, aged 48), supposedly caused by poor conditions in the prison.[867] He quotes: "there was no room in which the deceased could sit with a fire in it during his illness that was not at least six inches deep in water"; and

---

[865] Ibid., p. 15.

[866] Criticism of clinical conduct at the gaol did not cease with Bryer's departure. Joseph Honnibal had died as a result of ascites and pleural effusion and, at his inquest, both Mr Shorland and Mr Robertson testified that they thought Honnibal's life would have been prolonged had his ascites been tapped.

[867] Sim, 'Prison', p. 24.

uses this incident, together with the statement: 'In 1822, out of 600 prisoners in Ilchester prison, 400 were ill'[868] to support the conclusion that 'prisoners have always been a very vulnerable group, experiencing extremely high sickness rates'.[869] This last charge is easily dealt with: as has already been shown the sickness rate in any prison, as judged by the numbers of those reporting sick, was always high in relation to those actually suffering from significant disease. More reliable is Ilchester's mortality rate; seven deaths in the three years 1818-1820 from a prison population of about 250 (approximately 0.9% per annum) shows this was a relatively healthy prison, a conclusion supported by low mortality in a typhus outbreak (chapter four). The charge relating to the death of James Bryant can also be set aside. The evidence at his inquest makes it clear that floods badly affected the ground floor, making movement within the prison difficult.[870] When Bryant's normal room flooded, he was moved upstairs to a room where initially there was no fire. The surgeon ordered a fire in his new room the following day. The evidence given by Bryant's wife shows he was ill when committed. Evidence given by another prisoner (his nurse), a turnkey and the surgeon indicates that this illness continued intermittently and with increasing severity for his remaining two-and-a-half months of life. During this time he received ample treatment: bleeding, mercury, emetics, bark, acids, cathartics, and eventually a bottle of wine a day; methods used at the time on any patient in the community at large able to afford medical care. Bryant 'hinted a wish to have further medical advice' but not unreasonably was told this would have to be at his own expense. Mr Tomkins gave evidence: 'the disease was aggravated by walking through the floods, and that living in such a situation must greatly accelerate his death, which was produced by debility, originating from inflammation of the liver'.[871] In retrospect, it seems likely that Bryant was suffering from an incurable chronic illness when committed to the gaol. It is clear that conditions in the prison were far from ideal during this period of flooding (presumably similar conditions existed in most of the dwellings in the neighbourhood) but it is hard to see how prison surgeons could be blamed for this state of affairs.

---

[868] This from a claim made in the House of Commons by Mr Fowell Buxton: 'Out of 600 persons who had been confined in the gaol, no less than 400 had been attacked by sickness'. *Hansard*, (new series), VI (1822), p. 1079.

[869] Sim, 'Prison', p. 24. He also states 'in January 1810 there were 700 sick prisoners in Dartmoor prison hospital'. At that time Dartmoor contained only French prisoners-of-war and was grossly overcrowded. Sickness and mortality rates were certainly high but there is little point in trying to draw conclusions regarding the generality of English prisons from this example of a completely different type of prison.

[870] *Report*, PP, 1822, XI, 757, pp. 1-2. Elsewhere it is noted that the district in which the gaol was situated was low lying and 'subject to frequent inundations'. *Reports*, 1822, XI, 313, p. 212.

[871] *Copies*, PP, 1822, XI, 757, p. 2.

LEICESTER AND BIRMINGHAM GAOLS

Just after 1850, serious problems involving medical officers arose at Leicester county gaol and house of correction and at Birmingham borough gaol.[872] In neither was the environment at fault – Birmingham holding about 200 prisoners, opened in 1849, was described as '…spacious, airy and well-built …'[873] and as already noted the prison at Leicester holding about 100 had been remodelled in the 1840s. The authorities at both – and this was part of the problem – were firm believers in the separate system and of the importance of the deterrent value of a harsh prison regime. The main tool for hard labour was the hand crank and usually the resistance was set so high that: '… the labour at these machines, as it has been enforced in this prison, is a labour of a most severe and exhausting kind; so severe indeed, that practically there remained in the hands of the authorities no means of further punishment in case of its neglect or non-performance'.[874]

CELL, WITH PRISONER AT "CRANK-LABOUR," IN THE SURREY HOUSE OF CORRECTION.

A prisoner working the hand crank in his cell. Mayhew's *Prisons of London*, 1860.

The minimal diet was further reduced for unsatisfactory work with the result that:

> Numerous other instances also appeared in which the prisoners from weakness or exhaustion were excused from the crank labour, and supplied with animal food

[872] *Report of the Commissioners Appointed to Inquire into the Condition and Treatment of the Prisoners confined in Leicester County Gaol and House of Correction, PP. 1854, XXXIV, 197. Reports from Commissioners, Birmingham Borough Prison, PP 1854, XXXI, 1.*

[873] *Report (Birmingham), PP, 1854, XXXI, 1, p. iii.*

[874] *Report (Leicester), PP, 1854, XXXIV, 197, p. iv-v.*

and other restoratives and stimulants, in order to the regaining of their strength; and wasting of the flesh in some instances to the extent of several stone weight, excessive perspiration, paleness, and prostration of strength, were described to us as being the ordinary effects of the crank labour.[875]

These remarks were made with regard to Leicester but conditions were just as bad – if not worse – at Birmingham. At both prisons there was a high rate of attempted and successful suicides and it was one of the latter – a fifteen year old boy (Edward Andrews) who hanged himself – which brought these matters to light.[876] The evidence given makes it clear that Andrews was a disturbed child but it is equally clear that the unsympathetic and harsh treatment he received from the (full-time) prison surgeon, Mr J.H. Blount, may well have contributed to his death. There were many other examples of unsatisfactory conduct by Mr Blount and he, along with Lt. Austin the prison governor, resigned.[877] The surgeon at Leicester, Mr Benfield, had carried out his duties in a more satisfactory manner but: '[he] undoubtedly failed in an important part of his duty; for he knew what must be the physical effects of the system [crank labour]; he actually saw the serious ill consequences to health resulting from it, which called for his interference in no less than 118 cases in the course of two years: under these circumstances, he ought to have raised his voice against its continuance'.[878] Clearly, the Commissioners had become accustomed to expecting a more proactive stance than that shown by Mr Benfield and both he and Mr Blount were too intimately involved in the system of controlling prisoners.

It would be very odd indeed had there existed a uniform standard of perfection amongst prison surgeons but I think it is clear that most of them put the interests of their patients first, even when it came to confronting their social superiors – the magistrates – over the matter of diet. Quite clearly some fell below the mark, at least in terms of sticking strictly to the rules they were supposed to obey and also, in the case of Charles Beale, in making what can be a very difficult distinction – between the malingerer and the truly ill. However, the evidence I have provided shows that in most prisons, surgeons carried out their duties in a reasonably punctilious manner. Regular attendance and scrupulous record keeping are not essential to patient satisfaction and there is nothing to suggest that surgeons' occasional failure to abide by the rules, deplorable though this may be, resulted in significant harm to their patients.

---

[875] *Ibid.*, p. viii.

[876] *Report (Birmingham)*, PP, 1854, XXXI, 1, pp. v-xi.

[877] *Ibid.*, pp. xiv-xxxii and 307-314.

[878] *Report (Leicester)*, PP, 1854, XXXIV, 197, pp. xiv-xv.

8

CONCLUSION

The practice of medicine necessarily involves the exercise of power and control. A patient consulting a doctor implicitly surrenders certain rights: specifically the right to privacy and the right of custody of the body. He or she accepts the doctor's expectations that questions of an intensely personal nature will be answered – knowing that failure to answer those questions may well have an adverse effect on the outcome of the encounter. The individual is then likely to submit to medical examination of an intrusive nature. Invasive procedures – from the taking of blood to a heart transplant – are all to a greater or lesser degree assaults on the person. The patient accepts this surrender of power and loss of control, believing that some benefit will accrue. In return the doctor gives a guarantee (unspoken but nonetheless real) that he or she will endeavour to fulfil the patient's expectations.[879]

The relationship between prison doctor and prisoner/patient is not significantly different. It is true that the prisoner does not as a rule have the (often illusory) freedom to choose his or her doctor enjoyed by the free person – although, as I have shown, such freedom of choice was occasionally exercised by prisoners. It is also true that a prison doctor had power over and above that normally applied: the ability to order extra punishment to a recalcitrant prisoner. In practice this power was rarely exercised and then

---

[879] As formally expressed in the "Hippocratic Oath". Porter, *The Greatest*, p. 63.

nearly always to a category of patient (malingerers) who by lying had in effect broken the unspoken contract. The central question to be answered therefore, is not whether prison medical officers had power over prisoners – that can be taken for granted – but whether that power was used in a manner compatible with medical ethics as generally understood. That is, with both the intention and the result of benefiting their patients and I believe that I have shown that both of these intents were accomplished.

It should be borne in mind that we are looking at an age when, as the following statement shows, most of those in the stratum of society who became prisoners could barely afford any sort of medical attention:

> The apothecaries in the country charge so high for their attention that a poor distressed working man (if he be a few weeks in illness) dreads the consequence of employing them, as if he survives the illness he knows it will be an additional drawback on his labour (for perhaps several years) to get clear of the apothecary.[880]

Consequently, prisoners seem to have relished the opportunity of unwontedly free medical attention: '... sick prisoners were tended with a care and indulgence that sick workmen rarely enjoyed'.[881] They were able to summon more quantity of medical care – usually of at least equal quality – than they could when free. It has to be accepted that (then as now) much of the therapy provided was ineffective but equally it has to be accepted that (then as now) an indisposed individual usually feels benefit from medical attention – even in the absence of any objective merit in the treatment.[882] This is the prop on which the medical profession has leaned since human society first came into existence.

When Anne Hardy claims that 'Medical services to prisons were ramshackle until at least 1850' (chapter one) she is using he word ramshackle (meaning decrepit or rickety) quite unjustifiably in a pejorative sense. It is true that throughout the period there was no centralised control of the prison medical service and that, with a few exceptions, prison medical officers were part-time. I would assert that, in an era when most prisoners were incarcerated for relatively short periods, this provision of a service staffed by doctors closely involved in the local community was a positive advantage. The special needs of long-stay prisoners in national penitentiaries were catered for by full-time staff who, if William Baly and William Guy are archetypes, were of high intellectual quality.

---

[880] Loudon, p. 67. This was written in 1787 by a steward on a Bedfordshire estate.

[881] Clay, pp. 115-116.

[882] Dylan Evans, *Placebo: The Belief Effect* (London: HarperCollins, 2003), passim and particularly pp. 25-43.

A central question to be answered is that of control. The existence of social control is undeniable.[883] Prison doctors could not avoid being involved in this process. But were they involved primarily for the benefit of patients, or were they a conscious part of a system deliberately designed in order to render the already disadvantaged even more disadvantaged? Can it really be said that: 'The disciplinary strategies which lay at the heart of penality were legitimised by the interventions which Medical Officers made'.[884] And that:

> The emergence of the institution [of prison] and the professional groups who staffed it was built around discipline where the body of prisoners was broken down and fragmented into individual cellular spaces "thus allowing their control and ordering through routines and time-tables". The consolidation of medical knowledge reinforced this fragmentation, constant surveillance and individualised documentation became corner-stones in penality.[885]

It is of course true that (by a happy chance and even allowing for the fact that Howard and Paul exaggerated the risks) the separation of prisoners into 'individual cellular spaces' for reform purposes was important in achieving a reduction in common infectious diseases. But to conflate the fortuitous reduction in typhus and smallpox with the supposed breaking down of the body of prisoners, and to infer that medical documentation was somehow one of the building blocks of the whole system of penality are surely unrealistic propositions. Prison surgeons were more often criticised for failing in their documentation duties than for any excess of enthusiasm. And even in the later part of the period under study, when prisoners were routinely weighed, the results of such measurements were more often used in an attempt to improve the condition of prisoners than the reverse.

Sim asserts: '[prison medical officers] rather than operating from a perspective bereft of ideology and politics have been intimately involved in reinforcing the discipline of penality, attempting to create the well-adjusted individual from the undifferentiated mass of criminals living dangerously behind penitentiary walls'.[886] The evidence I have produced supports the conclusion that prison medical officers were not remotely concerned with these theoretical aspects of penality. Their concern was with the practice of medicine in the manner they believed to be right. It is also difficult to find any justification for Sim's statement: 'Those who have staffed [the PMS] from the late-eighteenth century to the present have built their position

---

[883] A.P. Donajgrodski, 'Introduction', in *Social Control in Nineteenth Century Britain*, ed. by A.P. Donajgrodski (London: Croom Helm, 1977), pp. 10-16.

[884] Sim, *Medical*, p. 40.

[885] Ibid., p. 9.

[886] Ibid., pp.179 & x.

on their unique access to, and surveillance of, the confined'.[887] As I have shown, those staffing the prison medical service probably did so because of a mixture of financial and philanthropic motives – the solitary example of a surgeon taking advantage of his position was the quite exceptional case of Mr Bossy on the prison hulks at Woolwich.

The claim that any improvement in health care in prisons was not the result of the efforts of medical men must also be met. The assertions made by Roy Porter and Anne Hardy that success in the prison reform process was not down to medical men (see chapter one) entirely disregards the efforts of Drs. Fothergill, Hartley, Good, Lettsom and others and to ignore the influence exerted by them on Howard and Neild. One of the objects of what Porter describes as the 'construction of perfectly regulated environments' was precisely that of controlling disease – a matter foremost in the minds of the reformers. Undoubtedly, such environments *per se* did much to control epidemic diseases such as smallpox and typhus (although less to control cholera, tuberculosis or typhoid) but it took the efforts of prison medical officers to see that these environments were properly maintained.

Diana Medlicotts's statement (see chapter one) to the effect that prison doctors were engaged in barbarism, '[colluding] in the generation of physical and psychological ill-health, [and] sanctioning cruel punishments …' is, as I have amply demonstrated, such gross hyperbole that, but for its association with such a prestigious body as the Howard League for Penal Reform, it could be ignored. Even Sim's more cautious assertion to the effect that: 'The will to discipline has had a profound impact on the level of medical care that prisoners have received since the end of the eighteenth century with deleterious and sometimes fatal consequences for a number of them'[888] is difficult to justify in the light of the evidence I have produced. Prison doctors were concerned to maintain as equable an environment within the prison as was possible, but they would have been equally concerned to maintain such an environment within a hospital ward or in the patient's own home. A disorderly patient, in whatever surroundings, is seen as a challenge to the doctor's authority, a challenge requiring action. Failure to respond to such provocation results in a lowering of the doctor's esteem in the eyes of all around, and esteem is an important part of the medical image – important to the patient also if he or she is to obtain maximum benefit from the doctor's administrations. Sim's other charge – of prison medical officers being responsible for causing deleterious effects to the health of their charges and even deaths

---

[887] Ibid., p. 10.
[888] Sim, *Medical*, p. x.

– is also impossible to substantiate in the light of the evidence I have produced.

Equally impossible to substantiate is Ignatieff's charge that 'the medical rituals that accompanied admission to the penitentiary had a latent but explicit purpose of humiliation'.[889] In fact if medical officers were to be criticised in this respect it was in failing to carry out these 'medical rituals' with sufficient enthusiasm. There was certainly no attempt to play a part in the state's power to subject the offender to control nor to destroy the identity of the prisoner. It seems quite clear that admission procedures were performed only to identify those individuals suffering from contagious diseases such as the itch, knowing that failure to do so would result in spread of the disease in the prison, with more suffering to their patients, extra work for themselves and damage to their reputation.

What has emerged is that prison surgeons were not motivated by a desire to be a part of some all-pervasive power structure devoted to the control and subjugation of the inferior classes. They were men doing the job for which they had been trained, and doing it to the best of their ability. It is doubtful if many of them harboured particularly benevolent feelings towards their charges, but as doctors they were perfectly capable of putting any such feelings to one side. As Fissell puts it: 'Health care was an economic free-for-all, an open market, an exemplification of the consumer revolution'.[890] Prison surgeons could not afford to risk their reputations by practising low standards: they were anxious to avoid criticism, if only in order to preserve the reputation they held locally and on which their livelihood depended. They were professionals, and were motivated by the ethos they had absorbed during their training: to look after those in their care – irrespective of background – in a professional manner.

---

[889] Ignatieff, p. 101.
[890] Fissell, *Patients*, p. 10.

BIBLIOGRAPHY

Primary Sources

Gloucestershire county record office, Gloucester (GRO)
Surgeons' journals:

Gloucester county gaol

1791–1799	Q/Gc 32/1
1809–1820	Q/Gc 32/2
	and 32/3

Gloucester city gaol and house of correction

1825–1837	G3/G8/1

Horsley house of correction

1843–1844	Q/Gh 12

Littledean house of correction

1806–1854	Q/Gli 18/1–18/3
	and Q/Gli/19

Northleach house of correction

1800–1841	Q/Gn 5/1–5/3

Other documents at GRO

Annual returns to the Home Office from prisons 1823–1849 (1835 missing)
         Q/AG 19/1–19/26
Felons' Register, Gloucester county gaol   Q/Gc 5/1
Justices' Journal, Gloucester county gaol   Q/Gc 1/1
Justices' Journal, Gloucester county gaol   Gc1/2
Justices' Journal, Horsley house of correction   Q/Gh 1/1
Justices' journal, Littledean house of correction   Q/Gli 1/1
Punishment Book, Littledean house of correction   Q/Gli 12
List of Criminals Hanged in Gloucester from the year 1786–1885 PS 17
Prisoners' Histories 1794–1800, Gloucester gaol   GMS 244
Register of Prisoners 1791–1816, Gloucester county gaol Q Gc 4

Lancashire county record office, Preston (LCRO)
Surgeons' reports:

Lancaster Castle

1 October 1823	QGR/1/5
16 October 1826	QGR/1/17
13 October 1828	QGR/1/22
1 September 1829	QGR/1/25
1 July–20 September 1830	QGR/1/31
27 June–30 September 1831	QGR/1/34

Other documents relating to Lancaster Castle

A table showing the number of diseases from 1822 to June 1829
         QGR/1/26

A table exhibiting the average annual cost of Medicine, Wine, Ale, Groceries, Milk and all other extra allowances for the different Prisons of the County   QGR/1/27

General Report of His Majesty's Gaol the Castle of Lancaster in the County Palatine of Lancaster (1828)   QGR/1/19

General Report (1829)   QGR/1/23

Governor's Journal Lancaster Castle   MF 1/37

To the Magistrates, Governor, and Medical Gentlemen visiting and acting for the Gaol the Castle of Lancaster   QGV/1/5

Surgeons' reports: Kirkdale House of Correction

3 November 1823	QGR/3/5
31 October 1824	QGR/3/10
7 November 1825	QGR/3/15
31 October 1826	QGR/3/18
31 October 1827	QGR/3/22
3 November 1828	QGR/3/26
5 November 1829	QGR/3/30
8 November 1830	QGR/3/34
31 November 1831	QGR/3/37
9 November 1835	QGR/3/38

Other documents relating to Kirkdale house of correction

General Report on the House of Correction at Kirkdale in the County of Lancaster QGR/3/11

Surgeons' reports: Salford House of Correction

Michaelmas 1824	QGR/4/11
Michaelmas 1828	QGR/4/21
Michaelmas 1829	QGR/4/25
Michaelmas 1828	QGR/4/26
Michaelmas 1829	QGR/4/30
Michaelmas 1830	QGR/4/29
Michaelmas 1831	QGR/4/31

Wigan Archive Service, Leigh
Surgeons' journals

Lancaster Castle gaol 1843–1849 MMP 12

Norfolk County Record Office, Norwich (NCRO)
Surgeons' journals

Norfolk county gaol and bridewell

1843–1850 MF/RO 576/1

Other documents relating to Norwich castle gaol

Keeper's daily journal, 1822–1835 MF/RO 576/1
Visiting Justices' Minute Book MF 880

Accounts of the Treasurers for the Prisoners in the Castle, 1734 MF /RO 581/7, 1735 MF/RO 581/8

Parliamentary Papers (PP)

Report from the Select Committee appointed to enquire into the state of Lunatics, 1807, II, 69

A Return of the Number of Prisoners who have died in the Hulks, 1810, XIV, 547.

Select Committee on Penitentiary Houses, First Report, 1810–11, III, 567. *Second Report,* 1810–11, III, 619

Select Committee on the Expediency of erecting Penitentiary Houses, and the State of Punishment in Hulks, 1812, II, 363

Report from the Committee on the State of the Gaols of the City of London etc., 1813–1814, IV, 249

Report from the Committee on the King's Bench, Fleet and Marshalsea Prisons, 1814–15, IV, 533

Report of the Committee appointed to examine the State of Newgate and other Prisons within the City of London and the Borough of Southwark, 1818, VIII, 297, and (Minutes of Evidence) 1818, VIII, 545

Report from the Commissioners appointed to inquire into the state, conduct, and management of the Prisons and Gaols of the Fleet and Other Places of Confinement, 1819, XI, 325

Reports of John Henry Capper, PP. 1819, XVII, 319

Reports from the Commissioners appointed to inquire into the state of Ilchester Gaol, 1822, XI, 277 and appendix, 1822, XI, 313. *Reports relating to Charges made against the Keeper by one of the Prisoners,* 1822, XI, 733. *Copies of Coroner's Inquests on two Prisoners at Ilchester Gaol,* 1822, XI, 757

First Report of the Physicians on the State of the General Penitentiary at Milbank [sic], 1823, V, 379 and *Further Papers (Correspondence),* 1823, V, 387. *Report from the Select Committee on the State of the Penitentiary at Milbank,* 1823, V, 403. *Report from the Select Committee on the Prison at Milbank,* 1824, IV, 407.

Copies of all Communications made to, or received by the Secretary of State for the Home Department, respecting the use of TREAD WHEELS, in Gaols or Houses of Correction, 1823, XV, 307, 1824, XIX, 165, 1825, XXIII, 567

Reports and Schedules transmitted to the Secretary of State, pursuant to Act 4 Geo.. IV. c. 64 and 5 Geo. IV. c. 12,

1828,	XX, 327
1829,	XIX, 1. 401
1830,	XXIV, 1
1830–31,	XII,1
1831–32,	XXXIII, 1
1833,	XXVIII, 1
1834,	XLIV, 225
1835,	XLIV, 225
1836,	XLII, 1
1837,	XLV, 1
1837–38,	XLIII, 227
1839,	XXXVIII, 17
1840,	XXXVIII, 1
1841,	XVIII, 1
1842,	XXXII, 1
1843,	XLIII, 1
1844,	XXXVII, 403
1845,	XXXVII, 417
1846,	XXXIV, 187
1847,	XLVII, 297
1847–48,	LII, 465

Reports of John Henry Capper (Hulks), 1829, XVIII, 315

Reports from the Select Committee on Secondary Punishments, 1831, VII, 519, 1831–32, VII, 559

First Report from the Committee of the House of Lords on the Present State of the several Gaols and Houses of Correction in England and Wales, 1835, XI, 1

Second Report from the Committee of the House of Lords on the Present State of the several Gaols and Houses of Correction in England and Wales, 1835, XI, 495

Copy of a Report made on 2ⁿᵈ July 1836, by a Committee of the Court of Aldermen to that Court upon the Report of the Inspectors of Prisons in relation to the Gaol of Newgate, 1836, XLII, 231

Reports of the Inspectors of Prisons for the Home District:

First 1836,	XXXV, 1
Second 1837,	XXXII, 1
Third 1837–38,	XXX, 1
Fourth 1839,	XXI, 1
Fifth 1840,	XXV, 1
Sixth 1841 Sess. 2,	IV, 1
Seventh 1842,	XX, 1
Eighth 1843,	XXV and XXVI, 31
Ninth 1844,	XXIX, 1
Tenth 1845,	XXIII, 1
Eleventh 1846,	XXI, 1
Twelfth 1847–48,	XXXIV, 373
Thirteenth 1847–48,	XXXV, 461
Fourteenth 1850,	XXVIII, 1
Fifteenth 1851,	XXVII, 1
Sixteenth 1856,	XXXII, 1
Seventeenth 1856,	XXXII, 329
Eighteenth 1856,	XXXII, 635
Nineteenth 1856,	XXXIII, 73
Twentieth 1857 Sess. 1,	VII, 1

Reports of the Inspectors of Prisons for the Northern and Eastern Districts

First 1836,	XXXV, 161	
Second 1837,	XXXII, 499	
Third 1837–38,	XXXI, 1	
Fourth 1839,	XXII, 1	
Fifth 1840,	XXV, 565	
Sixth 1841 Sess. 2,	V, 1	
Seventh 1842,	XXI, 1	
Eighth 1843,	XXV and XXVI, 249	
Ninth 1844,	XXIX, 227	
Tenth 1845,	XXIV, 1	
Eleventh 1846,	XXI, 483	
Thirteenth 1847–8,	XXXVI, 361	*(designated Northern*
Fourteenth 1849,	XXVI, 167	*District in the years*
Fifteenth 1850,	XXVIII, 291	*1848 and 1849)*
Sixteenth 1851,	XXVII, 461	
Seventeenth 1852–1853,	LII, 1	

Eighteenth 1856,	XXXIII, 1
Nineteenth 1856,	XXXIII, 385
Twenty-first 1857 Sess. 2,	XXIII, 1
Twenty-second 1857–58,	XXIX, 1

Reports of the Inspectors of Prisons for the Southern and Western Districts:

First	1836, XXXV, 269
Second	1837, XXXII, 659
Third	1837–38, XXXI, 177
Fourth	1839, XXII, 215
Fifth	1840, XXV, 721
Sixth	1841 Sess. 2, V, 177
Seventh	1842, XXI, 193
Ninth	1844, XXIX, 391
Tenth	1845, XXIV, 207
Eleventh	1846, XXI, 565
Twelfth	1847–48, XXXV, 1
Thirteenth	1847–48, XXXVI, 361
Fourteenth	1849, XXVI, 93
Fifteenth	1850, XXVIII, 579
Sixteenth	1851, XXVII, 669
Seventeenth	1852, XXIV, 1
Eighteenth	1852–53, LII, 113
Nineteenth	1853, XXXIV, 1
Twenty-first	1856, XXXIII, 485
Twenty-second	1857 Sess. 1, VII, 401
Twenty-third	1857–58, XXIX, 69 *(now called Southern District)*

Reports of the Inspectors of Prisons of the Midland and Eastern District

Thirteenth	1847–48, XXXVI, 1
Fourteenth	1849, XXVI, 1

Reports of the Inspectors of Prisons of Scotland

Twenty-first	1856, XXXIII, 659

Report of Visiting Magistrates of Warwick Gaol on Allegation in Petition of Messrs Lovett and Collins, 1839, XXVIII, 477

Correspondence relating to Treatment of W. Lovett and J. Collins, 1840,

XXXVIII, 751

Papers Relating to the Convict Establishments. Report of John Henry Capper, 1840, XXXVIII, 543

Two Reports of John Henry Capper, 1842, XXXII, 523

Report relative to the System of Prison Discipline, by the Inspectors of Prisons, 1843, XXV and XXVI, 1

Return of Health of Convicts in Pentonville Prison, 1843, XXIX, 377

Report to the Rt. Hon. Sir James Graham (Her Majesty's Principal Secretary for the Home Department) on the Case of Charles Beale and others, lately confined in the Northleach House of Correction, and the Management of the Prisons of the County of Gloucester, 1843, XLIII, 375

Report of the Inspector of Prisons for the Northern District on the Inquiry into the Treatment of Prisoners in the House of Correction at Knutsford, 1843, XLIII, 325; and *Further Papers with respect to the Inquiry,* 1843, XLIII, 355

Reports relating to Parkhurst prison, 1844, XXVII, 17

Report of J.H. Capper, 1845, XXXVII, 315.

Third Report of the Commissioners for the Government of the Pentonville Prison, 1845, XXV, 53

Second Report (1844) from the Inspectors of Millbank Prison, 1845, XXV, 1

Third Report (1845) from the Inspectors of Millbank Prison, 1846, XX, 1

Report from the Commissioners Appointed to Inquire into the Management of Millbank Prison, 1847, XXX, 1

Returns Relative to Hulks (Portsmouth and Gosport), 1847, XLVIII, 465

Returns Relative to the Deaths etc. of Prisoners on Board the Hulks at Woolwich, 1847, XLVIII, 465

Report and Minutes of Evidence taken upon an Inquiry into the General Treatment and Condition of the Convicts in the Hulks at Woolwich, 1847, XVIII, 1

Report on the Treatment and Condition of the Convicts in the Hulks at Woolwich, 1847, XVIII, 1

Report of the Manager of the Convict Hulk Establishment for the year 1848, 1850, XXIX, 1

Sixth Report of the Inspectors of Millbank Prison for the year 1848 and part of

1849, 1850, XXIX, 55

Report of the Inspectors of Millbank Prison for the year 1849, 1850, XXIX, 73

Reports from Commissioners (Millbank), 1852–53, LI, 1

Eighth Report of the Commissioners for the Government of the Pentonville Prison 1850, 1851, XXIX, 125

Reports of the Directors of Convict Prisons on the Discipline and Management of Pentonville, Parkhurst, and Millbank Prison, and of Portland Prison and the Hulks, for the year 1850, 1851, XXVIII, 1

Reports of the Directors of Convict Prisons etc. 1852, XXIV, 197

Reports from Commissioners, Convict Prisons 1854, XXXIII, 1

Reports of the Directors of Convict Prisons etc. 1854–1855, XXV, 33

Reports on the Discipline of the Convict Prisons etc., 1854–55, XXV, 435

Reports of the Directors of the Convict Prisons etc., 1856, XXXV, 1

Reports of the Directors of the Convict Prisons 1857 Sess. 2, XXIII, 65

Reports of the Directors of the Convict Prisons 1857–58, XXIX, 285

Reports of the Directors of the Convict Prisons 1857–58, XXIX, 483

Reports from Commissioners, Birmingham Borough Prison, 1854, XXXI, 1

Reports from Commissioners, Leicester County Gaol and House of Correction, 1854, XXXIV, 197

Public Record Office, Kew (PRO)

Convict Prisons: Quarterly Returns of Prisoners. Home Office, HO 8

Convict Prison Hulks: Registers and Letter Books. Home Office, HO 9

Domestic Correspondence: George III, letters to Lord Sydney. Home Office, HO 42/3, 42/4, and 42/5

Letter from Governor of Lancaster Gaol. Home Office, HO 20/1/53

Primary Sources: Books and Pamphlets

Anon., *Gloucester Bastille!!! Pathetic Particulars of A POOR BOY sentenced to suffer Seven Years solitary Confinement in Gloucester Gaol* (London: Holland, 1792)

Anon., *The Trials of Arthur Thistlewood, James Ing, John Thomas Brunt, and others, for High Treason before Chief Justice Abbott, Sir Robert Dallas, and special Juries, at the Old Bailey, London; which commenced on Saturday April 15th 1820 and closed Thursday April 27th 1820* (Leeds: Barr, 1820)

Anon., *The Trial of Mr Hunt, Mr Johnson, and others, For a Conspiracy at the Manchester Meeting, on the 16th August Last before Mr Justice Bailey, and a Special Jury at York which commenced on Thursday, March 17th 1820 and closed Monday March 27th 1820* (Leeds, Barr, 1820)

Arbuthnot, John, *An Essay concerning the Effects of Air on the Human Bodies* (London: Tonson & Draper, 1751)

Baly, William, 'On the Mortality in Prisons and the Diseases most frequently fatal to prisoners', *Medico-Chirurgical Transactions* XXVIII (1845)

Burt, John T., 'Results of the System of Separate Confinement as Administered at the Pentonville Prison', *The Quarterly Review*, XCII, (1852–53), 487–506

Campbell, John, *Thirty Years' Experience of a Medical Officer in the English Convict Service* (London: Nelson, 1884)

Chesterton, George Laval, *Revelations of Prison Life; with an Enquiry into Prison Discipline and Secondary Punishments* (London: Hurst and Blackett, 1856)

Clay, W.L., *The Prison Chaplain: A Memoir of the Rev. John Clay, B.D.* (London: Macmillan, 1861)

Creighton, Charles, *A History of Epidemics in Britain*, Vol. II (Cambridge: Cambridge University Press, 1894)

Dixon, Hepworth, *The London Prisons with an account of the More Distinguished Persons who have been confined in them to which is added a description of the Chief Provincial Prisons* (London: Jackson & Wilford, 1850)

Dornford, Josiah, *Nine Letters to the Rt. Honorable the Lord Mayor and Aldermen of the City of London on the state of the City Prisons* (London: Andrews, 1785)

Good, John Mason, *A Dissertation on the Diseases of Prisons and Poorhouses* (London: Dilly, 1795)

Griffiths, Arthur, *Memorials of Millbank and Chapters in Prison History* (London: King, 1875)

Guy, William A., *Results of Censuses of the Population of Convict Prisons in England Taken in 1862 and 1873* (London: Eyre & Spottiswoode, 1875)

Holford, George, *Thoughts on the Criminal Prisons of This Country* (London: Rivington, 1821)

Holford, George, *Third Vindication of the General Penitentiary* (London: Rivington, 1825)

Holford, George, *The Convict's Complaint in 1815 and the Thanks of the Convict in 1825* (London: Rivington, 1825)

Holford, George, *Statements and Observations concerning The Hulks* (London: Rivington, 1826)

Holford, George, *An Account of the General Penitentiary at Millbank* (London: Rivington, 1828)

Howard, John, *The State of the Prisons in England and Wales with Preliminary Observations and an account of some Foreign Prisons*, 1st edn. (Warrington: Eyres, 1777)

Howard, John, *The State of the Prisons in England and Wales with Preliminary Observations and an account of some Foreign Prisons and Hospitals*, 3rd edn. (Warrington: Eyres, 1784)

Howard, John, *An Account of the Principal Lazarettos in Europe together with further observations on some Foreign Prisons and Hospitals, and additional remarks on the present state of those in Great Britain and Ireland* (Warrington: Eyres, 1789)

Howard, John, *The State of the Prisons, etc.*, 4th edn. (London: Johnson, Dilly & Cadell, 1792)

Hunt, Henry, *Investigation at Ilchester Gaol* (London: Dolby, 1821)

Hunt, Henry, *Visits to a Prison: a Peep at the Prisoners; and a Description of the Interior of Ilchester Gaol* (Ilminster: Poole, 1821)

Latham, Peter Mere, *An Account of the Disease Lately Prevalent at the General Penitentiary* (London: Underwood, 1825)

Lettsom, John Coakley, *Memoirs of John Fothergill M.D.* (London: Dilly, 1780)

Lettsom, John Coakley, *Hints Respecting the Prison of Newgate* (London: Darton & Harvey, 1794)

Lind, James, *Essays on Preserving the Health of Seamen, with Considerations of the Gaol Distemper* (London: Wilson & Nicol, 1774)

Mann, John M., *Recollections of my Early Professional Life* (London: Rider, 1887)

Mead, James, *A Short Discourse Concerning Pestilential Contagion and the Methods to be Used to Prevent it* (London: Buckley & Smith, 1720)

Minshul, Geffray, *Essayes and Characters of a Prison and Prisoners* (Edinburgh: Ballantyne, 1618; repr. 1821)

Neild, James, *State of the Prisons in England, Scotland, and Wales, not for the debtor only but for Felons also, and other less criminal offenders* (London: Nichols, 1812)

Owen, Revd. Richard, *The Life of Richard Owen*, (2 volumes), (London: Murray, 1894)

Paul, Sir George Onisephorus, *To the Gentlemen of the Grand Jury of the County of Glocester[sic] at the Summer Assizes 1783* (Gloucester: Walker, 1783)

Paul, G.O., *Thoughts on the Alarming Progress of the Gaol Fever with Rules for the Treatment of the Disease and Means to Prevent Its Further Communication* (Gloucester: Raikes, 1784)

Paul, G.O., *Considerations of the Defects of Prisons*, (London: Cadell, 1784)

Paul, G.O., *An Address delivered to a General Meeting of the Nobility, Clergy, etc.* (Gloucester: Walker, 1792)

Paul, G.O., *Address on the subject of framing Rules, Orders and Byelaws for the prisons of the County of Glocester* (Gloucester: Walker, 1808)

Paul, G.O., *Address to His Majesty's Justices of the Peace for the County of Gloucester assembled at their Epiphany General Quarter Session*, (attached to which is an undated *Rules, Orders, and Regulations for the Controul [sic] and Governance of the Prisons of the County of Glocester*) (Gloucester: Walker, 1809)

Paul, G.O., *Doubts Concerning the Expediency and Propriety of Immediately*

Proceeding to Provide a Lunatic Asylum at Gloucester (Gloucester: Walker, 1813)

Pringle, John, *Observations on the Nature and Cure of Hospital and Jayl Fevers* (London: Millar and Wilson, 1750)

Report from the Committee of Aldermen appointed to visit several Gaols in England, (London: Nichols, Son and Bentley, 1816)

Smith, William, State of the Gaols in London, Westminster and Borough of Southwark (London: Bew, 1776)

Stow, John, Th*e Survey of London* (London, 1603, facsimile edition London: Dent, 1977)

Strype, John, *A Survey of the Cities of London and Westminster* Vol. 1 (London: Churchill, 1720)

Wakefield, Gilbert, *Memoirs of the Life of Gilbert Wakefield* (London: Johnson, 1804)

Law Reports

Buxton v. Mingay, 3 Wilson 70, Vol. XCV, XXIV

Villers v. Mosley, The English Reports, King's Bench Division, (London 1909), Vol. XCV

SECONDARY SOURCES: BOOKS

Andrews Jonathan, and Andrew Scull, *Undertaker of the Mind: John Monro and Mad-Doctoring in Eighteenth-Century England* (London: University of California Press, 2001)

Arthur, C., *Law and Marxism: A General Theory* (London: Intlinks, 1978)

Atholl, Justin, *Prison on the Moor: The Story of Dartmoor Prison* (London: Long, 1953)

Babington, Anthony, *The English Bastille: A History of Newgate Gaol and Prison Conditions in Britain 1188–1902* (London: Macdonald, 1971)

Bateson, Charles, *The Convict Ships 1787–1868* (Glasgow: Brown, 1985)

Bellamy Richard, *Beccaria: On Crimes and Punishment and Other Writings* (Cambridge: Cambridge University Press, 1995)

Blom-Cooper, Sir Louis, 'The Criminal Lunatic Asylum System Before and

After Broadmoor', in *The Health of Prisoners: Historical Essays*, ed. by Richard Creese and others (Amsterdam, Rodopi, 1995), pp. 151–162

Brockbank W. & F. Kenworthy, *The Diary of Richard Kay, 1716–1751, of Baldingstone near Bury: A Lancashire Doctor* (Manchester: Manchester University Press 1968)

Brodie, Allan, Jane Croom and James O. Davies, *English Prisons: An Architectural History* (Swindon: English Heritage, 2002)

Burt, John T., 'Results of the System of Separate Confinement as Administered at the Pentonville Prison', *The Quarterly Review*, XCII, (1852–53), 487–506

Bynum, W.F., Roy Porter and Michael Shepherd, (eds.), in *The Anatomy of Madness: Essays in the History of Psychiatry*, Vol. II (London: Tavistock, 1985)

Bynum, W.F., and Roy Porter, (eds.), *Companion Encyclopaedia of the History of Medicine 2* (London: Routledge, 1993)

Cadogan, Edward, *The Roots of Evil* (London: Murray, 1937)

Campbell, Charles, *The Intolerable Hulks: British Shipboard Confinement 1776–1857* (Maryland: Heritage, 1994)

Campbell, John Lord, *The Lives of the Chief Justices of England* (London: Murray, 1874)

Chisholm, Kate, *Fanny Burney: Her Life 1752–1840* (London: Chatto & Windus, 1998)

Clark-Kennedy, A.E., *The London: A Study in the Voluntary System, Vol. 1, 1740–1840* (London: Pitman, 1962)

Collins, Philip, *Dickens and Crime* (London: Macmillan, 1962)

Cousins, Mark, and Athar Hussain, *Michel Foucault* (London: Macmillan, 1984)

Crabbe, George, *The Life of George Crabbe: by his son* (London: Cresset Press, 1947)

Creese, Richard, W.F. Bynum & J. Bearn, (eds.) *The Health of Prisoners: Historical Essays* (Amsterdam, Rodopi, 1995)

Crosse, V. Mary, *A Surgeon in the Early Nineteenth Century: The Life and Times of John Green Crosse* (Edinburgh: Livingstone, 1968)

Dahrendorf, R., *Law and Order* (London: Stevens, 1985)

Davidson, L.P.S., *The Principles and Practice of Medicine* (Edinburgh:

Livingstone, 1954)

Davies, Mark, *Stories of Oxford Castle: From Dungeon to Dunghill* (Oxford: Towpath Press, 2005)

DeLacy, Margaret, *Prison Reform in Lancashire 1700–1850* (Manchester: Manchester University Press, 1986)

Dickens, Peter, Sean McConville and Leslie Fairweather, *Penal Policy and Prison Architecture* (Chichester: Bury Rose, 1978)

Digby, Anne, *Madness, Morality and Medicine: A Study of the York Retreat, 1796–1914* (Cambridge: Cambridge University Press, 1985)

Digby, Anne, *Making a medical living: Doctors and patients in the English market for medicine, 1720–1911* (Cambridge: Cambridge University Press, 1994)

Digby, Anne, *The Evolution of British General Practice: 1850–1948* (Oxford: Oxford University Press, 1999)

Donajgrodzki, A.P., 'Introduction', in *Social Control in Nineteenth Century Britain*, ed. by A.P. Donajgrodski (London: Croom Helm, 1977)

Dormandy, Thomas, *The White Death: A History of Tuberculosis* (London: Hambledon, 1999)

Driver, Felix, *Power and Pauperism: The Workhouse system 1834–1884* (Cambridge: Cambridge University Press, 1993)

Durkheim, Emile, *The Division of Labour in Society*, trans. G. Simpson (Glencoe, Ill.: Free Press, 1933)

Eliot, George, *Middlemarch* (London: Penguin, 1985)

Emblen, D.L., *Peter Mark Roget: The Word and the Man* (London: Longmans, 1970)

Emsley, Clive, *Crime and Society in England 1750–1900* (London: Longman, 1996)

Evans, Dylan, *Placebo: The Belief Effect* (London: HarperCollins, 2003)

Evans, Robin, *The Fabrication of Virtue: English Prison Architecture 1750–1840* (Cambridge: Cambridge University Press, 1982)

Finzsch, Norbert, and Robert Jutte (eds.), *Institutions of Confinement: Hospitals, Asylums, and Prisons in Western Europe and North America, 1800–1950* (New York: Cambridge University Press, 1996)

Fissell, Mary, *Patients, Power, and the Poor in Eighteenth Century Bristol* (Cambridge: Cambridge University Press, 1991)

Forbes, Thomas R., 'A mortality record for Cold Bath Fields', *Bulletin of the New York Academy of Medicine*, 53 (1977), 666–670

Forbes, Thomas R., 'Coroners' Inquisitions on the Deaths of Prisoners in the Hulks at Portsmouth, England in 1817–27', *Journal of the History of Medicine*, XXXIII, (1978), 356–366

Foucault, Michel, *Discipline and Punish: The Birth of the Prison* (London: Penguin, 1991) first published as *Surveiller et punir: Naissance de la prison* (Paris: Gallimard, 1975)

Garland, David, *Punishment and Modern Society: A Study in Social Theory* (Oxford: Oxford University Press, 1990)

Garland David, and Peter Young, *The Power to Punish* (London: Heineman, 1983)

Gattrell, V.A.C., *The Hanging Tree: Execution and the English People 1770–1868* (Oxford: Oxford University Press, 1996)

Gelford, Toby, 'The History of the Medical Profession', *Companion History of the Encyclopaedia of Medicine, Vol. 2*, ed. by W.F. Bynum and Roy Porter, (London: Routledge, 1993)

Hardy, Anne, 'Development of the Prison Medical Service', in *The Health of Prisoners*, ed. by Richard Creese and others (Amsterdam: Rodopi, 1995), pp. 59–80

Harwood, Ann-Rachel, David Viner and Martin Woodman, *Prison at the Crossroads: the House of Correction at Northleach* (Cirencester: Cotswold District Council, 1994)

Hay, David, *A Flickering Lamp: A History of the Sydenham Medical Club 1775–2000* (Andover: Hay, 2001)

Hay, Douglas, 'Property, Authority and the Criminal Law', in *Albion's Fatal Tree: Crime and Society in Eighteenth Century England*, ed. by Douglas Hay and others (London: Penguin, 1975), pp. 17–63

Hibbert, Christopher, *George IV* (Harmondsworth: Penguin, 1976)

Hibbert, Christopher, *George III: A Personal History* (Viking: London, 1998)

Higgins, Peter McRorie, 'Medical Care in the Prisons of Gloucestershire in the Early-Nineteenth Century' (unpublished master's dissertation, Open University, 1999)

Higgins, Peter McRorie, 'Medical Care in Three Gloucestershire Prisons in the Early 19th Century', *Transactions of the Bristol and Gloucestershire Archaeological Society*, 120 (2002), 213–228

Higgins, Peter McRorie, 'Genitourinary medicine and surgery in prisons during the period of reform', *British Journal of Urology International*, 95, (2005), 1192-1195

Higgins, Peter McRorie, 'The Scurvy Scandal at Millbank Penitentiary', *Medical History*, 50, (2006), 513-534

Higgins, Robert McRorie, 'The 1832 Cholera Epidemic in East London' *East London Record*, 2 (1979), 2–14

Hill, Christopher, *The Century of Revolution 1603–1714* (London: Routledge, 1980)

Hobsbawm, Eric, *The Age of Revolution: Europe 1789–1848* (London: Weidenfeld & Nicolson, 1975)

Horner, Stuart, and Meg Stacey (eds.), *Incarceration: Humane and Inhumane* (London: Nuffield Trust, 1999)

Howard, John, *The State of the Prisons* (London: Dent (Everyman's Library),1929)

Howard, Martin, *Wellington's Doctors: The British Army Medical Service in the Napoleonic Wars* (Staplehurst: Spellmont, 2002)

Hughes, Robert, *The Fatal Shore: A History of Transportation of Convicts to Australia, 1787–1868* (London: Pan, 1988)

Hutchins, John H., *Jonas Hanway: 1712–1786* (London: S.P.C.K., 1940)

Hutchinson, Herbert, *Jonathan Hutchinson: Life and Letters* (London: Heinemann, 1947)

Ignatieff, Michael, *A Just Measure of Pain* (London: Penguin, 1989)

Innes, Joanna, 'Prisons for the poor: English bridewells 1555–1800', in *Labour, Law, and Crime*, ed. by Francis Snyder and Douglas Hay (Cambridge: Tavistock, 1987), pp. 42–122

Johnston, Valerie J., 'Diets in Workhouses and Prisons 1835–1895' (doctoral thesis, University of Oxford, 1981)

Jones Colin, and Roy Porter, (eds.) *Reassessing Foucault: Power, Medicine and the Body* (London: Routledge, 1997)

Jones, David, *Crime, Protest, Community and Police in Nineteenth Century*

Britain (London: Routledge, 1982)

Kronenwetter, Michale, *Capital Punishment: a Reference Handbook* (Santa Barbara: ABC-CLIO, 1993)

Lane, Joan, 'The Role of Apprenticeship in Eighteenth Century Medical Education in England', in *William Hunter and the Eighteenth Century Medical World*, ed. by W.F. Bynum and Roy Porter (Cambridge: Cambridge University Press, 1985)

Lane, Joan, *The Making of the English Patient: A Guide to Sources for the Social History of Medicine* (Stroud: Sutton, 2000)

Lawrence, Christopher, 'Democratic, divine and heroic: the history and historiography of surgery', in *Medical Theory, Surgical Practice Studies in the History of Surgery*, ed. by Christopher Lawrence (London: Routledge, 1992)

Leonard, E.M., *The Early History of English Poor Relief* (Cambridge: Cambridge University Press, 1900)

Lewis, Griselda, *A Collector's History of English Pottery*, 5th edn. (Woodbridge: Studio Vista, 1999)

Loudon, Irvine, *Medical Care and the General Practitioner 1750–1850* (Oxford: Clarendon, 1986)

Macalpine I., & R.A. Hunter, *George III and the Mad Business* (London: Allen Lane, 1969)

McConville, Sean, *A History of English Prison Administration, Volume I, 1750–1877* (London: Routledge, 1981)

Medlicott, Diana, review of 'Incarceration, Humane and Inhumane: Human values and Health Care in British Prisons', ed. by Stuart Horne and Meg Stacey, (London: Nuffield Trust, 1999) in *The Howard League Magazine*, 19, 2001, 18

Morris, Norval, and David J. Rothman (eds.), *The Oxford History of The Prison: The Practice of Punishment in Western Society* (Oxford: Oxford University Press, 1995)

Nietzsche, F., *The Birth of Tragedy and the Genealogy of Morals*, trans. Francis Golffing (Garden City, N.Y.: Doubleday, 1956)

Pashukanis, Evgenny B., *Law and Marxism: A General Theory*, trans. Barbara Einhorn, ed. Chris Arthur (London: IntLinks, 1978)

Philips, David, *Crime and Authority in Victorian England: The Black Country 1835–1860* (London: Croom Helm, 1977)

Porter, Roy, 'Howard's Beginning: Prisons, Disease, Hygiene', in *The Health of Prisoners*, ed. by Richard Creese and others (Amsterdam: Rodopi, 1995), pp. 5–26

Porter, Roy, *The Greatest Benefit to Mankind: A Medical History of Humanity from Antiquity to the Present* (London: HarperCollins, 1997)

Porter, Roy, *Bodies Politic: Disease, Death and Doctors in Britain, 1650–1900* (London: Reaktion, 2001

Porter, Roy, *Blood & Guts: A Short History of Medicine* (London: Penguin, 2002)

Priestley, Philip, *Victorian Prison Lives: English Prison Biography 1830–1940* (London: Methuen, 1985)

Prout, Curtis, and Robert N. Ross, *Care and Punishment: The Dilemmas of Prison Medicine* (Pittsburgh: University of Pittsburgh Press, 1988)

Rabinow, Paul, *The Foucault Reader* (London: Peregrine, 1984)

Rose, Gordon, *The Struggle for Penal Reform: The Howard League and its Predecessors* (London: Stevens, 1961)

Rusche Georg, and Otto Kirchheimer, *Punishment and Social Structure* (New York: Columbia University Press, 1939)

Schama, Simon, *The Embarrassment of Riches: An Interpretation of Dutch Literature in the Golden Age* (London: Fontana, 1991)

Scull, Andrew, *Social Order/Mental Disorder: Anglo-American Psychiatry in Historical Perspective* (London: Routledge, 1989)

Sim, Joe, *Medical Power in Prisons: The Prison Medical Service in England, 1774–1989* (Milton Keynes: Open University Press, 1990)

Sim, Joe and Tony Ward, 'The magistrates of the poor? Coroners and deaths in custody in nineteenth-century England', in *Legal Medicine in History*, ed. by Michael Clark & Catherine Crawford (Cambridge: Cambridge University Press, 1994), pp. 245–267

Sim, Joe, 'The Prison Medical Service and the Deviant 1895–1948', in *The Health of Prisoners*, ed. by Richard Creese and others, (Amsterdam: Rodopi, 1995), pp. 102–117

Sim, Joe, 'Prison Health Care and the Lessons of History', in *Incarceration, Humane and Inhumane*, ed. by Stuart Horner and Meg Stacey (London: Nuffield Trust, 1999)

Sloan, Tod, *The Treadmill and the Rope: The History of a Liverpool Prison* (South Wirral: The Gallery Press, 1988)

Smith, Leonard D., *Cure, Comfort and Safe Custody: Public Lunatic Asylums in Early Nineteenth Century England* (London: Leicester University Press, 1999)

Smith, Richard, *Prison Health Care* (London: B.M.A., 1984)

Southerton, Peter, *The Story of a Prison*, (Reading: Osprey, 1975)

Standley, Anthony John, 'Medical Treatment and Prisoners' Health in Stafford Gaol during the Eighteenth Century', in *The Health of Prisoners*, ed. by Richard Creese and others (Amsterdam: Rodopi, 1995), pp. 27–43

Stockdale, Eric, *A Study of Bedford Prison 1660–1877* (London: Phillimore, 1977)

Thompson, E.P., *The Making of the English Working Class* (London: Penguin, 1991)

Thompson, F.M.L., *The Cambridge Social History of Britain, Vol. 1: 1750–1950* (Cambridge: Cambridge University Press, 1990)

Tobias, J.J., *Crime and Industrial Society in the Nineteenth Century* (Oxford: Alden, 1987)

Uglow, Jenny, *The Lunar Men: The Friends who Made the Future* (London: Faber & Faber, 2002)

Verey, David, *The Diary of a Cotswold Parson: Reverend F.E. Witts 1783–1854* (Gloucester: Alan Sutton, 1978)

Webb, Sidney and Beatrice Webb, *English Prisons under Local Government* (London: Longmans, 1922)

Whitfield, H.N., W.F. Hendry, R.S. Kirby, and J.W. Duckett, *Textbook of Genitourinary Surgery* (Blackwell: Oxford, 1998)

Whiting, J.R.S., *Prison Reform in Gloucestershire 1776–1820* (London: Phillimore, 1975)

Whiting, J.R.S., *A House of Correction* (Gloucester: Alan Sutton, 1979)

Wiener, Martin J., *Reconstructing the Criminal: Culture, Law and Policy in England, 1830–1914* (Cambridge: Cambridge University Press, 1990)

Wiener, Martin J., 'The Health of Prisoners and the Two Faces of Benthamism', in *The Health of Prisoners*. ed. by Richard Creese and others (Amsterdam: Rodopi, 1995), pp. 44–58

Williams, Basil, *The Whig Supremacy 1714–1760* (Oxford: Clarendon, 1962)

Williams, David Innes, *The London Lock: A Charitable Hospital for Venereal Disease 1746–1952* (London: R.S.M., 1997)

Wilson, A.N., *The Victorians* (London: Hutchinson, 2002)

Winston, Mark, 'The Bethel at Norwich: An Eighteenth-Century Hospital for Lunatics', *Medical History* 38 (1994), 27–51

Wright, Martin, preface in John Howard, *The State of the Prisons, Bicentennial Edition* (Abingdon: Professional Books, 1977)

JOURNALS AND OTHER DOCUMENTS

Bulletin of the New York Academy of Medicine, 53 (1977)

Cheatle, Thomas (surgeon), *Account Books 1820–1845*, (held in Tolsey Museum, Burford, Oxfordshire)

East London Record, 2 (1979)

Gentleman's Magazine, XX, (1750)

Gloucester Journal, 13 April 1818 and 11 May 1818

Hansard (New Series), VI, (1822)

Illustrated London News, 1861

Journal of the History of Medicine, XXXIII, (1978)

Lettson, John Coakley, *Letters of Prisons Collected in Four Volumes*, (held in Wellcome Historical Collection)

Medico-Chirurgical Transactions, XXVIII, (1845)

Medical History 10 (1966); 28, (1984); 38, (1994)

Parliamentary Journals, 1778, Vol. 36; 1779, Vol. 37

The Edinburgh Review, CXXVIII, (1836)

The Howard League Magazine, 19, (2001)

The Lancet, 1, 1823; 1, 1830–1831; 2, 1839–1840; 2, 1858

The Quarterly Review, XCII, (1852–1853)

The Times, 1823 and 1861

Transactions of the Bristol and Gloucestershire Archaeological Society, 120 (2002)

Wilts and Gloucestershire Standard, 9 January 1843 and 22 April 1843

Reference works

Lists of Members and Fellows of the Royal College of Surgeons, 1822 and 1825

The Provincial Medical Directory, 1847

Pigot and Co, *National Commercial Directory* (London: Pigot, 1830)

Victoria History of the County of Gloucester, Vol. IV: The City of Gloucester (Oxford University Press: Oxford, 1988)

INDEX

Abortion and miscarriage: at Fleet prison, 28; death from, 175–176

Abscess: psoas, 104; treatment, 40 and 118; in thigh, 183

Acland, Sir Richard (magistrate, Somerset): and Ilchester gaol, 228

Act for the better governance of prisons: passed 1850, n.6, p.2

Alcohol: allowance to nurse, 57, 58, 59, 61, 223; use in treatment, 73, 76, 78, 79, 89, 99, 101, 105, 110, 111, 129, 151, 172, 180, 181, 182, 229; excess, 146, 156, 172, 173, 190; prisoners work better on water, 197; effect of deprivation, 204; effect on Dr Hutcheson, 211

Amenorrhoea: cured by treadmill labour, 139

Amputation of breast: see Mastectomy

Amsterdam *Rasphuis*: work at, 12 and n.51, p.12

Andrews, Edward (prisoner Birmingham borough gaol): mistreated, 231

Anxiety, see insanity

Aperients: use of, 88, 102

Apothecaries Act of 1815: passing of, 38 and n.162, p.38

Apothecaries: see surgeons and Society of Apothecaries

Asiatic cholera: see Cholera

Asylum, lunatic: provision of, 141–143; transfers to Broadmoor, n.549, p.141; bowel complaints at Bethlehem, 169; use of cold bath at, 147 and n.587, p.153

Attacks on surgeons, 121–122

Attempted suicide: see suicide

Aylesbury (Buckinghamshire) county gaol: infirmary, 53; cholera at, 83

ISBN 142510153-4